# all because
## of
# henry

*Also by Nuala Gardner*

A FRIEND LIKE HENRY

# all because of henry

## My Story of Struggle and Triumph with Two Autistic Children and the Dogs that Unlocked Their World

## nuala gardner
### with Beth McDonough

BLACK & WHITE PUBLISHING

First published 2013
by Black & White Publishing Ltd
29 Ocean Drive, Edinburgh EH6 6JL

1 3 5 7 9 10 8 6 4 2    13 14 15 16

ISBN: 978 1 84502 707 0

ALBA | CHRUTHACHAIL

Typeset by Iolaire Typesetting, Newtonmore
Printed and bound by Grafica Veneta S. p. A. Italy

This book is dedicated to the children of Dale's generation who, like him, are now adults living with autism. There are incalculable numbers of adults that have not been as fortunate as Dale to have received the right education or support. Dale's desire is that this book will give his generation new hope to help them pursue a similar quality of life, like any other adult in society.

# Contents

# Preface

1991. Where were we? Dale, my three-year-old son, was trapped in his terrifying, autistic world and I was lost too. Yet, somehow, I had the maternal remit to rescue *him*. Desperate, I drove the thirty miles to Glasgow, seeking a new support group, wanting answers, needing to cling to the slightest chance of hope . . . any hope.

Well, I didn't find hope. I found this:

*My child is four years old and severely autistic. I've been told we have to fight for adult provision for him* now.

That night was the beginning of an incredible eighteen-year journey I would travel with Dale. He would emerge from that lonely world, with me battling beside him. After all, during those years I had the best teacher of all, a certain Henry – all four legs and tail – our beautiful, noble golden retriever. Everyone who knew him agreed. He was to become Dale's first real friend and he was the perfect gentleman.

This was no ordinary dog. He did the extraordinary: he gave me hope when I had none. It was Henry who freed my tormented son and it was Henry who would throw us both the lifeline we needed. Dale's autism was so severe that family life was extremely difficult. Any break in Dale's usual routine could cause severe tantrums, and we simply didn't know what to do, how to get through to our son and give him the help he so badly needed. Then Henry arrived and the bond he formed with Dale provided the breakthrough we had so desperately wanted. His arrival in

Dale's life helped bring my son out of his autistic world and gave us a way to communicate that simply had not been there before. Henry unlocked Dale's world and gave us hope for our son's future, which is the most incredible feeling for any parent. And led by Henry, I believed we had made it to adulthood, problem solved. I was able to see Dale's future; he would be a confident, fully productive, professional member of society. I thought him secure. Likely anyone reading my earlier book had every reason to believe that too. Would that it were to be that simple.

*. . . we have to fight for adult provision . . .*

Eighteen years on, that parent's words would come back to haunt me. Repeatedly. Dale had caught up with society, but had society caught up with him? We were about to find out. Those early adult years would become the most challenging of times. For both of us.

Easter Sunday, 17 April 2006 was the night Henry died. That beautiful dog had led not only his young master into the world but he had made our family life, well, a family life! How would his death affect my seventeen-year-old Dale's future? How would it affect all of us? Strangely, the one thing I needn't have worried about was how my son would cope with this most painful of losses.

As Henry lay dying, only a mature man could have done what he did. Just as Henry had helped Dale all his life, now it was Dale's turn to help him. My son assisted the vet, allowing Henry a comfortable and loving death. I stood back in awe.

"You're going to be all right now, Henry. This jag will make you feel better," said Dale.

With these heartbreaking words, I realised that my son was able to allow his precious dog to die, and more: I learned that Dale would never let slip the better future Henry had given him, however challenging that might prove to be.

"Mum, due to Henry I am not scared any more of being an adult. I have decided that for the rest of my life I am never going to let my amazing dog down, so that he will be proud of me, as I will always be of him."

This would not be Henry's final gift to my son, nor indeed to me and my daughter, Amy.

Amy was my millennium miracle baby, who had been diagnosed with moderate autism when she was only two years old. Thankfully, because of lessons learned from Dale and Henry, she was able to develop at an impressive rate. At five, she had already caught up with her brother. Both now are considered to have high-functioning autism. Unlike Dale at five, Amy's vocabulary was extensive and she utilised it well. Too well! She became The Interrogator! She could take ownership of any conversation and turn it around to her own obsession – horses. Once in control, she would question to her heart's content, whatever anyone else might think!

But what did anyone else think? Over these twenty-four years of bringing up two children with very different kinds of high-functioning autism (Autism Spectrum Disorder or ASD, as it has come to be known), I have seen change. I have seen society accept the condition as a recognised disability. So far, so good. But is it enough? Life should be fine by now, shouldn't it?

With the help of Henry, these are issues I have faced every day of my life as a mother, trying to find ways to help my children be all they can be and facing the challenges life throws at them every single day. But, of course, I am not alone, and with over half a million people in the UK affected, this is a major issue for our society. This figure includes Asperger's syndrome (AS), which is the highest level of functioning on the spectrum.

To help understand autism a little more, there are three main aspects that make it the lifelong disability that it is. The first of the triad is communication, and some will be unable to speak at all. All affected will have problems interpreting non-verbal communication, body language being completely incomprehensible to them. If that weren't bad enough, then there is the sufferer's literal understanding of language to add to the mix. Let me explain how that works using the true story of Philip, when he had to resit his driving test.[1]

Examiner 1: Can you read the number plate of the green car over there?
Philip: Silence.
Examiner 2: Philip, he is talking to you.
Philip: Oh, sorry!
Examiner 1: Philip, can you read the number plate of the green car over there?
Philip: Yes, thank you.
Examiner 1: Go on then.
Philip: I have.
Examiner 1: Can you read it for me, please?
Philip: I have read it twice already!
Examiner 2: Philip, would you please read out loud the number of the green car over there?
Philip: J123 VOS.

Is it any wonder that many with autism choose not to speak at all? As Dale revealed when he was a child, he would have chosen not to talk to us had we not communicated with him via Henry. To this day, Dale's remark chills me. What might not have been?

The second part of the triad is difficulty with social interaction. All social skills have to be learned; they don't come naturally, understanding the complexities of emotions, feelings and empathy. Sufferers have problems understanding social rules and how to navigate society.

Nowadays, we are also aware that many with autism endure the distress and discomfort of sensory-processing issues. When Dale was young, I suspected he was affected and adapted things as best I could. Thirteen years later, he told me about his sensory problems – the smell of some foods, the colour combinations, the textures – some of which were the catalyst for many of his most challenging tantrums.

The third leg of the triad is difficulty with social imagination, not being able to understand people's behaviour or abstract ideas, their thoughts or feelings, including in times of danger and crisis.

This explanation of autism is far from exhaustive, but again, this is never to be forgotten: anyone with autism can learn and develop with the right condition-specific education and support. Amy, Dale and thousands of their peers in society are proof of that.

Where were we?

Six months before Henry's passing, Dale had the foresight to acquire a puppy, and insisted on calling him … Henry! We managed to live quite normally with two golden retrievers in our home with the same name. It was amusing how both dogs responded with only the words *Wee* and *Sir* to distinguish them. Dale knew that Wee would never replace Sir, but he needed to hold onto that name. And quite rightly, too!

I didn't realise at the time, but I was beginning an extraordinary new voyage. I was to travel to places in the world, far further than I could ever have imagined. It was all because of autism. By visiting these places, I was able to continue the work that Henry had begun. Dale and Henry had shone a light in a dark place. That light was nowhere near ready to go out! Already, thanks to Henry, we were in a happier, safer place. Both my children were reaching out to consider exciting futures, just as their neuro-typical peers – others not affected by autism – were doing.

This is the story of our journey together into those futures. This time though, unlike my earlier excursions at the family helm, I would not be alone, and it would be no mystery tour. I was in the safest hands possible, with my strong, brave tour guide beside me, my now adult son Dale. However, to begin this new journey, as a family we had to get through the hardest day of all.

The first day without Sir Henry.

# 1

## *After Henry*

My husband Jamie was awakened by a damp nose nuzzling his face, a paw nudging – by someone who was not about to be ignored! Wee Henry (or Henry, as he was now) had slept in Dale's room since puppyhood when Sir could no longer manage the stairs. By the time his elder had gone, Wee Henry knew with certainty that he was Dale's dog.

Returning from his morning constitutional, Henry demanded his breakfast. He refused to settle without a full stomach – 6 a.m. or not – just like his namesake. It felt strange to hear Jamie call "Henry" now, even though the youngster seemed to have accepted his reformed name. Suddenly, I heard loud sobbing from Jamie.

"What's wrong?" I asked.

"It's Henry. He won't eat his breakfast. I put his bowl on Sir's step. He just won't do it."

We had let Henry eat there to show him he was now the top dog, but there he laid, head between paws, big brown eyes staring and depressed. No amount of reassuring or coaxing interested him. I placed his bowl on his usual table. Wolf! He devoured his meal in seconds, followed me back to my bedroom, and joined me in bed.

An hour later on that Easter Monday and Henry wasn't my only bedmate. There was Amy, fast asleep. I can't say it was a surprise to see her there. Regularly, she ended up in between Jamie and me, just as a younger Dale had done (but at least he hadn't sneaked in until later). In good faith, we always started her off in her own bed, in her lovely horse-decorated bedroom, with that all-important routine, but it didn't take long for her to limber up for her marathon – up and down, all night. After numerous failed attempts to return her to her own bed, one of us would climb into her wee bed to try to settle her there. Some nights the musical bed routine was so shattering that by the morning one parent was with her in our double bed, and the other would be camped in her single one. We could hardly remember how or when it happened, but happen it did! No wonder we called it the "Bed-a-thon"!

I was aware she had heightened sensory issues. Even as a baby, she sought comfort by playing with my hair, which lulled her to sleep. In a sense, she had perhaps "over bonded" with me. Now she was six and I felt I had exhausted all means to get her to stay in her own bed. No, we were just exhausted! Well, the tide didn't stop for Canute, and the business of the Gardner household day wasn't going to stop just because of mere parental burn out!

Now that Henry was awake, Dale was too. Looking for comfort, he came in. I reckon Sauchiehall Street was quieter that morning! His dad gave him a big, manly hug, and set off, hoping that work would take his mind off Sir's death. As Jamie left, I suggested Dale pop in whilst I made all of us a pot of tea. Thankfully, we had a king-size bed! Henry was sprawled out, sleeping deeply, on a third of the space. We all squeezed together and enjoyed the security.

As Dale and I sat up, sipping our comforting cup and musing sadly, suddenly we heard a familiar voice. From the middle of the duvet we learned . . . The Interrogator was awake!

"Nuala, what's Dale doing in our bed?"

Amy called me by my first name, and had done so since she was four, when I taught her the rules of conversational turn-taking. I explained that she needed to wait her turn to speak, and then say the person's name. I should have known better! Autistic children learn in a literal way, and Amy applied this rule exactly. "NUALA!"

Now she was wide awake, bolt upright between us, and she needed answers.

[ 2 ]

"Nuala, what's wrong? Why is Dale sad?"

I cuddled her, warning her that I had sad news. Sad news usually meant that someone or something had died. We shared our saddest news of all over breakfast in bed.

Eventually, I suggested we needed to move on, to get out of the house. We weren't in the mood to do anything special but had to get through this, so we headed for Glasgow to buy Dale his first tailored suit. He had already been to a couple of funerals in hired suits, and I thought for future job interviews and the like it was time he had one of his own. Having dropped Amy and Henry off at her grandparents', we headed off to Glasgow's famous tailor, Slater's. The shop assistant was very helpful and understanding when we explained why Dale was getting his first suit. Having a grandson of his own with a profound disability, he grasped the real significance of this event.

I saw my son emerge from the changing rooms, and my soul swelled. What a handsome grown man he had become! Remembering that lost and lonely child, that child who had spent days rocking in a corner of a room, unable to communicate or relate, I thought, Wow! Look at my incredible, handsome son now!

Dale chose the most expensive outfit on the rail – the designer suit. I realised I was going to take the financial hit when, as he modelled it, the assistant explained that a famous local footballer had chosen that very one. Dale had learned how to "fit in" by following good role models, so when he heard someone successful had bought the same suit, there was never any choice!

Suit bought, Dale declared he was hungry. That was always a good sign! We headed for a Chinese restaurant, ate ravenously and headed home.

That night we all sat watching television. Henry was cuddled up beside Dale on one sofa, while Amy sat snug between her dad and me on the other. Life seemed quite normal again, but I reflected on what she had taught me in bed that morning. I had assumed because horses were her world, she would be less affected by Henry's death. So wrong! On that first morning without our beloved Sir, Dale and I sat listening to our personal Interrogator.

"Amy, Dale and I are sad because, when you were sleeping, Sir Henry died and he is now in Heaven."

I hugged her tightly, while we braced ourselves for her response.

She screamed. "Buy another one! Please, please, Nuala, buy another one!"

Her body shook, distressed. She shouted this phrase, repeatedly. You might well conclude that she was a ruined, unfeeling little girl, simply wanting a replacement for a broken toy. Again, so wrong. Calming her, I extracted more information. She clung on, burying her head in my chest, unable to look.

"Nuala, I will miss Sir Henry – my dog Harry – and my special horse has now gone."

Immediately I understood. "Harry" was the name she had given Henry when she was a toddler with emergent autism. Henry was Dale's dog, while Harry was Amy's. Now, I was confused regarding her special horse, until she explained. "Nuala, Harry was sometimes my special horse that I liked to play with."

At three, when Amy adopted horses as her main love and obsession, I watched her groom Henry with her horse kit. She would attach a horse lead rope to his collar and walk him around the house. At the time, I thought that she was simply using her horse kit in a literal way with the dog. After all, she was unable to tell me otherwise. It never occurred to me that she was role-playing, and at that young age, showing the green shoots of imagination. Then, I believed she had none.

It was not the only time I underestimated my daughter. Amy nurtured her equine obsession at the Ardgown Riding School. In the centre of the estate there was a one-hundred-year-old oak. During her pony walks, Amy would be led around it a couple of times, blank-faced, expressionless, and uninterested in her walk and the environment.

Despite this, she went every Sunday for years. Visiting Ardgown five years later, Amy was upset to discover that the tree had been felled.

"Nuala, Nuala. I am so sad ... because my big tree is gone! I liked to pretend I was on a real horse carousel when I went around my tree."

At the same age, Dale had adopted a similar big, old tree which, miraculously, gave him his first word. I have learned that children with autism have extraordinary, albeit different, imaginations. We must embrace their obsessions, use them in a positive way to connect with them and teach them. That is why we need to take time in observing the child with autism at play. The pace and type of play may differ, but never doubt it: that child is learning and exploring.

After Amy's upset, I consoled her. It was good that she had played with Sir, her special horse. If she wanted, I told her, she could make Wee Henry her special horse instead. Hearing this, she seemed to settle, reverting to her usual happy self. Bereavement for any child, let alone a child with autism, is such a major transition that I had prepared her, years before, to give her an idea of Heaven and loss.

I had found a children's storybook, *Heaven* by Nicholas Allan, and I introduced it to her as soon as she took a fleeting interest in books, when she was about three. I already admired his other stories, which also appealed to Amy. She never tired of hearing his tale *The Queen's Knickers* (She was particularly fond of when the Queen wore her extra-padded riding knickers!). *Heaven*, being about a dog's death, helped her understand loss, and it would enable her to cope with the memories of Sir yet to come. As I had done with Dale, I adapted – indeed, I completely vandalised – books to suit our purposes. I had removed pages of *Heaven*, still allowing the story to shine out. I had taped over the text to hide it, for future release when Amy was ready to learn to read. By doing so, the book's sensory overload had been reduced. Naturally, I hid the part which considers the possibility of The Other Place. After all, that was never going to happen to our dogs! This book was a real godsend, as it helped Amy prepare for this eventual outcome we were now facing.

In the days that followed, Dale was to receive condolence cards from friends and family – this had been no ordinary dog. As a special thank you, we gave a framed portrait of Sir to his vet, Nigel Martin, drawn by Dale in those last weeks. The portrait was for their staff room, as a wee reminder of an extra-special client and for all they had done, both for Sir and for Dale.

At home, our Wee Henry was still an upset and lost dog. A couple of weeks on, as I watched Amy playing in the garden, I was distracted by a whimpering and barking from upstairs. I investigated immediately. Henry's distress was coming from Amy's bedroom. As I entered her room I was pleasantly shocked! There stood Henry, completely captured by Amy, wearing a pink horse head collar from her life-sized toy Shetland pony, and with a lead rope tied to the handle of his stable. If that weren't bad enough, she had put a pink saddlecloth on his back, and he wore brushing boots! God knows how long Henry had tolerated this before eventually letting me know he had had enough. I laughed quietly and rescued him, but I was relieved too that although Amy had been able to grieve for her "horse Harry", she was now moving on.

There were days thereafter when I would think of Sir constantly, and others when he entered my thoughts less, a normal part of the grieving process, including that for a dearly loved pet. For years to come, though, my grief would surface at the most unexpected moments. When laundry day arrived, I'd lift Dale's pillow and I would just sit on the bed, tears flowing. Sir's collar was tucked inside Dale's pillow, where he had put it on the night he died. Writing this seven years later, I know it's still there.

Day by day, life had to go on. After Easter, Dale hoped to begin a career in early education and childcare, in a mainstream nursery setting. At Gourock High, he had had a week's work experience in Carousel, a local private nursery. He received an exceptional report from the nursery staff, so much so that I remember the secondary's assistant head commenting that it was exceptional for a pupil to get such a good nursery placement report. During that week, Dale discovered he had a real understanding of how to connect and engage with children. He told me, "Mum, I remember what made me happy in my childhood. I understand how the children feel when there is an adult playing with them that really knows what makes them tick."

In common with so many others, Dale's autism had given him a photographic memory and his childhood recollections were vivid. Often when I have wondered at his ability to cope, he has explained that he can remember the bad and the good times in detail. He has even told me, "Mum, I'm really shocked that I behaved the way I did when I was a child, but I saw things so differently, and many things happening around me were so scary when I was young."

In order for Dale to follow this career path, I had to ensure he understood what it involved for him because of his autism. Probably, he would be one of the first people to have had autism which had been classed as severe in childhood, who wanted to have a career in this area. We had major concerns. So, when Dale was seventeen, his father and I sat down to talk with him about his choice. The conversation we had and the issues we had to raise were both devastating and depressing. His dad and I felt we had no option but to make him face the reality of his situation, the potential barriers, and the problems he would encounter if and when he qualified. We needed to help him realise how hard it would be to find a suitable job with a supportive, working environment, one that would be right for his autism.

In order to gain the necessary understanding from staff, he would need to let employers know about his condition. Already Dale had concluded that because he had autism he would have to prove himself *more* and be *more* able than his non-disabled peers.

Motivated to overcome this perceived prejudice, Dale took on voluntary work as a support worker with Barnardo's Scotland. He worked with a group, aged five to eighteen. The children had a diverse range of disabilities, including autism. He volunteered at an out-of-school holiday play scheme and helped support disabled children in a weekly drama group. Barnardo's require in-service training of all their volunteers in areas like child protection, so Dale had to learn about challenging behaviour, know and understand many other disabilities and their effect on child development. He became familiar with issues like health and safety, first aid, seizure procedures, safe administration of emergency medication, life support and more. These new topics and skills were relevant to his chosen career, and we discussed them all. We assured him that Barnardo's was such a long-established charity that his volunteering would be a really strong, positive aspect of his curriculum vitae. Or so we thought!

A very focused Dale told me, "Mum, I know it's going to be really hard work, but I am determined to prove to myself and others that I have got what it takes. I'm not going to let having autism ruin my life!"

Hearing this, I helped him appreciate that there were more positives than negatives in his career choice. Obviously, his talents in art and music would be an advantage, but even more: his was a unique and incredible insight into autism. Indeed, this is where many of the children emerging on the autistic spectrum would be first recognised, and this was where their early intervention would be implemented. Dale's personal journey would prove an asset in any nursery.

We talked about how he would avoid discrimination. We didn't like discussing this subject, but he had to know. Together we considered what barriers he might face, whilst trying to keep things upbeat. We reassured him that as he would be working in an area where autism was now so common and was on the syllabus, he would certainly have understanding, supportive colleagues. Sadly, with improved diagnosis, it would reasonable to assume that there would be at least one child (probably more) with ASD in every nursery. Undoubtedly, working there, Dale would give hope to parents, whilst simultaneously giving staff a unique insight into autism. He had made a great career choice.

At the time, I had spoken to a few girls who were qualified practitioners, working locally. They said that the profession was trying to encourage more males into nursery education careers as positive role models for vulnerable children, and a good influence on many children from single-parent families. So far, so good.

We explained, in detail, that there was legislation in place to protect him, the Disability Discrimination Act 1995 (DDA), as it was then.[1] Under this Act, he should not be treated less favourably because of his autism. Dale had the right, like any other person, to apply to his local college and take part in any course he desired, assuming he was a suitable candidate.

And Dale was a suitable candidate ... because of his voluntary work, his good work experience report and the right Standard Grades! Importantly, under the Act, college staff had to take reasonable steps to ensure that Dale accessed the curriculum fully, in a similar way to the adjustments which had already been made for his school exams. He would have additional time at exams; instead of note taking he would receive classroom notes from lecturers, addressing his processing difficulties and poor fine-motor skills. Under the DDA, it was unlawful for a person to "harass or victimise a person because of their disability". We talked at great length and felt optimism for his future. Really, there was no reason he shouldn't pursue this course. How much more suitable could he possibly be?

Understanding the difficult and extraordinary journey Dale had made already and knowing how much good he would bring from his childhood experiences, after much deliberation his dad and I decided that no matter what we would support him in his pursuit of this profession. He was returning to a system which had helped him be the person he was today, and that was huge.

About a month after Sir's death, I was deeply touched to discover that Nigel the Vet had hung Sir's portrait on a main reception area wall. He told me that his staff really respected all that Dale had achieved with Sir, and it was only fitting that the portrait be enjoyed by all the clients. If only all the people to have involvement in Dale's future would be as understanding and supportive of his achievements.

Meantime, there was something else I needed to do for both my children. I compiled memory photo albums of Henry. When Amy saw Dale's album, immediately she drew a picture for Dale to insert. The drawing was clearly Sir – happy-faced, wearing his bright blue collar – with the words *"To Dale, Sir Henry went to Heaven on 17/4/06 and was a good dog. From Amy"* written underneath.

This gesture truly moved us, reassuring us that Amy showed the beginnings of empathy, a concept that takes years for many with autism to grasp. Indeed, some will never be able to do so. With Sir's passing, I was to learn so much from Amy as well as from her brother about the complexities of their condition. However, for now, we were still coming to terms with the past that was Sir Henry and the future challenges that lay before Dale as he moved from his familiar world into the big wide world beyond.

# 2

# *Awareness*

"I believe that language for many people with autism is like trying to understand the handbook of a computer software package that is in computer code when you are not computer literate. Why do we say things that we don't mean? I can remember my father telling me to make friends. I knew how to make rice pudding, but I did not know how to make friends."

— Lawson, an adult with ASD[1]

"My son does not tell me when he is being bullied. I have to figure it out sometimes from bruises."

— Parent of a child with ASD[2]

Deep below the duvet, something – or someone – was fuming.

"Nuala, Nuala! I could kick a horse!"

There was no pony-hating monster in the room. Far from it! This was our six-year-old, horse-mad Amy, expressing her fury as only she could. Let's listen to her again, because sometimes what a child with autism says is not what we are first able to hear.

"Nuala."

As ever, Amy followed this mode of address with the literal precision that hallmarks autism, despite all my carefully structured words – "Tell your dad something", "Ask your gran", and the like. As I write this, and look at my now secondary-school-aged daughter, it still remains an all too rare treat when she chooses to call me Mum. In her Primary 1 days, it simply wasn't a name she used.

"Nuala! I hate horses!

Certainly, she was angry. I was to learn that Amy's emotional responses were three-tiered. The first layer would manifest itself when she was slightly annoyed. She would scream, "Shannon hates horses!" (Shannon, Amy's best friend, was a great horse lover.) When moderately upset, she upgraded to, "I'm going to kick a horse!" But worst – at maximum, high-volume anger – she would stomp and jump around, yelling over and over, "I'm going to kill a horse!" What more powerful images were there for Amy than her beloved horses?

She would repeat these statements until diverted and consoled, as we directed her to a better emotional response. These outbursts became such a part of our normal life that my close friends started to include them in our banter! Many's the glass of spilled wine that one of us has shrieked over, "I could kick a horse!" Throughout the years of managing my children's autism, my sense of humour has helped me cope, stay sane and keep positive. Autism provides a plethora of amusing scenarios, and has given me and my friends so much life-lightening laughter. That laughter is always with my children's autism, never at it.

Anyone overhearing Amy's terrible remarks might laugh, but in so doing would add to her distress. It was a scenario we knew all too well. Some people would be visibly shocked and respond by ignoring her. How I helped Amy recover doubtless horrified many. Bystanders might have thought I was simply condoning bad behaviour in a girl of six, who was, after all, old enough to know better. It was so easy to see a spoilt brat, just as had so often been seen when I had been out with a younger Dale.

Perhaps this helps explain that Amy's high-functioning autism, with its attendant verbal skills, was no easier for any of us to deal with, least of all for Amy herself. Verbal and able or not, my girl needed an education which was both mainstream and condition-specific. In her mainstream school, she had the advantage of being surrounded by positive role models, free from communication or social difficulties. Her friends (the

Famous Five), without understanding exactly why, accepted that Amy was different. From the word go, as she started school, she was beginning to learn how to adopt her peers' social skills. Equally, the Five were fast becoming adept at using Amy's obsessions to engage with, motivate and include her. Just as it had proved in nursery, this was already proving to be a key to her success.

Fortunately we had recognised in time that it was crucial that she had support similar to that which she had previously received in nursery. Supported by this structure, she was given the social tools she needed. That support is vital, not just for Amy, but for any child with ASD or AS who is attending a mainstream school. Sadly, for many children, the provision of this remains far from ideal.

Yes, Amy was already nearly six in the autumn of 2005 when she started school. Importantly, she had had a deferred school year, making her the class eldest. This initiative lessened both her social pressure and the developmental gap with her peers. It was a tactic which had already worked brilliantly for Dale. Further, we had the support of all of the Five's parents. Parents try everything to ensure their children reach their full potential, to protect them from harm, but these issues are compounded when your child has ASD. Autism is an unseen handicap, devoid of physical or outward features. Like so many, Jamie and I debated about when we should introduce others to our children's condition.

There is no single, easy answer. In situations like Scouts, we had always disclosed and explained Dale's autism, for many reasons. It helps those in charge understand and support the child better, and gives them protection under the existing legislation. Now it was Amy's turn as she started Brownies. Unquestionably, it was the right path to take as it enabled those in charge to make the adjustments needed to help both Dale and Amy enjoy full inclusion, and simultaneously ensure safety for all. Everyone had a good time. Of course, Amy's idea of a good time wasn't always the same as other people's!

In the early spring sunshine of 2006, Amy was in her favourite place, the stables, and she couldn't believe her luck! She spotted the farrier, whom she hadn't met before. He was hard at work, shoeing a big mare. The young yard girls, sitting relaxing over lunch, started nudging each other. They had prime viewing as Amy cornered her new victim.

"Hello! What's your name?"

"Scott. What's yours?"

"Amy! What are you doing?"

Everyone at the yard already knew that Amy had an in-depth knowledge of horses and farriers. Everyone, that is, except Scott. She went full throttle – the whys, whens and hows of her hundred questions unfolding. He took it all in his stride, answering everything, and he still managed to shoe three big horses throughout the onslaught! I went to retrieve her, to explain her autism and thank Scott for his incredible patience.

"So what! Her knowledge of horses is amazing!"

I jokingly offered to bring her down the following week for a repeat performance.

"Any time! She's something else!"

During the Easter holidays, Amy couldn't believe her eyes when she saw Scott again. This time I decided to distract her, but it was too late. He got in first.

"Hello, Amy! Nice to see you again. Fire away!"

Back at school for the summer term, Amy continued to improve, benefitting hugely from a little social group which had been in place since the start of the session, the Gingerbread Group. The Group included several neuro-typical kids from the school. Amy's teachers gave her peers an explanation of her autism and why she behaved the way she did – with the positive effects of that chat greatly outweighing the negative. Inevitably, a few children tried to exploit her, but they were doomed to fail. Amy had taught strategies and a bevy of well-educated peers as protection!

The Gingerbread Group focused on the big issues, like bullying, but it also taught Amy basic social skills: how to sit in a chair properly, to look and listen, engage appropriately within a group. It let her practise problems and solutions in a safe, controlled environment. At the school gate, she proudly showed me her sticker. "I asked a good question today!"

To ensure she understood how pleased I was and to encourage her success, I reacted with my OTT, Oscar-winning response. "Amy! Well done!" I leapt up and down, gesticulating madly. "Congratulations! That's brilliant!"

A nearby parent added to the congratulations, asking what exactly the occasion was. With Amy in earshot, I had to show off her sticker, and . . . well, I know, it sounded so lame.

"Er, that's lovely. Well done, Amy."

And the parent shuffled off, shooting me an over-the-shoulder look. Written all over it was *Go get a life, wummin!*

Never mind, I knew what I meant, and at home, her dad did too. Most importantly of all, Amy knew! That visual reward and the positive reinforcement of praise worked.

After school, there were regular, shared times in the Five's homes and gardens. Occasionally I would take the friends out, as a gesture of appreciation. Although their parents protested that this was unnecessary, it was a pleasure. Without her friends, Amy's quality of life and progress at school would have been very different. Even in that very first year, that was apparent.

One day, as the school bell rang, I saw Amy, holding Shannon's hand, with Regan following. Amy's happiness was obvious – Shannon was being hugged and kissed to bits. Clearly, however, Shannon was uncomfortable with the exuberance of Amy's affection! As I intervened, Amy's reply was unforgettable: "Nuala, it's okay. I know what you mean. I don't want people to think that Shannon and me are gay!"

Trying to keep my belly laugh under wraps, I asked. "Amy, what does gay mean?"

"Nuala! Do you not know? Simon in my class told us. It's when a man loves a man, and a woman loves a woman, and they can get married as well. Simon is good at telling you things."

Aye, so he was!

"Amy, everyone is different and that's okay!"

Just then, Shannon and Regan grabbed Amy's hands and shouted out, "Come on, Amy! Giddy up! Let's get to Funworld!"

Of all the challenges and social barriers a child with ASD has to face in life, from a parental perspective, perhaps the most heartbreaking is to witness your child's social isolation, day after day after day. My children have been lucky, but many parents have to cope when their child has been unable to establish that most basic of human needs, friendship. Never underestimate it. For those affected by autism, having a friend is every bit as important as it is to anyone else, yet it is possibly the most complex challenge of all. Friendship, after all, imparts social belonging and is inclusive in a real and meaningful way. Which of us could live without our friends?

Both my children have often told me that they hated the isolation when they couldn't engage or integrate socially. Both have told me that in an attempt to cope, they would withdraw more into their autistic world, immersing themselves further into their obsessions as a substitute for company. I repeat: never underestimate the need of anyone, anywhere on the spectrum, for friendship. It may be their greatest aspiration and, for some, it is underscored by the harrowing knowledge that they are different. One child with Asperger's asked his parents if there was a shop called Friends Are Us where they could take him to buy a friend. How much we neuro-typicals take for granted!

In 2010 the NAS (National Autistic Society) Our Impact Report revealed that over 40 per cent of children with autism have no friends. Unsurprisingly, these socially vulnerable children and adults make easy targets for bullying. Some traumatised children have needed to move from mainstream to additional support needs (special) schools, in order to ensure they are protected from further bullying.[3] Amy was one of the lucky ones. Her teachers at Moorfoot knew how to work with her autism in a positive way. Small but constructive adjustments made a huge difference. The award of a horse sticker instead of a star, being allowed to draw horses in her busy book on completion of classwork or work well done, all these little things add up. Amy was following a similar pathway to Dale, except Dale's educational motivators had been trains and dogs.

Together with the positive use of her equine obsession, Amy benefitted from an excellent Individual Education Plan (IEP), with realistic and achievable objectives. Some of the adjustments were so simple but essential, where and with whom Amy would sit in the classroom, for example. The right seating position allowed the teacher to prompt Amy and minimise distractions. This showed a real awareness of her sensory integration issues. This is a particularly important issue for almost everyone on the spectrum, and it needs to be unpacked here.

Practitioners now understand how sensory stimulus can overload an environment. Sensory issues alone can have a direct affect on the person's ability to cope with situations, and it can completely undermine their receptiveness to learning. Like many others, Amy had numerous sensory difficulties. Her senses could be heightened or reduced with a marked effect on her overall perception. As a child, Dale had also had many such problems, but his difficulties were harder to discern because he was unable to tell me. Amy could tell me, and it shocked me to discover that her sensory difficulties were greater and more varied than Dale's had ever been. It seems likely that in her greater awareness of her world, Amy was more vulnerable to this particular shaft from Hell.

Consider the sensory stimulus in a classroom: the glare of strip lights, the wall displays of paintings and projects, all the colours and endless information. We absorb about 70 per cent of our information from our environment visually. With all the other energy involved, is it any wonder the child with autism has problems deciphering? Think of the sounds and smells of a classroom, the feel of the seats and desks! No wonder they become overwhelmed. Add people into the mix. Think about the chattering and echoing and how that distorts the auditory ability to process verbal instructions. Have you any idea what a fire alarm does to someone with ASD?

Even to this day Amy still struggles, particularly with food, let alone with the environment in which she is eating. For example, one day not too long ago, as I was crunching away at my cereal, she said, "Nuala, eat your breakfast in another room. The noise hurts my ears and the look and smell of it makes me feel sick."

Compounding this problem is the sufferer's differing spatial awareness. Amy often uses her peripheral vision and she appears to squint. Seeing this, you might sometimes conclude she wasn't paying attention. In a busy mainstream school overflowing with people, is it any surprise that many children with inadequate or no support struggle? How many are wrongly excluded from the life of the class because their problems have been misunderstood or not recognised?[4]

Something else which amazed me about Amy's autism was that her obsession with horses was even fiercer than any of Dale's childhood obsessions. Unbelievable! Even Dale's ten-year affair with *Thomas the Tank Engine* wasn't as intense as this. Already as a six-year-old, Amy was able to manipulate anything and everything to bring horses into the equation, and she honed these skills throughout her primary years! From nursery days onward, Jamie had been in the habit of taking her to the local shop every Saturday to buy a *Daily Record*. He thought the paper was for him. One windy Saturday, in the summer before she started school, he was to discover otherwise. As her dad handed over the paper to be scanned, a full-blast Amy blurted out, "Jamie! Remember and keep The Punter for me!"

"The Punter" was the name of the paper's horse racing section. Amy would make collages from the few pictures of horses that were in it, but then she would create horses from anything – leaves from a tree, food on her plate! As a bold seven-year-old, she even managed to capture a bricklayer who was working in our garden.

"Rab, do you have any spare cement I could use?"

With this and other materials so artfully gained, Amy built Brickie the Horse! Rab left a gap at the back of a couple of bricks, allowing Amy to complete her sculpture with the final flourish – a tail robbed from a nearby bush! Brickie was duly painted to her exact specifications and stood in our patio for three full years (with regular replacement tails, naturally!).

Using my children's obsessions creatively has always worked. It works every bit as well in professional settings, as good practitioners know. When Amy displayed a new or different type of behaviour where the underlying reason for it and for her resultant distress was unclear, I had to figure out the trigger, Amy couldn't express what was wrong. This was the iceberg effect. With the iceberg effect I had to decipher if there were any sudden changes at school or in her home environment. Because the behaviour was abrupt and new, I had to consider if there was an underlying medical reason. A child with autism has difficulty interpreting pain and, undetected, this can cause serious problems.

Amy's obsession with horses was already extreme, at both school and home, but that had its uses. As every mum knows, the beginning of school is a time of scraped knees, bugs and illnesses. Amy certainly had her fair share of all that. For more than a week in the May of that first year, she was unsettled and unhappy, repeatedly telling me that she had a sore eye. As a nurse, I could see that her eyes were fine. Nevertheless, I kept reassuring her. Eventually as the week went by, her behaviour became more erratic and challenging. She insisted her eyes were really painful. I drew on her obsession.

"Amy, how sore is your eye? Is it a walk, trot, canter or gallop sore?"

Immediately she understood, screaming at me, "Nuala! It's a gallop! It's galloping sore!"

Now I knew that she was in real pain. I had a doctor check out her eyes, ears and throat. To my horror, the doctor confirmed she had a severe middle ear infection. With Dale too I had been able to use the colours and numbers of his *Thomas* trains to help him express his pain and anxiety levels. Similarly, in his early school years he used colour charts or traffic light systems. He even had a red card when he needed to stop or take time out.

It is essential that mechanisms are put in place to allow a child to communicate and express their negative feelings or needs. Failing to do this is disastrous. What is a child to do? Some may scream, have tantrums, others may cry intensely and some may self-injure. I know of children and adults with ASD, experiencing the severe pain of acute appendicitis and the like, who were almost on the brink of death before their physical symptoms were recognised. Because of their autism they were able to mask their symptoms and were unable to express what was wrong. Their pain confused them. How dangerous.

Amy was lucky, and with a course of antibiotics her problems soon cleared up and before long she was back at school, enjoying summer-term life with her friends. There were terrific activities too – Brownies, drama, gymnastics – and, of course, her weekly fix of horse riding. So with Amy settling in, it was time to focus on Dale, who had an exciting agenda of his own.

# 3

## *Transitions*

So what was that agenda for Dale? He wanted to attend Duncan Currie College, where he would study for a National Certificate (NC) in Early Education and Childcare. Back in 1991, I would have never dreamed that would be possible. Then, of course, Henry intervened and provided Dale with a precious lifeline which helped him communicate. Dale also had the advantage of being able to tap into our useful friends' expertise. Kenny Whylie taught Dale how to use a mobile phone. John Turner (whom Dale described as being as funny as Charlie Chaplin) enhanced Dale's love of music, and played to his sense of humour! Without these wonderful people and more, Dale's first seventeen years of life would have been very different. But Henry had been the best teacher of all. He alone spoke directly to his master.

That same year, 2006, Jim Taylor, the then head teacher of Struan School, explained this to us. When I found Henry for Dale and horses for Amy, we had recovered their lost jigsaw pieces, and those lost pieces can be found at any age. For anyone.[1]

We were as determined as Dale was to help him access college. When he qualified, he would have the same rights to employment as any others of his generation, but to get there, Dale had many more hurdles to overcome than most. Firstly, he had to cope with and integrate into a big college environment. Then, if he safely cleared that, there was money to understand and all the other trappings of the adult world. Our real work together was only just beginning!

Dale was eighteen when Henry died, and adulthood loomed large. I was determined that my son would attain real independence, but this was not something we could achieve alone. I must stress that he needed the many specialised skills of a variety of integrated services. In those fifteen years since his diagnosis I had come across a very extreme range of professional abilities and aptitudes. Some seemed to have almost no understanding of the implications of autism – for the individuals, for their families – and their contributions were utterly useless. Thankfully, most involved with Dale demonstrated that vital in-depth knowledge that we needed. These exceptional people had a life-changing input.

One such person was his local transitional social worker, Joyce Docherty. Her remit was to ensure that Dale received the support he needed to transfer from school to college. She would give him the toolkit to access all his state benefits so that he had an adequate income for his journey towards full financial independence. Dale had much to learn about the complexities of money, its value and how to manage finances responsibly. He was not going to be subsidised by his family forever. Working with me alone on this would have been something of an own goal. We needed the right professional, in a separate place. Joyce was a shining example of how real awareness makes all the difference.

She arranged to see Dale at home, with me there. I reassured him that it was better for him to work with Joyce independently. I explained that his autism was a legally recognised disability, and how, as an adult, he would be able to find the right professional support for himself and his sister. I knew that the day would come when he alone would be the next of kin, responsible for Amy's well-being. He needed to know where to access support and services for both of them when we were no longer around.

Dale accepted all this and was completely comfortable meeting Joyce for that first time. Like any good practitioner, she took nothing for granted – always the best policy when supporting an adult with autism. After this successful icebreaker, she invited Dale to meet her for a coffee, so they could get to know one another better. Secure in this setting too, Joyce was able to explain in detail how she could help him access his benefits. This worked ideally for Dale, who might have felt quite differently in a busy, clinical office. Not only that, but he experienced a successful social outing, which did wonders for his self-esteem.

Alas, outwith Joyce's control, the road to financial independence was to be bumpy and frustrating. You'd have hoped that accessing state benefits would have been made easier for Dale, given his circumstances and the support of the DDA, but it proved far more difficult than even I had feared. Dale needed what was then Incapacity Benefit, but to qualify he had to attend an assessment. This was a generic, one-size-fits-all medical to determine if Dale's autism matched their criteria. His diagnosis of a lifelong condition meant nothing. Joyce liaised with Prospects, an autism-specific adult support service run by the NAS. They provided autism-trained support workers and advocates for clients like Dale, helping them through the process. He was accompanied at his medical by Anna Williamson and Billy Docherty of Prospects, to help speak for him and explain any of the ambiguities certain to occur. The NAS was aware of hundreds like Dale failing this medical. Truly, the failure did not lie with these young adults. The system failed them. To this day, medical assessments are carried out by doctors and nurses employed by Atos Healthcare, a private company funded by the Department of Work and Pensions.[2]

Dale's anxieties on the day threatened to overwhelm him. He told me later that, without the advocacy of Anna and Billy, he would never have coped. Without them, it would have been three people behind a big desk, him, and no explanation whatsoever. By his own account, it was intimidating and scary. He explained the extent of his embarrassment and his demoralisation, being bombarded by demeaning and obscure questions.

Can you answer the phone?
The ever-literal Dale replied, "Yes, I can."

I thank the heavens for Anna and Billy. Unquestionably, without them Dale would have been added to that enormous pile marked Failed. On and on for an hour, more ambiguous, unrelated questions, as some doctor's tick-box sheet filled up. Perhaps the final straw of so many final straws that day was this:

How long have you been sick?

On Wednesday, 10 May 2006, Dale was lucky enough to be awarded his benefit.

In 2008, the government took steps in recognising the system's flaws, stating "no one should be written off," and changed Incapacity Benefit to Employment Support Allowance. Allegedly, this was giving "more money to those facing barriers to work and more support to those seeking work". A great initiative in principle, but unfortunately, this new template still doesn't fit adults with autism; it excludes and discriminates them still more.[3]

Benefits in place, however, and with Joyce's support – a couple of coffee meetings on – Dale had a decent income for college. Her next task was to help him get a travel card for subsidised public transport use, allowing him greater freedom, without worries about costs. Dale began to socialise more with this. He'd nip into town to browse and shop; he'd take the train to see his best friend Ryan, and he was no longer dependent on us for that twenty-mile trip.

The NAS campaign Think Differently about Autism proved timely for Dale. Launched to raise awareness of autism among the general public, one of its principal thrusts was: should an adult with ASD find themselves in a crisis situation, in public, they would have a support strategy. In partnership with The Scottish Society for Autism (now Scottish Autism) and related organisations, they launched the Autism Alert Card. Carrying this proved a godsend for Dale and his peers, providing real reassurance in potentially precarious situations – in the event of police involvement, for example. Each individual's card is registered with a resource centre and endorsed by the police. It details the difficulties the card carrier experiences through their autism and the official dealing with the adult can contact the resource centre to access any information and support required.

Thankfully, in the five years that Dale carried his card, he never actually had to put it to the test, but simply having it made an enormous difference. As his parents we never subsidised Dale at all. He bought all his own clothes, DVDs or CDs. He paid for Henry's food and insurance. Boy, he learned the value of money, as well as how to manage it responsibly, and quickly!

Within months, Dale went from having little understanding of money to miserdom! Shopping to buy his own snacks, sweets and drinks, he became adept at finding the best deals. Often, he'd comment on prices. If I had to borrow money from him to pay the window cleaner, Dale would hound me until I repaid him. What a turnaround! For years, I had never needed to reimburse him, because he would simply forget, money had meant nothing to him.

Having helped Dale bridge his financial issues, Joyce's next challenge was to support the crossing between school and college life, a major transition. Some transitions are so simple – painting a classroom another colour, a changed room layout, new furniture, the arrival of a different teacher. However, major transitions like leaving the familiar secondary school to the navigation of a big, college environment had to be addressed and planned months ahead. The NAS recommendation for anyone with autism about to experience a major transition is "that the seed be sown and strategies implemented a full year before the actual event". Accordingly, I always took simple steps early with both children to help them accept significant life events. The year before Dale went to secondary school, I drove him past Gourock High, showing him the building's exterior and explaining that this was the big school, where he would go after Primary 7, with all his friends. Periodically, I would stop, letting Dale observe the hoards flowing out of the massive buildings at the day's end. He commented on things like their different uniform and how many more pupils there were there. Similarly, in preparation for post-school study, at fourteen Dale enrolled in a junior car mechanic leisure course – two terms at Duncan Currie College. The course itself was the least important aspect of that. Most importantly, he became comfortable and familiar with the college. Thus, without pressure, Dale learned that this college was likely to be the next stage after school. Taking these measures was not a substitute for adequate planned transitional strategies between the school and the college staff. They happened too!

Again, Dale was privileged, being a client of Prospects. Although Joyce's involvement with Dale had concluded, she would ring him occasionally, checking his progress, reminding him she was always there. Furthermore, she liaised with the Prospects Students' Support Service Officer, Anna – just in case!

Presently, the NAS has secure funding to sustain four Prospects employment consultancy centres in the UK, in London, Manchester, Sheffield and Glasgow. It is designed to help adults with high-functioning autism and Asperger's syndrome handle difficult situations like the transition into further education, and issues arising during college and university study. Another vital role is the provision of a unique, internationally renowned service, assisting adults with ASD secure permanent employment. Prospects was established in recognition of the wealth of talent available at the higher end of the spectrum, the "Undiscovered Workforce". Dale and his ASD peers have so many exceptional skills, making them potentially ideal employees in certain specialist fields.

Dale observes in great detail, identifying errors neuro-typical people might miss. Usually, people on the spectrum are blessed with an excellent memory. They tend to be conscientious and persistent, often achieving tremendous results. Someone with ASD may be better at a particular job than someone without it! My own son has exceptional insight into how children develop and learn to communicate, and his is a unique empathy for the child with a disability – yes, I believe, more than many of his non-autistic work colleagues!

Many high on the spectrum are very intelligent and well educated. Dale and his peers are meticulous regarding routine, rules and accuracy. Generally they are reliable, hardworking, with the potential to excel in professions like accountancy, engineering and computer sciences. Others like repetitive tasks, both basic and complex, and so are capable of succeeding in areas like IT and administration. Prospects has strong evidence that people with ASD are often motivated workers, thriving in structured, well-organised workplaces. They have great attendance records, potentially lower staff turnover rates. Adults like Dale have the capacity for lengthy, undistracted task focus, following policy to the letter. Dale has never been late for work – actually, he's always early! Merely being on time would induce too much anxiety, so just starting on time for him means . . . being late! This group could never wrongly phone in sick or take a day off. The pressure of lying would be overwhelming. Imagine a world and workforce with all these personal and business qualities! How many millions might that save employers and our economy?

Prospects is committed to supporting the employee, and the employer. Before its establishment, the success rate for their client group in securing long-term work was dire. Even now, only 15 per cent of UK adults with autism are in full-time employment, and only 13 per cent in permanent employment in Scotland. The NAS has revealed that 51 per cent of the UK group has been unemployed without accessing state benefits. Appallingly, 10 per cent of this figure has been in this position for a decade, or more. Compounding this, 61 per cent of those out of work say they want to work, and 79 per cent of those adults in receipt of Incapacity Benefit say they would prefer to be working.[4]

If this continues, what is the future for Amy and her peers? Despite early intervention and improved condition-specific education, is society setting up that generation to fail? Prospects is helping lessen that gap but, as always, funds are insufficient to meet needs. In the past five years, enquiries seeking their support have increased by 300 per cent. Formal referrals have doubled. The effect on the Exchequer generated by Prospects includes reduced benefit payments, income tax and national insurance contributions, accumulating to over £500,000 saved! Many of Prospects' clients have secured permanent employment, becoming highly valued workers.

Dale was lucky. With one-to-one support from them, Prospects ensured he suffered no discriminatory practices. We were to discover later that plenty of organisations have found legal loopholes. Blatant discrimination is still rife.

All this was still far out on the horizon for Dale. Studying at college and working two full days a week in a mainstream nursery, Dale needed to learn good work ethics. The support he received from Prospects was vital. Thanks to Joyce, Dale had the financial security. Now he had to navigate Duncan Currie College!

Prospects Students' Support Service took Dale through every aspect of the transition. Step by step, Dale learned the differences between the two learning environments. They worked on details like his college rising time, his journey, lunchtime arrangements, where he sat in class and study plans. Visual timetables and support notes were formulated – again, nothing was left to chance. With Anna's help, he met the staff at the college beforehand. As a result, one of the tutors offered a great initiative to help Dale's confidence and one that would ensure that he was 100 per cent certain that he wanted to study in that area.

To give him insight into college life and allow tutors to get to know him, Dale became part of a National Certificate class. The college tutor arranged for him to participate informally in the NC class for three months. I felt so hopeful for his future at college. Despite his initial anxieties, the transition was effortless and such a success that with

Prospects' help he was accepted to start on the NC course in September 2006. Dale was probably the first person with recognised severe autism to study on this course. Indeed, we suspected the first in this field, in the country.

To ensure that he was fully prepared for college study and nursery placements, Prospects put him through an intensive, six-week Personal Development Programme. Again this was a huge commitment, highly detailed, covering many aspects of personal progression. He learned team-building and workplace health and safety, the management of his own condition and issues involved in disclosing his autism to an employer. He was made aware of equal opportunities and his rights under the DDA 1995. He was taught, in depth, workplace relations and effective communication skills.

Dale, like many affected by ASD, would have to face many anxiety-inducing situations, therefore Prospects taught him coping strategies, so much so, that I found that he managed crises better than I did! Often when I lost the plot, Dale took control, calming the situation. Everything was covered: interview success skills, how to dress, greet people, awareness of non-verbal communication – everything!

In effect, Dale, aged eighteen, was given personal skills and work ethics that many neuro-typicals would envy. He was provided with visual handouts for reference and future revision. Prospects gave him all the strategies he needed to thrive as a successful team member. He was able to identify and manage potential problems: an unhappy parent's complaint, staff meetings, the consequences of not passing on important information, and more.

Lastly, Prospects gave Dale an appraisal. Unsurprisingly he had excelled: "Dale fully completed both courses and throughout his referral period, he showed that he is extremely hardworking … evident in the way he applied himself to all the coursework. He was punctual throughout and showed a level of maturity and consideration for others beyond his years. 16 March 2006."

Additionally, he received help from the College Learning Support staff. All the DDA adjustments that Dale had received at Gourock High School for exams and curricular access would be implemented by the college, or so we thought! These were: extra time in exams, a scribe and a prompt if needed. Spelling and grammar mistakes were not to be taken into account, presuming the factual content was accurate. These learning adjustments, according to the college policy, would be provided, agreed and noted within a Learning Support care plan. He would receive a copy of this.

Throughout those two terms, Dale never did receive his copy.

This would be my first major mistake with the college. It was less important during his NC course; he had my support and problem-solved well, but by taking my eye off the ball, there were to be devastating future consequences. Supporting and fighting Dale's corner all those years, I had taken nothing for granted. For the first time ever, I thought I could relax! Never again! At the time, juggling a home, nursing, dealing with a second child with autism, helping other parents, I slipped up. Big mistake! Yet, so many good things were happening.

Dale's friends also attended the college. Scott, David and Matthew met up with him at breaks, and they would go into town together for lunch, just as they had at school. They formed a rock band, practising in a local community recording studio. A rock band in the habit of using our home to test its soundproofing! Dale continued to spend time with his "autism friends" too: Ryan, his best friend since St Anthony's Communication Base days, and three other classmates, Frank, George and Simon. All these boys had been every bit as challenging and affected as Dale had been, but had benefited from the same condition-specific education. They too were now fully communicative, leading productive, independent lives.

Ryan was studying engineering at an internationally renowned corporate organisation; Frank, art and design in Glasgow; George, music and production; and Simon was in sound production (he also worked voluntarily in a local radio station). All these boys accessed support from Prospects. Unsurprisingly, all thrived. Dale balanced his two very different sets of friends and, socially, he never stopped. Dale's ASD friends were so mature. Comfortably acknowledging their autism, they called themselves The A-Team, after the TV series! They also formed a rock band but struggled to find a name – and were seriously annoyed that another band had grabbed the name Spectrum! During one practice, a delighted Dale told me that they had, at last, agreed on a name. I was forced to intervene. These lovely boys were sometimes let down subtly by their ASD.

"Mum, we've decided to call ourselves Out of Depth!"

I replied that that was interesting, but did they know the meaning of the expression? Dale replied, "No, Mum, we just liked the sound of it."

Diplomatically, I explained that the phrase might have negative connotations. All five were relieved. Soon they became Perfect Criminals, very rock band!

The A-Team Saturday visits became so regular that I often left them alone whilst I shopped with Amy. The first time I did this, I remember pausing, realising that I had left my home in the hands of five autistic adults. Unlike leaving five neuro-typical teenagers, however, I could trust all the lads completely, because of their autism. Every one of them had the advantages of excellent parenting and good condition-specific education. It was not lost on me that if these five boys hadn't had autism I would have felt differently.

Dale's involvement with the two bands meant he went to many rock concerts with both sets of friends. Ironically, much of their musical taste leaned towards classic rock from my era – Alice Cooper, Zebrahead, Journey and Iron Maiden – in addition to contemporary bands like Less Than Jake, Blink-182 and The Killers. I loved The Killers too, and even through my hard times, I have always enjoyed new music, and Dale has loved sharing his music with me.

All five of these incredible, successful boys, as children, had been locked in autism, terrified, unable to communicate or cope with our world. Eighteen years on, they were all enjoying a normal quality of life, fitting in, contending with difficulties like the enormous crowds, noise and sensory overload of massive rock concerts. All five were determined to find permanent future employment. Undeniably, they are living proof of the merits of early diagnosis and the right education – intensive, expensive, but worth it! When society and governments recognise this, how different life could be.

Dale was fortunate; he accessed extra home support for his studies from an organisation called Lead Scotland, who provided a learning support adult. Luckily, the young woman assigned, Sandra Miller, already knew Dale and was a real asset. On a weekly basis, she helped him study, plan, and present coursework and assignments properly.

Throughout the early part of the course Dale seemed to be adjusting well. His two-day work placement was in a privately-run nursery, Rising Fives, within Moorfoot School. This was Amy's local school and a mere ten-minute walk from home. The nursery head, Karen, and her staff really embraced Dale as a student, understanding his autism and recognising his success and progress. Secure in their support, he became an important team member.

Out shopping one day, I met Karen, who went out of her way to tell me how well Dale had fitted in, how pleasant and hardworking he was. She was delighted to have him in tow, and even more significantly for us, the children had really bonded well with him, with his calm and patient manner. We were humbled. Dale would often create his own play resources for the children, spending hours devising them at home. Once, as part of a healthy-eating activity, he bought a selection of coloured cardboards, to let the children choose fruit cut-outs for colouring, for a fruit bowl collage. Jamie and I sat for ages, helping Dale draw and cut out. He regularly made play dough, adding food colouring and glitter. This delighted Amy, because he would make extra for her so she could make her horses. My kitchen was a bomb site, but I didn't mind. It was a treat, just seeing Dale in his element.

Another time, when we walked Henry at Greenock's Battery Park, we heard a little voice shouting, "Dale! Dale!" A hundred metres away was a very excited little girl, determined to get his attention. Recognising her as one of the Moorfoot children, he gave her a big wave.

A different time, in a local shopping mall, a shy girl was so determined to say hello, and I saw first-hand how natural he was with her, immediately kneeling down to her eye level, telling her calmly that it was nice to see her, and how he liked her lovely dress, A happy wee girl left, saying, "Bye-bye, Dale! See you at nursery."

Things seemed to be going so well. Dale was studying hard and had a natural understanding of child development and disability awareness. A major aspect of early years childcare is the support of children with additional support needs. Dale's Prospects education enhanced his innate understanding; additionally, he continued to volunteer for Barnardo's, which held regular training sessions in these areas. Barnardo's also gave him training in delicate subjects like challenging behaviour and child protection, including sexual abuse – considerable assets in his course. During school holidays he helped at their play schemes as a volunteer support worker. The children ranging in ages from five to eighteen each had a recognised disability – undoubtedly some had autism.

Dale's first Barnardo's summer play scheme was a trip to Glasgow Green. He came home, totally knackered and collapsed on the sofa.

"Mum, please, don't disturb me. I was partnered with a child with autism today, a bolter. The kid never stopped all day. Please! Please! Let me sleep."

Before his head hit the cushion I couldn't resist! "Well, Dale, now you know how I felt. Every day."

Struggling to stay awake, he replied, "Mum, I don't know how you've done it. It's really hard work and . . ."

Before he could finish, he had drifted off into a deep sleep!

Despite his exhaustion (and big wake-up call), Dale continued to help out at other play schemes, becoming a regular volunteer support worker at Barnardo's weekly drama group. The children had a similarly diverse range of disabilities, but thankfully for Dale, they were all under one roof. As he appeared to be coping well, in the run up to Christmas 2006 I was able to take a back seat in supporting him. This felt good. Anyway, there was an important project I had been involved in, and it was about to go public.

When Dale's severe autism was recognised in 1992, I wanted desperately to try to make a difference to the cause and to help other parents in my situation. I had always been heavily involved in support groups, awareness campaigns for the NAS and for Scottish Autism. It was all a great experience but my efforts never seemed to reach the masses or achieve as much as I would have liked. The work and commitment involved was overwhelming. Nevertheless, it was always worth it.

Dale and Henry's story broke in 1995, when I won a short story writing competition. I could never have dreamed how it would change all of our lives forever – and not just ours, but the lives of thousands of others affected by autism. At the time there was vast media interest in Dale's story, eventually leading to one of the best projects I would ever participate in, one which would raise autism awareness to 6.5 million people in the UK mainstream alone.

For the next nine years, I worked closely with the screenwriter, Lindsey Hill. Nine script drafts later, *After Thomas*, the ITV drama of our story, emerged. Henry's name had to be changed to Thomas as there had been too many film industry projects called *After Henry*. The production company at Hartswood films, together with the incredible passion of the producer, Elaine Cameron, secured the first airing, on Boxing Bay 2006, going head to head with *Pirates of the Caribbean*!

I was the sole autism adviser and story consultant for the script and I was thrilled my efforts were recognised in the credits. I will never forget that night, excitement tinged with horrendous anxiety. I downed a bottle of wine, knowing the enormity of the night. This needed to raise awareness appropriately amongst the mainstream audience, yet please the autistic world too.

The broadcast exceeded all my expectations. *After Thomas* was adored by the press, the mainstream and the autistic world. Hartswood was inundated with emails from parents complimenting the accuracy of the portrayal and how it had, at last, helped raise awareness for their own children. Professionals in the field also contacted Hartswood seeking copies for teaching aids. The film received Best International Film at the Shanghai Film Festival, and due to the press reviews and public demand, came out on DVD.

I received a nominal fee for my work on the film, but did not feel entirely comfortable in profiting from it. Everything the drama achieved meant so much more. Nevertheless, it was good to be able to donate a little sum to the two major autism charities. Then I realised that Amy and her school friends could benefit too.

In Amy's school, I noticed the playground, once lined out with hopscotch games, netball court and cycling track, had become faded to the point of being barely visible. So with some of my fee, I arranged to get the whole school playground revamped, giving the children some new motivation to play games again. Amy and her chums loved the results! It felt great, giving something back to Amy's peers, her fantastic role models.

I'd be lying if I said it was all good, though. There was one fly which kept surfacing in the ointment. I could sense that Jamie didn't share all of my joy. Was it too much of a public periscope on our family life? After all, we'd had years of people pointing us out in the street when Dale was tiny and one of those autism incidents happened. Why was it always in a busy street? Maybe that was it ... I kept trying to reason – too much, just too much. We all need privacy, after all. Maybe it was too great an invasion. I tried to sort it out in my head, and I tried to ask him, but some evenings the paper was up, like some barrier between us. The sports section seemed to take an awful lot of reading. Maybe

I was imagining it. We were both really tired, after all, and sometimes it was getting a bit like that scene in *Gregory's Girl*. We were passing each other on the stairs having hardly seen each other some days. "Yeah, Jamie, we must catch each other. What about a chat, say breakfast, the kitchen table, tomorrow?" We were just too busy. Far too busy. I pushed it to the back of my head, with the potato peelings in the sink and the never-ending to do list. As usual, what was to be done? I got on with it. The ripples from the film were unstoppable.

With the screening of *After Thomas*, Dale's neuro-typical friends, Scott, Matthew and David learned for the first time – in the five years of knowing him – of Dale's autism. Not only were they disbelieving that Dale had autism, they were shocked, and they took some convincing that a drama had been made of his story.

Dale's best friend Scott commented, "Nuala, Dale was a nightmare when he was a wee boy!" I know he used much stronger words to Dale, personally!

With the story in the public domain it was so reassuring that his group of his friends remained the same. In fact, they were really proud of him and impressed by all that he had achieved. Dale understood that a major part of his success was down to these superb boys being his friends in the first place. We owe them that, forever.

# 4

# *Calm Before the Storm*

January 2007. Dale was thriving at college, but for one niggle. His course included an optional Higher, with the necessary adjustments: extra time and a scribe to allow for his poor fine-motor skills. His confidence was such that he decided he no longer needed a scribe for the exam, but on the big day, a despondent, frustrated Dale sloped home.

"What's wrong, Dale?"

"Mum, the questions were meaningless. I had to guess what they were asking."

Rather like a bilingual student, Dale had yet to master some of the subtleties of written English. Unlike them, however, he was not allowed to bring a dictionary into exams. Often, he would struggle with a word for ten minutes and more, then make a wild guess.

His worst fears materialised. He received no award for that Higher. We were advised that no individual adjustments in the exam wording could be made, but that he should appeal on the basis of his successful prelim. It seemed odd that we were left to instigate this procedure, but nonetheless we did it. Unsuccessfully.

Thankfully, he didn't need the Higher for his overall qualification, and it neither stopped his progress nor dampened his enthusiasm. The garden was rosy indeed. On his last day at Rising Fives Nursery, Dale was so present-laden he could barely totter through our front door! The staff was generous, and the children had made a big card. It did wonders for his self-esteem. There were even individual handmade cards from the little ones, and the parents joined the avalanche of good wishes. Dale blossomed. He was a team member, his value recognised. All this, and he had his NC qualification to boot!

His next hurdle was to progress to HNC level, in order to qualify him for work in mainstream nurseries. The interview process geared up, and we waited for Dale's call ... and waited. In the final weeks of the session, his mood changed. He grew withdrawn and depressed. It was difficult to open up the conversation. When I did, I was unprepared for his bombshell.

"Mum, one of the tutors has been talking to me for a while, suggesting that I shouldn't apply for the HNC course. It feels like I'm being picked on."

I needed to know more. I opened my mouth, already formed with the name "Dale", ready to ask, but I wasn't the first.

"Dale, why do you feel you're being picked on? Dale, is it your clothes? Is it that shirt? Is it something on the shirt? I don't think that's okay."

It could have been funny, but it wasn't. I needed to hear Dale, and this wasn't the time for an Amy interrogation.

"Amy, have you seen The Punter this week? It's on the table."

"I'll have to see it, but, Nuala, Dale, what was she picking? Nuala, what ..."

Thank God I'd that new horse book at hand. Thank God. I don't think I'd ever have heard her brother. This was important. I scurried Amy off to the kitchen.

Dale was still there, waiting, head down. "She says I have come as far as I can at NC."

It transpired that the tutor had interrupted a lecture, pulling Dale out into the corridor for a chat. What Dale was hearing was that the HNC would give him problems with self-confidence because of all the extra support he required! She suggested that he would be well advised to seek a position as a support worker in a private nursery, as he'd cope better with that level of responsibility. Poor Dale accepted her judgements. I was pleased that he was opening up, but I certainly wasn't taking it!

Who had done what he had? Who had his knowledge, his experience? I reminded him of exactly where he had started, and told him that no one was about to take away his future! I ensured he would receive more comprehensive learning support, assisted by Prospects' Students Support Services. To try to resolve matters, we met with the college staff, and were reassured to hear Mr Ross, from the Learning Support Department, encourage Dale to apply for the HNC, with all the backup and adjustments he needed. It was going swimmingly until . . . there was a loud knock! Enter that same tutor who had been speaking to Dale! Having apologised for her interruption, she began to put in what she termed her "tuppence worth". That "tuppence worth" was a repetition of her talk to Dale!

We gave her our time, and our unanimous thumbs down! Dale sat, calm and composed throughout. He was by no means the least able in his class, and he knew it! Why then was he the only one not offered an interview? I was relieved when she left. Mr Ross gave Dale a copy of the HNC placement manual, saying, "It's very confusing and difficult to decipher exactly what you're meant to be doing, but I am sure you will get help."

It was easy enough to encourage Dale that he was on track, and yet, when he came home that day: "Mum, when you left, the tutor spoke to me again and gave me the same talk, but I remembered what you told me and just ignored her, but it angers me. I think this is all because of my autism."

Naturally, despite our efforts, he was still unsure whether or not to apply for the course. We sought help from Anna Williamson, who informed the college of her role and how Prospects would assist. The situation being precarious, she attended Dale's informal interview, recording: "I met with Dale before the interview, and he was very anxious [. . .] considering some of the issues [. . .] arising, regarding staff commenting on his suitability for the course."

She explained he could be helped by a student support practitioner, and helpfully outlined all the support available – on the wording of assignments, getting notes before classes, obtaining software and equipment, and he would have help with his presentation skills. Further, he would have additional support on placement, and autism awareness training would be made available from Prospects, should staff there wish it.

Anna's summary of their meeting showed a return to confidence for Dale, but it included a chilling note. She observed that, though Dale knew he had not managed sufficient detail in his written answers: "I wonder whether this had been raised with Dale earlier on in the placement ... He would benefit from regular feedback and encouragement, moreover from these sorts of problems [might be avoided if] ... highlighted earlier on."

Indeed! Anna put her promises into action, ensuring that Dale received Disabled Student's Allowance. The support plan in place, we looked forward to a happy summer break. There were three big events in the offing:

The first was the publication of my book, *A Friend Like Henry*.

The writing had not been easy. The emotional journey was draining and challenging. It took everything, but I was determined – and that was just the storyline!

I had no idea how to use a computer, and everything I know now was learned on that job. Thankfully, Jamie helped me, but I felt guilty knowing that I tested his patience. He was Mr Technology, a keyboard whizz. He tried but became increasingly frustrated by my ineptitude. We argued. We argued more. Cracks in our relationship were certainly appearing. I started to acknowledge painful aspects of our life together that I had never faced, going right back to the time of Dale's birth. I needed him to get me and my book where we needed to be. I had years to expose, people to reach. I plugged away. We needed to pull together. We couldn't. Every page was hell. No, every comma, every full stop, was hell. Somehow, I don't know how, it was there, in print, in covers on shelves. We made it. Just.

You cannot imagine how I felt, seeing my book in print. Or perhaps you can.

Almost immediately, the response overwhelmed me. It became a *Sunday Times* bestseller and was celebrated by the mainstream, autistic and dog lovers' worlds alike. I received so many letters and emails. Telling Dale's story had made the difference we had hoped. And it was worth every curse over every comma.

The next few weeks were a whirl of promotions, conferences, signings, TV appearances and talks. Professionals in the field told us the book had changed their practice. Quiet Dale proved a natural with an audience, his personality and humour shone out. As the praise and empathy poured in, I felt life couldn't get much better.

Our second big event was an opportunity for Dale to broaden his horizons, in more ways than one! Isobel, a local minister and family friend, put his name forward for selection for the Stavros S. Niarchos crew, part of the Tall Ships' Youth Trust. Dale was up for it! He was selected after an interview with Inverclyde Community Learning Team. Thrilled, we pulled out all the stops to make certain he raised the £1,000 needed. Fundraising was a compulsory component of the project. Everyone rallied round, and we raised the entire sum in one night, which was also an excuse to have a rare, fun time with close family and good friends.

We had a social night at home, but not with tea and buns or cheese and wine – no, we tapped into the array of talents and the kindness around us. Our Pirate Party! Free entertainment, food and drinks, but with a catch! Everyone had to dig deep for the raffle and there was an open bucket for donations. Dale's lifelong "social role model", our close friend John Turner, took charge. It ran like clockwork.

Cleared of seats, the lounge grew a dance floor, while the kitchen became a proper bar area, from which guests were banned! Everyone queued to be served by John's two teenage sons, in suitably piratical gear. There was a wee sign: Please tip the poor students. Those boys earned their chest of doubloons! Friends of ours who played in successful bands gave their time and we put their fee in Dale's bucket – a great start. Another friend, local shopkeeper Christine Gunn, donated many high-quality prizes, and raised £500 at her store. The fundraising even made the *Greenock Telegraph*, which had once upon a time covered Dale's childhood story.

On the big night, our house was a pirate's haven: the band blared out great music and even the non-dancing Dale danced! Mid-evening, he joined the band with his guitar for an impromptu cover, earning him massive applause. The in-house comedian and compere was, of course, John, who commandeered the mike like a professional. His lovely assistant was my dear friend Eleanor, and between them they worked the floor!

Later, Amy donned her French chef's apron with matching hat and I silenced the room. She announced, "Ladies and gentlemen, the buffet is now being served. Please eat up, or the chef will be upset."

Amy and the other kids carried trays like little waiters, doing us proud. What a night! More importantly, it raised £927.54, so his total fundraising total overran by £400. However, by donating all the money, another young crew member benefitted.

A few weeks later, we waved Dale off at Newcastle to sail to Cherbourg. Only the ship's staff was informed of the autism, allowing them to make adjustments and ensure his safety. He was a member of the "White Watch" and had to pitch in at mealtimes, scrub decks, and participate in night duties. Everyone was expected to attempt to scale the rigging to the crow's nest. Naturally, they were kitted out with safety harnesses, but the bold Dale reached the top without batting an eyelid! On other occasions, he climbed the masts' steep ladders, harness-free but wearing a life vest, to unfurl sails. With one slip, he would have been in the sea. Thankfully, had that happened, he was able to swim like a fish! With his determination to succeed and to fit in, he fulfilled all that the captain required. His crew member's assessment from the chief officer confirmed: "Dale is a key member of the watch, who is always on hand to help and has been up for all the challenges that a sail training vessel provides."

He was scored well for effort, his attitude to supervision, and for his reactions under pressure he was deemed *Satisfactory*. He was similarly valued as a team worker and praised for his communication, learning, problem-solving and team management. What a report for anyone, let alone someone with all his challenges! And what a boost to his confidence.

Dale brought back an interesting tale from his voyage. Prior to the trip, I had donated a signed copy of my book for the raffle which was won by a young crew member. The girl read it in her time off, and was pleasantly shocked to discover how severe Dale's autism had been. She was astounded that Dale was one of the crew. The significance of that was not lost on any of us.

The third exciting event for our family was the arrival of our long-awaited golden retriever puppy. Wee Henry had, by now, enjoyed two years of being top dog, but we felt the need to have a second dog in the household, and knew that the canine company would be good for Henry too.

We called the newcomer Thomas, not only after the train, in line with our Henrys, but also after the drama of our story. He was cute, with such a winning face, but from day one we discovered he was quite a different character! Unlike his dependable train namesake, this Thomas couldn't be trusted! My belief is that when selecting a dog for a child with autism, puppies should be avoided, and Thomas was proof in a fur coat. A fully mature dog with a suitable temperament should be introduced to the child, to fit the family's life. This reduces all the hassle and avoids worrying, unpredictable puppy behaviours. After the publication of my book, many parents contacted me, having bought a puppy. Invariably it would prove disastrous, and many puppies were returned to their breeders. Thomas educated me on how difficult a puppy can be, but we adored him. While he became the most affectionate golden retriever I have ever known, he was also the most troublesome, badly behaved dog in the world!

As ever, the first problem was house training. As both Henrys had mastered this within a couple of weeks, we had high hopes, but we endured six long months of intensive toilet training before Thomas's penny dropped. Then there was an added nightmare.

Thomas had an irritable bowel and we were on tenterhooks whenever he ate. What went in came out at high velocity less than an hour later. Many veterinary visits, innumerable stool samples, and trial and error dietary changes later, Nigel confirmed that Thomas had rare metabolic protein intolerance. He needed a specialised, and very expensive, dry food to manage his condition. Thankfully, for the atmosphere in our home and for what remained of our carpets, the food worked. Worth every penny!

Thomas created more havoc and mischief in his first eighteen months than the two Henrys ever had. It was akin to parenting a nightmare child. We told everyone he had the same gene pool as the famous Labrador Marley. Had we been able to obtain an ASBO for him, we would have done. In fact, we'd have sold him on eBay! That one-dog vandalism team cost us a fortune! However, he was also the cuddliest, most emotional sponge of a dog we had ever owned. He stayed and we coped, with a large dollop of humour! He was family. He kept us in stitches, and was a willing workhorse for the ever-resourceful Amy.

Once, I became aware that she was in her room "playing" with him. He was sitting contentedly inside her toy stable, with the door firmly bolted. She, meanwhile, had absconded to the garden! On his head, he modelled a pair of her shocking pink knickers, allegedly resembling a racing horse's headgear. He seemed to find them quite fetching. He was quite happy to bolt, adornments still in place!

He was also the worst chewer and digger we have ever known – nothing was safe. From the outset, like Amy, he over bonded and couldn't cope alone, despite having Henry around. He thwarted all my efforts. Nothing worked. Left for even ten minutes, Thomas would find something to destroy. His targets included letters, newspapers, shoes and socks, but his real favourites were knickers (clean or worn), my makeup and brushes, or anything else from my dressing table. Perhaps his pièce de résistance was his theft of the toilet bag containing my sanitary products. I discovered its disappearance when I went to the back garden. Thomas was enjoying a party, chewing the contents, one by one. How lovely for my neighbours to see that, despite my mature years, I was still fertile!

Spectacles were another special – designer ones were a blast! Amy's horses or stable dolls – nothing was out of bounds. Eventually, everywhere I went, Thomas went too. This got around the problem, but solved nothing. It certainly didn't cover his fun with food.

Before I cooked, I had to round up utensils from wherever Thomas had secreted them. If a visitor arrived, the fiendish hound would retrieve a carving knife from his hoard and run around excitedly, the blade protruding from his mouth, sideways. He found everything, and ate anything! A whole frozen chicken, a 12" spicy pizza, a whole box of chocolates. You name it, that dog devoured it! Christmas and Easter were particular feast days for him. He left nothing but a trail of foil!

It scares me to think about the amount of chocolate he's consumed over the years, as human chocolate is extremely toxic to dogs. To feed his addiction, he acquired another skill – that of a master locksmith. He opened bedroom and wardrobe doors, sniffing out his treasures. I never did find a kitchen bin that was Thomas-proof. But somehow we adapted.

Out and about, I began to address the dogs as "the boys". Soon, both would return together when I shouted, "Boys." (It meant dinner or a biscuit, usually!) Dale had trained Henry to a high standard and we were amused to discover that that dog had developed a fine brain, too. There was real rivalry between the boys, jealousy even, but Henry ensured he was in control. Whenever Thomas was the centre of attention, Henry would retrieve a toy, tail at full throttle. He knew his rival would be distracted and take the toy. This let the senior dog move in and bask in the attention. Henry's tactic has never failed yet!

Curiously, Thomas's vandalism reminded me of the positive power a dog can have with an autistic child. When Dale was young, he tolerated Henry stealing his trains, even when the occasional one was damaged. We were never allowed that! Similarly, Amy became distressed if I moved one of her horses. As Thomas could find anything, he often helped himself to a toy horse or stable doll. Despite being sad at the loss of a beloved horse, or worse, Scott the farrier doll (who met a spectacularly gruesome end with the devil dog!), she coped. Intrigued, I had to ask them why.

Dale explained. "Henry stealing my trains and toys didn't upset me because I trusted him completely. His trusting face and all the qualities he had being a dog, like his soft fur, his gentle character, made me really comfortable with him. He didn't have all the complexities of unpredictable human faces, with their changing personalities."

Or as Amy told me: "It was because Thomas was a dog. I didn't want to upset him by being angry. But I would get angry with people, because they were grown-ups and should know how to behave better with my things."

One incident stands out. Years of dog ownership have given me a practical approach to interior design. I accepted emulsion walls everywhere. Dog drool and muddy tail marks were wipeable. We had a large drab hall and I decided, for once, I wanted something stylish. There was a beautiful designer paper I really liked. It was washable! No sooner had I lassoed a decorator than my hall was transformed. A fortnight later, I was rushing to collect Jamie from work. For once, I didn't take Thomas. He only had twenty minutes alone. On my return, Henry immediately caught my eye as he made his swift getaway to

Dale's room. He had his tail between his legs with a worried look on his face: *It wisnae me, and I'm oot o' here!*

Momentarily, I found this odd, and then I opened the door fully. The hall floor was knee-deep in large and small shredded pieces of my precious wallpaper. Two of the walls were completely stripped back to the emulsion. As I waded through the mess, screaming, the culprit was nowhere to be seen. When I entered the lounge, he was lying in the middle of the floor, with a large piece of wallpaper draped over his head. He continued to chew his way through even that, like an advert for a certain famous toilet roll.

I yelled again. "THOMAS, what have you done?"

Still trying to work out how he managed this devastation, his response was to make his way to the dog cupboard in the kitchen, sit, tail wagging in anticipation of his usual treat. No way – not on your life, pal!

When we investigated how he had managed to become a professional wallpaper stripper, we discovered that, as the paper had been pasted onto emulsion, the paste had been absorbed into the walls, leaving little dry, upturned corners. Enter Thomas!

Clearing up and eventually seeing the funny side, we tried not to catch sight of the mournful pooch, lying with a bemused look in his eyes. *Well, you would leave me on my own . . .*

Fortunately, we managed to get the same paper and Jamie even remembered the batch number. My hall was restored to its former glory. It was expensive, but truthfully the problem was easily resolved. A pity the same couldn't be said for Thomas's brain!

# 5

## *Eye of the Storm*

In September I attended the tenth anniversary celebration of Inverclyde Barnardo's Family Support Services, where Dale had been volunteering for eighteen months. His drama group was performing and I was invited as a service user, having benefitted from their befriender and sitter services, lifelines to us for so long. This event gave me some time out, meeting parents I hadn't seen in ages. It was great to catch up – and enjoy the superb buffet. While I was grazing, the father of a young boy told me how fond his son was of Dale, detailing what a change his support had made. Dale had become quite famous at Barnardo's. There was real appreciation that he wanted to return something for all he had received. He was inspirational!

Whilst there, I had the further joy of witnessing Dale support a physically disabled lad playing guitar. I was moved to see him guide and interact with the boy, while mindful to support the whole drama group as they entertained the audience. Truly, I thought he had the makings of a good teacher. As I waited for the performance to begin, I became aware of a shadowy figure a couple of rows behind – one Mary Smith, a spectre from fourteen years earlier. She had been Dale's educational psychologist and professional team leader when he was just two and a half. I was well aware of the pathway Mrs Smith and her ilk intended to pave for my son. What a quality of life that would have been! According to that lady, Dale was a child at risk of abuse from me. In Mrs Smith's view, he shouldn't have been allowed any future in my care.

*Mrs Gardner, I think you want your son to be autistic.*

She informed the local paediatrian that I had diagnosed Dale myself. Maybe I had. After all, who else managed? Accessing the right help in 1991 was the hell which nearly broke me.

That was twenty years before; surely conditions have changed. Sadly not. In November 2010 the *Sunday Times* uncovered the terrible tale of Elliot's family, in Hull. The parents of Elliot and Mason (five and two years old, respectively) moved their family from Hull to the East Riding of Yorkshire in a nightmarish three-day period in order to avoid Elliot being removed from the family and taken into care. The Hull authority used terms like "emotional abuse" and "bad treatment" by his mother, "resulting in developmental delay". Enquiries in the East Riding exonerated both parents, and their reading of their son's autism was confirmed diagnostically. Thankfully, with condition-specific education and one-to-one support, Elliot then thrived.

It is far from unique. I cannot count the letters and emails I have received, essentially outlining the same plight. And it shows how difficult and intractable this issue remains. We all love our children. Of course we do! Yet, somewhere in that exhausting, endless struggle to secure the basics when dealing with autism, it becomes hard to enjoy them and share that love. You don't need me to tell you that is wrong.

Before the performance, Martin Crew, Director of Barnardo's, gave an uplifting speech about their Inverclyde work. He was presenting awards, in recognition of staff commitment. Among them, to my delight, was our Barnardo's babysitter, Joanne, recognised for her ten years of dedicated service. There was one prestigious award left, the Volunteer of the Year. The recipient had to be nominated by a senior staff member and the competition was always of a very high standard. The award winner was a great example of all that Barnardo's stood for, of their ethos, encompassing diversity and inclusion – "giving children back their future". The winner was giving back his time, and channeling the adversity he himself had experienced. Barnardo's was privileged that he had chosen them.

"So without further ado, it gives me great pleasure to present this year's Volunteer of the Year award to ... Dale Gardner!"

The room exploded! I was bursting with pride and shed tears. However, knowing Dale didn't like fuss, I kept a low profile!

As he was about to embark on his HNC, with this on his CV, his career was beginning to take shape. It was no longer just a vague hope, somewhere. If this award gave me confidence in my son's future, I cannot begin to think what it did for him. Filled with that, and the knowledge that he was truly on his way, there could have been no happier winner that night.

In mid-September Dale started his course. I accompanied him to Motherwell College in Glasgow for a detailed assessment of his autism-related barriers in accessing the syllabus. Importantly, the evaluation would determine how these difficulties could be overcome, with specialised software and staff support strategies. The teacher assessing had a superb understanding. Watching, I was shocked to discover the extent to which his condition impacted on his learning ability. I learned so much that day, and both my children would benefit.

We had always known that Dale's poor fine-motor skills affected his writing, but I had never considered the difficulties he encountered in lectures. Note taking was nigh impossible because of his information processing difficulties. Whilst concentrating on his writing, he lost the understanding of the words. Copying from the whiteboard was another stumbling block. Dale would copy one word at a time, and fall behind in class. This was such a problem that at home he would rewrite his lecture notes. It was recommended that he should be given relevant notes in advance. A simple but effective adjustment.

He was given help sorting his course information and study planning to address his problematic organisational skills. Thankfully, Sandra (from Lead Scotland) continued to support him at home, and he had guidance from Prospects' Student Support Services. When accessing the Internet, some of the text on certain sites was a barrier. He was supplied with software developed for dyslexia. He was able to purchase all of this, including home training on the software, a Franklin System speaking dictionary and thesaurus, with his financial award from SAAS (Students Award Agency Scotland). However, of all the DDA learning adjustments highlighted that day, there was one paramount recommendation. Dale was awarded a generous package of extra human support, to ensure he suffered no disadvantage whatsoever. SAAS approved the employment of someone qualified to HNC level in early years childcare as a proofreader, and employed four hours of general support each week. The college could employ anyone – even a newly qualified student. There were plenty such people needing work. Alternatively, SAAS would pay any of the college tutors willing, at the same hourly rate. It was recommended throughout, should he need to take long lecture notes, he should have a note taker.

With these support measures identified, Dale and I felt he would cope. All staff would be made aware of his barriers to learning and be copied into the adjustments – there would be no confusion. Teaching staff were to be lenient regarding spelling, grammar, and the structure and style of his work, the emphasis being on the factual content. Dale could contact his tutors by email or by prior appointment to go over the contents of lectures or assignments. He was to receive all lecture handouts and information in electronic format, with time to read them. If he did not get the information beforehand, he was to be able to make photocopies of the lecture notes after. He would not have to ask for notes.

Dale was to be given a copy of his A4 placement folder electronically, giving him backup papers for all eventualities. The extra human support would help him decipher his assignments and understand what was required in his nursery tasks. For exams he was to have 25 per cent extra time, an interpreter, prompt, reader and scribe. He had flexibility in submitting assignments, providing he gave the lecturer forty-eight hours' notice should he be likely to miss a deadline. He would receive his assignments early, which would be proofread prior to marking. In total, Dale was awarded a comprehensive package of £5,199.49. Included in that sum, Duncan Currie College was granted £3,897 to utilise that funding.

With that support, I told Dale, there was no reason not to do well. It was up to him to study hard. In retrospect, I wish that I had scrutinised his adjustments in more detail and ensured they were being implemented. Had I taken the time to go through them properly with him, it would have avoided much of what he was to face, but he was doing so well and wanted greater independence . . . I took just a fleeting interest. The adjustments were formally documented. What could go wrong?

Waiting for the college to implement this, he purchased all the equipment, and a lovely lady, Annmarie, trained him on the new software. Well worth the £1,028 from the overall figure. However, it wasn't the start of things going well for Dale. Instead, he was in the eye of a storm.

At first, everything seemed to be going well. Sandra continued to visit weekly, helping Dale set out assignments and the like. That funding soon ran out. Officially she was unable to help, but she continued in her own time, as a friend. She knew that with the right guidance he could qualify, and she was adamant that his chances would not be compromised by a funding issue. Her generosity was to be a lifeline. Without it, Dale would have been unable to carry on. We will always be thankful for Sandra's integrity.

Prospects' Student Support Services complemented her support. Dale regularly visited a student support worker who helped him with study timetables and similar problems. His next hurdle was fitting into a new nursery placement two days a week. He was allocated a staff member there as his trainer, to guide him through the tasks in the confusing and difficult to decipher manual.

Nevertheless, with the human support, those problems were manageable. As Dale was a qualified NC childcare worker, he was, in turn, expected to support NC students on his placements. I thought this would be stressful, but he told me, "Mum, I don't mind helping new students, because I know how they feel. I'm used to working with new volunteers at Barnardo's, so I know I can deal with helping NC students and I already have."

Inverclyde has abundant local authority preschool nurseries, and many private ones. Gourock is a couple of miles out of Inverclyde's catchment area, and around fifteen miles from its furthest nursery. As Dale had already acquired practical experience in Rising Fives Nursery, a private provision, he needed to broaden his skills in a different environment. It was expected that he, like any student, would be placed near his home. However, at a meeting with Anna Williamson and a member of the learning support staff, one issue in particular troubled us: the proposed nursery placement. Dale was to be sent to a large local authority provision, in a socially challenged area, fifteen miles away. How was he to get to this placement on time twice a week? It would entail rising around 5 a.m., leaving forty minutes later, taking a bus to the train station, the train to Port Glasgow town centre, yet another bus, then a walk to the nursery! Anyone would be stressed travelling to a strange area, hoping all the transport connections would synchronise. Imagine what that would do to Dale, before arriving at a challenging environment to carry out a full day of responsible work?

It was suggested that providing him with (entitled) free transport might help, a local taxi for the whole journey. We were annoyed. Apart from the needless waste of public money, it undermined his hard-won independence with his travel card. The situation was unreasonable for any student, so we bore down on the tutors to provide an alternative. Eventually, Dale was assigned to another large mainstream local authority nursery. Glynhill, in the east end area of Greenock, was about eight miles away. Again, it was an area with many social challenges. We were all concerned that he had been given such a demanding placement. Whilst he was required to adapt to the situations children from various homes bring, he needed a nursery where he would not have added pressures. There were plenty such nurseries in Inverclyde.

Nevertheless, he was determined. He arrived at Glynhill punctually and ensured he kept up his perfect attendance record. This meant a rise at 7 a.m. sharp, although he did not start until 9. He kept strictly to his routine of a daily shower, and I ensured his royal blue college polo shirt was clean and ironed. Like many people with autism, Dale had a slight obsession with hygiene. Sometimes, when stressed, he would shower twice daily, until the hot water ran out. It helped alleviate some of his anxiety. Anyway, showering in a teenage lad was preferable to the aversion some have!

He left home at 7.40 a.m. on the dot for a bus to Greenock Town, then a connection to Glynhill. We gave him taxi money to ensure he got to Glynhill with time to spare, and reduced pressure. Weeks later, he chose to tell me that he walked the two miles from Greenock Town to Glynhill, only taking the taxi on rainy days. He pocketed the money, which I thought a fair cop – most astute!

It was such an exciting autumn for all of us. From my perspective, the positive book reviews continued and I received letters, both heart-wrenching and uplifting, from parents and professionals. But things between Jamie and me grew increasingly frustrating. Sometimes, Jamie would hand me over a batch of mail, wordlessly. I tried to show him the letters, let him see how Dale's story had touched these people, and how, in turn, their tales were touching me. Sometimes, he just didn't seem to want to know. Somehow that wasn't as bad as it seems now. I simply didn't have time to be hurt . . . or perhaps, more truthfully, I didn't have time to know I was hurt. There was too much to do. Too many painful stories. Too much hurt everywhere. Too many people who needed help. People who needed me.

A regular feature of the mailbag was correspondence from parents seeking advice on how to find and use a dog to help reach their own child. I advised them as best I could. Curiously, I had never really considered the strategies I'd used with Henry and Dale. I just did it!

That October, I became aware of a real need for some kind of dog-autism programme. As I wondered how to devise something suitable, I received an email from a friend who had stumbled across the Autism Assistance Dogs (AAD), run by Irish Guide Dogs for the Blind (IGDB) in Cork. This charity was placing purpose-trained, mature dogs with families of children with severe autism throughout Ireland. I was intrigued, and checked their website. What I was to discover hooked me. I phoned Neil Ashworth, their autism assistance dog training manager.

As fate would have it, Neil had read my book and he was planning to contact me! We both wanted to develop ideas, with Dale's guidance, knowing we had an advantage: he could explain exactly why Henry worked! His recollections, both good and bad, were vivid. How was it working in Cork?

Their model was derived from the Canadian programme, National Service Dogs, developed around 1997, in which dogs were assessed and trained to a similar standard to a guide dog. The temperament of any working dog has to be exceptional, and autism dogs were trained, specifically, to cope calmly with the difficult home environments and extreme behaviours that accompany a child with severe autism. Amongst his many duties, the dog has to keep the child safe outdoors and in public places with their parents; he must assist at busy road crossings – many children with autism have bolting behaviours and no sense of danger. They may throw themselves to the ground, and more, much more – just as Dale had done.

The (fully registered) AAD dog is trained to stop at the kerb and maintain a strong anchored "stand" position until given the command to move. The child is safe because he or she wears a comfortable belt with a lead attached to the dog's harness, and so the child stays too. Neil explained this model was now being adopted in many countries, including England. This was not how Henry and Dale had worked, but I saw we had much to share and learn together.

Then ... the invitation I couldn't refuse! Neil was about to attend an Assistance Dogs International Conference (ADI) and wondered if I'd be interested in also attending. The working dog field throughout the world was gathering. In Frankfurt! I wanted to learn everything from them – it would be crazy not to! They had decades of experience. When Dale's autism exploded in February 1991, the radio reported that a young American non-verbal autistic boy had been taken swimming with dolphins. He spoke for the first time. This may be integral to our current understanding, but then it was revolutionary! Certainly, I have always been aware of animals' therapeutic value – indeed that has been known for centuries. Throughout my childhood, cats, dogs, goldfish, mice were part of our household – even the occasional injured wild bird was nursed back to flight. Back in Dublin, visiting my mother's childhood home, our domestic zoo was expanded by chickens, donkeys and rabbits, stray cats and dogs. A regal cockerel stood in charge of the yard. He was also the household 6 a.m. alarm! My parents couldn't lavish me with toys and luxuries, but instead we had the joyous benefit of all sorts of animal contact. What a legacy!

Now, I understood my challenge. I had to develop a programme encompassing not only the child, but the whole family. It had to be both inclusive and individually tailored. However, I was determined not to lose sight of another important figure in all this! I had been meticulous with Dale, ensuring that Henry's needs were met. His dog was a living, sentient being, for no matter the severity of the human condition, an animal is no cuddly toy. I didn't know where this would go, but I was putting my pack on my back for the journey, and was both thrilled and privileged. The possibilities flooded ...

Henry's legacy had begun!

A week later, I caught the plane from Glasgow to Frankfurt Hahn. Neil would meet me. My flight was quiet, so I had privacy and time for reflection – enhanced by a couple of glasses of red wine! I thought of my wonderful parents, my saviours throughout the hellish years. Now, as a guest of the Irish Guide Dogs staff, I felt my mum's Irish strength touch me. This was fate!

Neil and I greeted each other like old friends, yet he seemed a little stressed. In our taxi, he warned me we were in for quite a drive – 125 miles! No wonder he was flustered. When we arranged our flights, we both assumed there was only one airport in Frankfurt. Neil had arrived at Frankfurt International and me at Frankfurt Hahn. Hence the epic cab journey!

While we cruised through the small hours, Neil told me he had spoken to Dale, and he was amazed at what he had learned. Aware of the two-airport problem, Neil phoned my home and Dale answered. During the call, Dale interrupted Neil, with an apology, and said goodbye. Neil overheard Dale saying, "Dad, I think you should talk to Neil. I think there's a problem."

Neil was stunned. He hadn't explained to Dale about the mix-up, but he had recognised from his tone that something was wrong. My son's perceptiveness was not lost on him.

The journey whizzed by as we discussed the possibilities for my programme and ways to enhance the Irish one. On arrival, we grabbed a couple of hours' sleep before the three-day conference began. Later, as the hotel foyer filled with delegates, I thought how much Dale would have loved all this – because I did! There were many professionals but there were also delegates with their own assistance dogs. What a catalogue of canine working dogs, golden retrievers, Labradors, Lab retrievers, German Shepherds, Inuits and even the occasional small variety! I was so excited; I'd a real sense of belonging.

Suddenly, Neil greeted a couple, Alberto Alvarez-Campos and Jane Kefford. They had known each other for years, having worked together in England. He introduced me, and I sat beside Jane, knowing that the guys had a lot of catching up. Jane explained why they had come. Both had worked for twenty years as guide dog trainers in England, where they met and married. A year ago, they moved with their two young daughters to Zamora, Alberto's hometown, in Spain.

I felt an increasing affinity. The passion and professionalism just oozed from her. Alberto had over thirty years of experience working with assistance dogs, and he had also trained animals for films, drug searches and the police. She understood my anxieties and excitement, having herself been thrown into the deep end. She had so recently adapted to life in Zamora, settling her family, learning Spanish, and she had missed her own career terribly. Just as Henry came into my life, changing it forever, a friend of Jane's offered their family a beautiful Golden Retriever. It was apparent immediately that it would make a wonderful guide dog. Seeing Alberto's passion and enthusiasm for the dog, Jane saw that their lives were about to change forever. That was the seed that was to grow to become their new charity, PAAT (Spanish for: Dogs for Assistance & Animal Therapy). Just as I was on a mission for Dale, PAAT were on a parallel journey. They had had years of observing the positive impact that dogs had on their clients' lives, but perhaps they had witnessed something more, cases where dogs had shown the ability to master new skills spontaneously, skills for which they had never been trained!

Jane recalled partnering a man with his first guide dog. His young son suffered from severe asthma, yet he had boundless energy. The dog absorbed the boy's excess exuberance during his playtime and he even slept in the lad's room. His parents noted he settled better in that situation. One night, as the boy's parents slept, the dog entered their room, barking furiously, pulling at their bed covers until they responded. They followed the dog to their son's room to find him in the middle of an acute asthma attack. Had the boy not received the medical help he needed then, he would certainly have died.

Another story affected them profoundly. A female client had a son with communication difficulties, on the autistic spectrum. He needed specialised schooling, and his mother told Jane of her sadness: the only time he ventured outdoors was to get his school bus, and only then because it collected him at the gate. Jane got thinking. Perhaps the boy would walk outdoors, firstly to the shops with the dog in tow. She knew this might be possible, providing both dog and "user" were properly instructed. She put her theory into practice. Soon, it became evident that a strong bond had developed, without significant input from her. When the mother and son, dual-role guide dog in tow, successfully ventured to the shops, Jane recognised the milestone. Here was a life-changing effect on the quality of life for not just the child, but for his whole family.

I sat, riveted. The reason PAAT were at the conference was to expand their work: purpose-training dogs for autistic children! Something magical was in that Frankfurt air! All of us wanted to utilise the dog in its widest possibilities. Our shared aim was to get the maximum benefit, the best quality of life and independence possible for every child.

For the remainder of the conference, Neil, PAAT and I stuck together. During those days I attended fascinating workshops and learned so much about how guide dogs were trained to help clients with sight loss. I thought I would feel like a fish out of water, but I was wrong. I already knew visually impaired patients often had an innate or acquired heightening of their other senses. This is not dissimilar to the sensory experiences of certain people with ASD. Further, sight loss clients had similar spatial awareness difficulties. Such invaluable learning when I came to develop my own programme! However, it was a lecture on the final day that really blew my mind, a lecture given by the eminent English dog psychologist Daniel Mills.

I was transfixed from the start, as my experience rang true. Daniel then revealed his latest research, leaving me desperate to talk to my son. Daniel projected images, showing that all dogs have just five recognisable facial expressions. This was stunning. Unknowingly, Dale had described Daniel's science perfectly already, as he had summarised in my first book:

"Henry had a wise look on his face. I could understand Henry's feelings from looking at his eyes. Henry's face only had slight changes with his expression so I understood them."(From "In His Own Words", *A Friend Like Henry*.)

After the four days with my new friends, I struggled to leave. Jane told Alberto she wanted to take me back to Spain. Talking to me had had the effect of a light bulb exploding in her head! I was expressing feelings and thoughts she had carried for years. I gave them a copy of my book and we hugged each other, exchanging their traditional, two-cheek goodbye kiss. I hoped that we could stay in touch – we were soul mates already – but deep down I wondered if we would.

I secreted a lovely hand-painted ceramic horse bank in my luggage for Amy, and dashed for my homeward flight. She was to find it inspirational in her own drawing . . . and I had a lot of mental unpacking to do!

I began immediately. When I told Dale all, I left out one important issue. Whilst I was thrilled by all the positive coverage of my book, I was becoming increasingly frustrated by a regular comment of this nature: "We don't know why dogs have this effect on autistic children." Dale had explained it beautifully already! After Frankfurt, I could now clarify, but Dale's explanation was a world first. Today, there is abundant supporting evidence.

There was a little experiment I had to try, courtesy of Daniel Mills. Without telling him why, I asked Dale to draw the facial expressions he recognised in Henry. He produced pencil drawings, showing four Henry expressions – happy, content, excited and worried/sad. Perplexed, I queried, "Dale, did you recognise only these four expressions?"

"Yes, Mum. That's all I remember, although there could be an angry/snarling face, for some dogs, but remember, Mum, Henry was a golden retriever!"

This correlated with everything Daniel Mills had found, and fitted with all that Dale had told me earlier. It was no surprise that both my children, and others, would find it easier to connect with animals. Whether it was Dale and Henry or Amy's horses or dolphins, unthreatening, non-verbal animals were easier for people on the spectrum to interpret and predict. Add in their wonderful temperaments and patience, and why should it be a surprise that animals can provide a key for some children with autism that we neuro-typicals can hardly approach. Is it not time we tried to learn?

Now with family life resumed and Dale settled, I started to write down ideas from all I gleaned in Frankfurt. Once again I mused on that German magic. Was it by chance my path had crossed with PAAT, or was it something more?

Life was zooming on and Christmas approaching fast. Dale's "monthly progress indicator" assessments at Glynhill showed that his timekeeping and attendance were, of course, *Highly Satisfactory*, but in other areas of his assessment his progress was recorded only as *Developing*. When Dale returned to college and Glynhill in the New Year, I observed a daily deterioration. His well-being began to trouble me. He had stopped acknowledging me when he came home, going straight to his room. Hours later, I would go up to check if he was all right. Throughout these early weeks, he did not express any concerns to me or to anyone, but clearly, something was very wrong.

One day I disturbed him in his room and noticed there were course papers strewn all over his bed. Was he attempting to complete an assignment? Four hours would pass, and he wouldn't or couldn't take a break. After a couple of weeks of worrying terribly, I interrupted: "Dale, is everything all right at college? Do you need help?"

His reply relieved me, but was grim. "Mum, I'm really tired and finding college work totally confusing and difficult. My tutors have noticed I'm struggling in class and at Glynhill. It's so bad they have been advising me to think about leaving."

I've seen my son in some bad places over the years. This was as dire as it came. For the first time in Dale's difficult life, I really feared for his health. He was so fragile. I sat on his bed, with him staring at his laptop screen blankly, as if the words on the screen were written in Chinese. It broke my heart, seeing my amazing, intelligent son in such turmoil. Yet, even in that despair, I could tell he didn't want to be beaten.

"Dale, it's okay. No matter what the problems are and how you feel about college, you will never fail in my eyes, nor anyone's. Please let me help you get things sorted. Please, talk to me."

He opened up, but his tutors' "advice" began to trouble me more.

"Dale, why didn't you let me, or someone from Prospects, go with you to the meetings you were having with college staff?"

His reply stunned me. "Mum, I didn't know the tutors were going to talk to me – twice in the last two weeks. A couple of tutors just cornered me, advising me that I should think seriously about leaving."

Trying to absorb this, I reassured him that while he was capable of making decisions and having impromptu discussions with his tutors, I thought it was unfair for him to be approached without notice and unreasonable that he had been given no opportunity to discuss such a serious matter with Prospects, or me, first. I told him to forget any pressures in his academic work and at Glynhill. If he was spoken to again, he was to inform the tutor that he wanted to discuss the situation in the proper context before doing anything. He was not to worry; I would contact Anna Williamson. Once she had fully investigated this, with his full involvement, then and only then would he leave the course. If that was his choice.

Dale knew Prospects would intervene and guide him to the best outcome. In the first week of February, while waiting, his behaviour deteriorated dramatically. He came home from Glynhill disheartened and anguished. "Mum, the children's behaviours at Glynhill are very difficult to manage. Staff are constantly challenged, keeping them under control."

I reminded him that the children had problems caused by their environment. They needed a similar approach to some of the children he met at Barnardo's. He understood that it wasn't their fault, and that

[ 62 ]

the lack of positive parenting affected many. Trying to reassure him to keep going, things reached breaking point the night before he returned to college.

I tossed and turned in my bed, just as, undoubtedly, Dale had done too. I heard him cough all night. I tried to help him with what sounded like a dry, irritable bark. I made him take regular sips of water, offered to make him a cup of tea, gave him cough linctus. Nothing worked. I knew this was caused by anxiety, though I didn't tell him so. This happened in his early adulthood when he was stressed, but this was the worst bout yet. In the morning, I worried as he set off for college, his eyes dark and sunken, blinking furiously. He could barely talk for stammering. He had started to tic.

Like many with autism, Dale has periodic autistic tics similar to the involuntary muscle movements suffered by a person with Tourette's Syndrome. On the rare occasion it happened, it was a serious sign he was in autism crisis.

The phone rang in the afternoon. It was Dale, in desperation: "Mum, I can't cope any more with this pressure. One of the tutors wants me to meet her after lunch to discuss my assignment."

I suggested that he try not to be obstructive. As the meeting was about his assignment, I told him to see the tutor, reassuring him that Anna was contacting me soon. I felt dreadful, telling him to meet the tutor because I knew he was at the end of his tether. When he came home, he approached me, deeply distressed, fighting back tears. He just managed to utter, "Mum, I'm really sorry to let you all down, but I can't take it anymore. I want to leave college. Mum, I'm beat! Please help me get out of there."

The sobs racked him. Hugging him, I was gutted to see my strong, determined son so defeated. He felt a failure. I told him how much I loved him and how proud I was of him, offering him his solace of choice: a cup of tea. Since childhood, tea had worked magic. So often, a brew saved the day.

Afterwards, calmer but still down, he explained, "Mum, I went to see the tutor, and she began to discuss where I had gone wrong in my assignment. Then during the meeting, another tutor came into the room, and both advised me it would be better for me to leave the course, because I can't handle the work."

I was shocked. Angry. I was the one who had coaxed him to go to that meeting, when deep down, Dale knew he would be coerced into leaving. I felt sick.

"Dale, please don't worry about any of this any more. Enough is enough. This is going to get sorted out for you, I promise."

As he was due back at Glynhill for his external assessment, I told him, "Dale, go to Glynhill – just to get your progress reports. I guarantee, you will not be going back to college or Glynhill until we meet with Anna to sort out this mess, whether it means you leave college or not!"

# 6

# *Maelstrom*

How much is the young mind and body meant to endure, the super-human efforts of an athlete in training; the musician practising into the night towards perfection? I can't answer that, but I know that these months pushed my son way beyond his physical and mental limits. His health remained fragile as the stress tolled. He'd stopped eating, he scarcely slept. The autistic tics continued, draining him. We watched, desperate yet powerless. For the rest of that hellish week, somehow he managed to attend Glynhill, but he returned at breaking point: "Mum, I've made up my mind. I'm definitely leaving college. I can't work at Glynhill. Enough!"

I made several attempts, but it took until evening until he was settled enough to talk and share his assessments. Seeing the three reports for the first time, I began to understand. Dale had benefitted from a good trainer early in his placement, so he thrived until Christmas. However, in January, he was assigned someone else, who voiced that she was having serious problems interpreting his task manual. What on earth was going on? A trainer who didn't understand her job? A trainer who didn't understand autism? Her confusion prevented him from completing tasks on time. For five weeks, she did nothing to address the problem. Instead, she left him, fending for himself in the nursery, falling behind and with tasks undone.

All three reports were confusing for anyone to interpret, let alone for Dale. Each practitioner skill category had four boxes, the student being: *Highly Satisfactory, Satisfactory, Developing* or *Unsatisfactory*. The first assessed how Dale used observations, and another how he consulted with staff regarding planning. Two boxes were ticked simultaneously, indicating that he was *Developing*, but also *Unsatisfactory*! Professionals working with autistic children or adults must know that those with ASD perceive and learn in a literal way. No wonder he was upset and perplexed! These reports were both negative and ambiguous, and were consequently bewildering and upsetting. In the interim report there was a statement in bold: "If the student's performance is *Unsatisfactory* in any aspect of the interim report, the student will be given a second attempt in another placement."

While this policy seemed harsh, it was fair. As I read the reports, I could see what was going wrong. His over-monitoring began on Tuesday, 6 February 2008 and concluded on Wednesday, 14 February. Dale had been formally "assessed" three times within six working days. Subjecting him to such scrutiny would have been of dubious worth to the tutor, and was a disastrous pressure overdose for him.

The more I looked, the more horror I found. What had not been done for my son. In accordance with the Motherwell adjustments, all involved were to be aware of Dale's autism. That wasn't so difficult! His life was so much in the public domain. Everyone concerned should have known the requirements and implications of his DDA adjustments. Instead, joint decisions were made, blaming Dale's autism for his failure to progress at Glynhill and at college.

At least in his February report, Dale's areas of strength were recorded: "A very pleasant and willing student who is anxious to please and has a lovely manner with the children." Again, two boxes were ticked describing him as *Developing* and *Satisfactory*. Still confusing, but positive at least. Only six days later, two indicator boxes were ticked, again showing Dale's practice was *Developing* but also *Unsatisfactory*! Adding to this strange soup, the tutor wrote: "Dale has a good rapport with the children and interacts well." He was "eager and enthusiastic about what he was doing".

It was noted that his preparation, implementation, recordkeeping and evaluation of practical tasks were all *Unsatisfactory*. This was, at that time, an accurate description of this aspect of his work. However: "The change of trainer feels Dale needs help to understand what he is doing with his tasks, as he finds paperwork very difficult."

This was clarified further: "Dale can carry out activities, but doesn't fully understand why he is doing them."

I smelled an extremely nasty rodent.

"Dale, why are you still finding your task manual difficult to understand? Under your Motherwell adjustments, this was all sorted."

I had really touched a nerve.

"Mum, what the hell do you mean? It's not just me that's confused. My new trainer doesn't understand my task folder either!"

What could he mean? I pushed on. Frustrated by his attempts to make me understand, Dale stomped upstairs. Perhaps I had gone too far. Minutes later, he returned, carrying an A4 notebook. He pushed it into my hands, with a terse command: read it, and understand!

The notebook contained a handwritten letter, dated 6 February 2008, from the new trainer to the tutor who had assessed Dale that week: "After speaking to Dale's tutor about his progress [. . .] I explained to her that I am finding it difficult to understand what exactly Dale is expected to do for his tasks 4 & 5 [. . .] I am getting really confused. I feel I can't support him properly until I fully understand myself what is expected of him. His paperwork is very hard to understand e.g. what his main aim for the day actually is [. . .] Could you please keep me informed on a weekly basis of what Dale is working on in the playroom and outdoor play, which he seems to be focusing on for his Task 5. Thanks very much."

"Dale, with your adjustments, you're supposed to get your task folder adapted for you, in electronic format, and someone to help you understand exactly what is expected of you."

By now, sadly, his reply did not surprise me. "Mum, I was given the electronic disc in January, but got no help to understand what I was supposed to be doing. I've tried to work it out myself."

The assessment tutor had discussed Dale's failures with him in full, and in tandem with the so-called trainer, had compounded his already lowered self-esteem. No wonder he was in such a state. How was it possible that he could have been so mistreated by professionals who should have known better? Those same professionals, at the diagnostic forefront, who were spelling out that condition-specific education must begin in nursery! Dale would have read the tutor's comments. How distressing must it have been for him, particularly in the context of his Barnardo's experiences and the respect that he was accorded there. Worse, Dale had to contend with being repeatedly spoken to by the "tuppence worth" tutor and several others. I began to see that he had tolerated ongoing similar treatment since his return to college and to Glynhill. It broke my heart.

"Dale is not working satisfactorily at HNC level. Dale would find it difficult to take responsibility as a registered practitioner. There is no guarantee of Dale's final results. At this moment, it would be difficult to see Dale as a qualified member of a child care team."

And the tutor and the new trainer agreed: "Dale needs an awful lot of support and direction from staff. Placement staff feel he needs extra time if he has a possibility of achieving his HNC."

Ironically, they were right. Dale was, after all, entitled to extra time and human support under his Motherwell adjustments. Support that had never been implemented. *Thud!*

"The tutor in the college was to document and explain within the notebook what practical tasks Dale was to complete."

*Thud, thud!*

"Dale must communicate better with staff."

Everything was clear. Suddenly I became focused, my anger found its direction. I told his dad to make us a cup of tea. Tea! Once again, our saviour! As the kettle boiled, I retrieved a copy of the Motherwell adjustments, adjustments I hoped had been sent to the college.

Tea in hand, calmly, I went through the adjustments, one by one. Dale's reply became a mantra. "Mum, I work the same way as the other students."

I had the evidence that his adaptations were not being made, but to what extent?

"Dale, who is the person [paid by SAAS] to proofread and spend time with you, for all your coursework?"

"Mum, I don't understand what you mean. How many times do I have to tell you: I'm treated the same as any other student in the class. There's one tutor, Gwen, who spends extra time with me, and tries her best to help me, but she has nothing to do with my SAAS award."

Surveying the absence of support, I was astounded that he had managed to cope at all. That night I vowed that I would never again take his progress for granted. The Disability Discrimination Act of 1995 was meant to protect him. He sat motionless and quiet. Despairingly, he said, "Mum, I now understand why Prospects teaches adults like me to understand our rights. I thought discrimination would never happen to me because of the career I chose."

Something of the old Dale was beginning to re-emerge.

"Dale, if we can improve things for you at college and on placement, would you still want to leave?"

"Mum, I like working with the children. If things can get sorted, I won't give up, but I feel I can't go back to college, ever again."

Oh, son, I was in awe of you then. I still am.

Finally, he relaxed, and made his way to bed, knowing we were going to fight for his right to be treated fairly, to have the same chances as any other student! For the first time in weeks, he even slept!

We had fought similar battles for Dale in the past and won, but this one was to be our ultimate crusade. Facing another war, we would need new armour, fresh defences. Whilst our fight was for our son, we knew that our eventual victory – and we never doubted that we would win – would be not just for him, but for the waiting, deserving masses out there, all those with improved diagnoses and the benefit of condition-specific education. This was huge. What we could not see was what the three years of combat would do to Dale.

All that was the future. We had to deal with the present. As Dale was considered *Unsatisfactory* in some areas, we understood that he would be moved to another nursery. We all felt that a change would work. The prospect didn't worry him, as he was aware of other HNC students in a similar position – it had helped improve their practice, and they had qualified, successfully. Yet . . .

"We recommend that Dale remains at Glynhill."

That thud again. How much more was he to face? It seemed to have been with him forever, obstacle after obstacle, unfair punch upon punch. Like over 40 per cent of autistic children today[1], Dale had endured the torment of bullying at school. When would it stop?

These early adult months battered his mental health, his confidence and self-esteem to an all-time low. It was time to see our GP, Roddy Grose. He had a good understanding of autism and great empathy. Dale was signed off for a month, recognising that his future was in the balance.

Dale and I met with Anna, of Prospects, to discuss how to move forward. I was saddened to learn that his experience was quite typical. She had done her homework. The college staff had indeed received copies of the Motherwell adjustments: "Yes, we do have a copy of Dale's Motherwell Report, and staff are aware of his requirements."

Anna understood the extreme delicacy of Dale's emotional state. She arranged to meet us informally at Prospects, under the guise of a casual lunch and chat. It worked. He relaxed, as she reinforced what we had already put in place. A sandwich, and yes, that cup of tea on, I saw Dale's determination, his conviction that he was not to be beaten, to return. Thank God!

Anna outlined the option of moving Dale to another college, while ensuring all adjustments were implemented. Prospects could provide a college support person who would be there throughout the day, including at break times; he would have someone who understood his anxieties and he wouldn't be isolated in his new environment. This support mechanism had worked very successfully for other students in similar situations. However, as Dale was halfway through his course, we needed to address what had actually occurred, and we needed to investigate the possibility of completing his course at Duncan Currie as an Open Learning student.

In this format, Dale would study at home for the entire course, which would be supplied in manuals. He would also access tutor support. Ironically, the entire course could be made available to OL students in a straightforward format – the very format he hadn't accessed, in line with his DDA adjustments, when he attended that same college!

For what seemed the hundredth time in a lifetime of composing fighting letters, we were once again taking days to perfect that all-important letter for Dale's future. Parenting a child or adult with autism is a sufficiently demanding task, but ask any of those parents to try to count the desperate hours spent on computers, researching and learning about their children's rights, the days and nights sweating over letters, possibilities, impossibilities, hopes – well, ask them! There's no way any of us can quantify that.

We had sheet after sheet of notes spread out on the table, comparing, cross-referencing, contemplating, comparing again. You name it, we reckoned we'd done it. That was until we came down one morning to find Amy had already laid all the notes out on the floor in the shape of a horse. Yes, a very large horse. Luckily, we found them before Thomas did. Sometimes life didn't need her creative input.

In addition to Anna and Prospects, I spent ages on the phone to the Equality and Disability Rights Commission for guidance on what to include in our letter. However raw our feelings, it had to be the most professional letter possible. We forced points from the DDA. This wasn't Dale's failure, but the college's failure: "To make reasonable

[ 71 ]

adjustments", "[Dale] . . . should not be treated less favourably because he has a disability." We quoted the college's "Disability Equality Duty 2005". The college staff were to endeavour to: "Eliminate harassment of disabled persons that is related to their disability", "Take steps to take account of disabled persons' disabilities, even where that involves treating disabled persons . . . more favourably than others."

While we waited to hear about the outcome of our efforts, Dale continued his work with Barnardo's. He attended a course in March, giving him the skills to carry out emergency life support. He had possibly acquired superior skills to his student peers, because of the intensive training given by Barnardo's and Prospects. Sadly, no one at the college ever acknowledged these assets. Undoubtedly, though, the children and their parents managed to see Dale's unique qualities.

On 13 March, we received a reply from the college vice principal, requesting that we meet with the Director of Business and Customer Relations. On the appointed day, Dale was very worried, despite our support. Whatever was not happening for Jamie and me at home at the time, there was no question. We were together on this. We were Dale's parents, and on this, if increasingly on so little else, we were a unit and we were not about to be shaken. We were taken into a grand office suite on the top floor. There were no other staff present; we three sat together on the sofa, with the director across from us, alone on another chair. He began by emphasising to Dale how sorry he was for the situation. Dale tried his best to speak and to acknowledge his apology, but his anxiety was all too evident, his voice was shaking and his eyes were blinking furiously. The apology was lost on all of us. The Director launched into a speech reiterating how professional his staff were . . . Enough!

"If your staff are so professional, why didn't they implement Dale's adjustments, and we wouldn't be sitting here now?"

His response was worthy of any politician. Skirting around the facts, he repeated, endlessly, that his staff were professional, always. Conceding that we were getting nowhere, as he jotted down notes, I asked, "Why didn't the college apply for the extra human support Dale was to receive?"

No one could have anticipated the reply which I can recall: "We didn't think anyone would have taken the job."

"At twenty-five pounds an hour, you're telling us that a newly qualified unemployed HNC person wouldn't have grabbed the opportunity?"

Bizarrely, even this seemed lost on him. All his energies were directed at defending his staff. We focused on the only option left: for Dale to try to complete his course as an Open Learning student. In fairness, the director was concerned about Open Learning, because the chances of a student passing the course were, statistically, very poor. Regardless of his nerves that day, Dale was adamant: "The thought of being in classes causes me so much worry. I know I would panic, and I won't be able to cope. I would rather leave than go back into classes again!"

We ended the meeting, agreeing that he would take the OL option. Luckily, the very helpful Gwen turned out to be the tutor! Dale had so much respect for Gwen that this clinched the deal.

A few days later, he received a letter confirming an action plan, which would allow him to complete his course: "Many thanks for raising the issues with college management and I apologise for causing any stress to you."

Dale would have access to the College Supported Learning Department, in particular for proofreading his assignments. While this seemed a helpful mechanism, the purpose of the department was to ensure inclusion and to help him, and indeed anyone with a recognised disability, access the syllabus. This was not a luxury but a right. However, in Dale's adjustments, he required the support of a person qualified in and familiar with his coursework. This was why SAAS awarded so generously. Thankfully, Sandra, as a senior social worker, had a good knowledge of most of Dale's syllabus, and knew the standards expected in his assignments.

This wasn't wasted on me; what would Dale have done without his own learning support in place? Our fears were confirmed only a week later, in a letter from the college: "Assessments will be marked and cross-marked, following the same procedures used for full-time classes, and as with full-time students, you will be allowed two submissions of assessed work."

Within a couple of weeks Dale received the complete course syllabus in manual form, which, remarkably, was quite easy to decipher. Gwen was to sort out the problems with his graded unit, so that he fully understood what was required. As he needed a new placement, it was decided that the best environment for him was the college nursery, where support for students in the past had enabled them to qualify. As the nursery was on campus, it allowed him seamless support. Helpfully, it was arranged for Dale to visit beforehand, meeting the Head and the allocated trainer.

On 7 May 2008, a less anxious Dale ventured into his new placement. We let Anna know he had managed to return and that he was feeling quite relaxed and motivated again. When he came home, he was our Dale again, the autistic tics gone, he was sleeping and eating well, and he looked so much better. The relief for us all was immense. Our hopes resurfaced.

We all didn't know at the time, but the maelstrom he had survived was going to keep swirling in his future.

A few days later, an upbeat Dale explained how much happier he felt in his new placement. I was pleasantly shocked when, casually, he mentioned a factor which had made his first day a real success. In a strange quirk of fate, his trainer, Marie, knew him well. When she was newly qualified, she had worked at Hillend Nursery, which Dale attended as a child. She really appreciated how far he had come, in view of the severity of his childhood autism. I couldn't help but wonder how Marie must have felt, meeting him again fifteen years on. What a wonderful woman! From day one, Marie was an exceptional trainer. She was generous with her praise, a great benefit to any learner, and doubly so to one with autism. She would write lovely comments on his task paperwork, knowing that the few minutes invested would be soundly returned in her student's progress.

Her ability to evaluate Dale's practical tasks, both constructively and with respect for his autism, allowed him to learn and to grow in confidence. She was truly a remarkable professional and person. Her support allowed Dale to progress as any other HNC student might.

A few weeks later, Dale received news that he had been nominated for the college's Adult Learner of the Year Award, a surprising but very welcome initiative, and one more for his already admirable CV! Yet again, Dale had hope for his future, hope when he needed it most. We all understood the chances of success for him as an Open Learning student were precarious. However, his determination to succeed was back. He wasn't going to be defeated – autism or no autism!

# 7

## *Progress*

Secure under Marie's wing, Dale thrived, despite some unanticipated "additional support". Within five minutes of getting down to work, the bedroom door would fly open. Enter the boys! Henry would curl up to sleep, wedged under the computer desk, warming his master's feet. Meanwhile, Thomas claimed two-thirds of the bed, sprawled out, snoring drunkenly, tail thudding as he dreamed. However long Dale worked, neither moved an inch until he had finished.

The boys' attendance became part of the study routine. They never flinched, even when we spread paperwork on their torsos! Dale told me their presence gave him a feeling of well-being; their deep restful breathing had a calming influence, which helped him work longer. Even as a child, he never stopped until all his homework was completely finished. Eight years later, here we were again, with him studying for an HNC, two massive dogs by his side. With the dedicated assistance of Sandra and Prospects Student Support, he grafted hard and his willpower remained strong.

After Frankfurt, I was bursting with inspiration, and so began to develop transitional resources for an educational programme, fully aware that the autism and the assistance dogs' world would have to merge. Assistance and support dogs for clients with ASD were nothing new. What was new was what the working dog world had shown me. Suitable training programmes could make the dogs far more beneficial and functional. My thoughts were confirmed in an NAS magazine: "We found having a dog and training the dog in road safety, etc., helped reinforce better behaviour for our quite severely autistic son when he was a child [ . . . ] Our non-pedigree dog lived to the good old age of twenty-one and gave our son a great gift: the breakthrough of communication, friendship and devotion." – Maureen Erdwin.[1]

Maureen's son was now forty-five years old. I had seen this too, with added illumination from Dale, unpacking what had been his own severely autistic mind. In 1994, when I prepared my son for Henry's arrival, my great concern had been the dog's welfare. Dale, on some level, had to understand that Henry was a fellow being. His dog, like him, had emotions and needs; he was no cuddly toy! My programme had to recognise how a child with ASD learns. By seeing, hearing, doing with repetition, people with ASD learn in a literal way. Everyone involved with them must be consistent, and use minimal language. The six-second rule is golden. This means that when engaging verbally with a child you allow six seconds for them to process information before they reply. The child must be rewarded when they have understood so the child learns communication works!

When Dale's autism emerged, I had sought guidance from Jim Taylor of Scottish Autism. He stressed that it was essential to get the educational approach right, and never deviate from it. And so it is with dogs. Years before, my dad had explained canine training: first get the dog's attention by saying its name. Be consistent. When the dog obeys, give treats as rewards accompanied by verbal praise (positive reinforcement). These unbreakable rules made sense, and with patient persistence, our family dogs were core trained. In 1991, Jim's advice rang true; the principles were the same.

Henry's arrival had been a major transition. I engineered it that the dog became my son's ultimate obsession. Weeks in advance, I was teaching him all things dog related, the process I now call "dogifying". This means exposing the child to suitable games, books and DVDs in order to make that needed connection. Jim emphasised that this phase

[ 77 ]

should take two to three months, and in keeping with the literal learning pattern, social stories and pictures needed to be realistic.

My programme would have to address individual needs, with appropriate short- and long-term educational objectives. Interventions would be planned, implemented and evaluated with accurate indicators covering improved communication, imaginative and social skills. Ultimately, it sought the greatest possible independence for each child. Using the dog in this way addressed the triad of impairments, and simultaneously mirrored the school's approach.

The resources I developed were basic and articulated without dramatic changes. There was another vital function. I felt strongly that siblings should be involved. I tapped into my father-in-law's drawing skills. He produced line drawings of the "stand", "sit" and "down" positions as language and colouring resources, to be introduced one at a time. The educational potential for each resource was nigh endless and gave meaningful language opportunities well ahead of the homecoming.

I took pictures of dog equipment; perhaps most importantly, several of the raised feeding table, showing two full bowls – dry food and water. Using a table was better for the dog's digestion and the height and stability was easier and safer for the child to use when feeding and replenishing water. Additionally, the table gave the positive social rule that people, like dogs, eat at a table. There were pictures of the dog's fleecy bed, brush, comb, toothbrush, toothpaste, all reinforcing that the dog has the same needs of care.

A fun, quacking furry duck was also part of the package, which I hoped would be a good language and sensory resource. It was also more appealing and easier to manipulate than a ball. Like children, dogs want to play with toys. The duck's main purpose was to allow me to research a particular interest of mine. If the child saw the dog repeatedly fetch, would the child also engage in the game? This was an ambitious goal, as a simple game like that is difficult for a child on the spectrum. He needs to understand the vocabulary, and his lack of imagination and social awareness would be problematic. Hand-eye co-ordination, poor motor skills, spatial awareness problems and difficulties in understanding social timings added to an already volatile mix. Yet, Dale and Amy had managed with Henry. I needed to find out.

Finally, I incorporated a rubber Kong, which is good for dogs to chew; the child learns to fill it with food and to give it to the dog themselves. The Kong offered learning and interaction, and so much more.

When the child became familiar with each picture, the images worked into a story and the parent and teacher could be certain that the child understood all the dog's needs. There were line drawings of the equipment too, for fine motor and language work. Three dog songs were downloaded onto CDs – "Who Let the Dog Out?" even had real barking noises! I found uncomplicated dog storybooks, which could be "vandalised" and adapted, just as I had once done with the *Heaven* book.

I also wanted to explore if introducing a preferred colour would help increase bonding. My own children, like the majority on the spectrum, had postive colour connections. The range of colours was potentially as varied and individual as the children themselves.

Dale's was "Thomas Blue", which he adopted, aged two, on the very day he found the train. At the same age, Amy took ownership of red, and at six she told me it was because she loved Winnie the Pooh's jumper! At St Anthony's School, it was easy to recognise the paintings on the walls. Dale's were always shades of blue, while his friend Ryan's were predominantly pink. I saw the possibilities! Henry wore a blue lead and collar, with his master's picture attached. Now, taking this further, I designed a harness with a hook at the top for the child's lead, and with another at the bottom, suitable to attach toys, pictures or little bags or purses. I ensured there was the opportunity for all sorts of progression without unnecessary and intrusive change. From the international dog model, I learned that the child holds onto a long handle attached to a harness. However, as the child grows this approach would need to change – a handle is far from a standard lead, and wouldn't be practical indefinitely. I found a range of coloured leads made from broad nylon webbing with a second hook at the hand loop, to enable the lead to be made half size and form a secondary loop, just like a handle. Later, the half lead could be unhooked again to form a full lead. I wanted the lead to be special, as many of the children play with ropes or plastic tubing to reduce anxiety. So, it had uses even without the dog.

By extension, I had to discover if using the child's obsession would help the bonding. I had utilised Dale's obsession with Thomas the Tank Engine until it ran out of steam! Henry's treats were stored in a "Thomas" tin, as were his master's! That dog had a sound reason for his name!

As I worked, Jim Taylor's advice to keep things real kept coming up. I had used a little soft yellow Labrador toy, in tandem with real equipment, for weeks on end with Dale. We brushed and fed the toy, sang dog songs daily, as if the toy was real. From this I created what I now call "The Cuddly Pack". This was developed with the help of another unique autistic mind . . . Amy's!

We set off to IKEA to view their permanent range of these toys and their extensive pet department. Our first purchase was the dog. I opted for the little one. Wrong! Amy retorted, "Nuala, you need the big one. He's the right size."

I pondered; the big one was two-foot long and floppy. She clinched the deal. "Nuala, you could put more stuffing in him so he makes a good . . . Golden Pillow!"

Often during Dale and Amy's childhood, I would find them both fast asleep using a comatose Henry as a pillow. Their heads would be resting at his heart, and neither would budge for hours. Amy called this her "Golden Pillow". Until she was eleven she struggled to sleep and her "Golden Pillow" worked every time. I realised the dog had some positive sensory stimulus for them. Aged ten, my daughter explained, "Nuala, I like the feel of the dog's soft fur, and it makes me feel good to flick his ears. The noise from his heart and him breathing up and down helps me sleep." This made sense. I thought the "Golden Pillow" was unique to my children. However, in the future, because of Henry, I was to learn to the contrary.

With the cuddly thing sorted, I bought the equipment I'd shown in the resources and put it together, with a key ring picture of Dale as a child, attached to the collar, to demonstrate that the cuddly toy and its things belonged to him. I added a blue towel, sewed on a paw print and put on an elastic loop to make hanging it up easier. This would help teach the child to take care of his or her dog, and learn to hang up their own coat.

I included a pink lead for any potential sibling. Siblings would be fantastic role models for the child in learning to share and play with the pack. The pack's uses educationally were endless. Consider the fear a child with ASD has when faced with the purchase of new shoes or clothes. The "dog" could be dressed appropriately for the trip, even shod! The potential for fun, imaginative and educational play was clear and long lasting. All this geared up to the arrival of the child's real dog, and all that equipment would be transferred.

The toy's fleecy bed would be a liner for a plastic tub bed. It was so important that the dog had its place for time out and rest during the day. I was determined that the dog would not be subjected to constant working or handling, and so I downloaded pictures of a sleeping yellow Labrador. I hoped the cuddly pack would help the child connect with the real dog, increase social and emotional skills, address sensory issues and introduce meaningful language for the child. No small aim in one wee package!

Just as I had done with Dale, all the teaching would be done through the dog. I wanted the commands to be a platform of core language for the child. I modified the assistance dog training commands, mindful not to overload the child with language. Using the word "toilet" for the dog transferred naturally to the child. For crossing the road: "We stay. No cars, we go!" It was building up. I used the same Makaton signs I had already used with my own son. Makaton is an internationally recognised sign language that uses hand signals with the spoken word. It helps the child understand and learn to communicate. Therefore, to be consistent with the child and the dog, I used the same hand signals from the Makaton system for "sit", "stand", "here", "come", "eat", "leave" and "fetch". Learning from his dog, I used to ask Dale to "fetch" his coat, "eat" his dinner, and "leave" things that were dangerous.

The more my programme evolved, the more my approach deviated from that of the working dogs. Guide and assistance dogs are trained with strict boundaries. My programme gave the dog free run of the house. I felt the dog should feel comfortable with the child, even sleep with the child if it helped, be it on the sofa or in the bedroom. Let's face it, almost anything if it helped the child improve or become calmer. I wanted the child to take ownership and care for their dog. I wanted to enable them to transfer the skills they needed to be able to take care of themselves.

As the weeks passed, a four-stage programme emerged which would take the child through life transtions until the dog's demise. In order to help the comprehension of these life events, I adopted the traffic light system that is often used in schools.

Red Stage: Stop and prepare the child for what a dog needs.

Yellow Stage: Wait and prepare the child for the real dog coming.

Green Stage: Go for using the dog as an educational facilitator and motivator in its wildest sense!

For later, hopefully much later, the Blue Stage: The child learns the dog is old and finds out how to let go. All this was timely.

Dale's Open Learning course was going well and remained blessedly uneventful until February, when the February mid-term holiday of 2008 offered us an enjoyable, but unconventional, break. Neil Ashworth arranged for us to visit Irish Guide Dogs, in order to see their Autism Assitance Dog Programme and share ideas.

The boys were booked into The Happy Hound Hotel, a luxurious boarding facility in Port Glasgow. They shared their own bedroom in a basement of a big country house. Their room had toys, water on tap and real sofas to sleep on. They had access to acres of hills, with panoramic views of the River Clyde. They also had the option to mingle with the other canine guests!

Meanwhile, we stayed at the impressive, purpose-built Guide Dog Centre in Cork, Ireland. Neil and his staff made us so welcome. Some had read my book and were delighted to talk to Dale. What an abundance of stunning dogs – Labradors, Lab-retrievers, Golden Retrievers, Goldendoodles. Oh, we could have run off with any of them! Enough! We weren't here for dog rustling!

Knowing that she was in a kind of school for dogs, Amy had questions. She was keen to learn how sight loss affected people: what was the Braille signage on the bedroom doors? She understood some of the dogs would work to help children with autism, just as Henry had helped Dale. What she didn't know at the time was that *she* had autism. That was something she worked out for herself later on. It's difficult for a parent to decide where and when to inform their child they have autism. For the majority of children, the day arrives when, having gained insight into themselves, they begin to feel they are different from their neuro-typical peers. For Amy, she had the bonus of understanding that Dale had autism, because of my book, and her realisation was to come about a year later, at age nine. When she asked me, "Nuala, do I have autism?" I sat with her and asked her what she thought. She confided that she thought she might have it, because of some of the things she said. I confirmed it, and told her that, like Dale, she had support at home and at school through it all, no matter what. But all that was yet to come.

At the Guide Dog Centre a year earlier, the hospitality from the friendly kitchen staff was superb. We were fed with copious, hearty Irish breakfasts and bucket-loads of tea. I sat with Neil and explained the reasoning behind the resources, and how they might be useful to the Irish model. He understood my thinking exactly, and he then invited us to see a trainer work with a potential autism assistance dog.

We drove to a quiet housing estate. The harness was put on the dog. The trainer had control, with a long lead attached to the collar. Training? We suddenly realised we could make this session real! With Amy! Being small-framed for an eight-year-old, she was perfect. With the Canadian dog model, the child has to be ten years or under so the dog can counteract the child's strength.

The dog was big, strong and stunning, with a beautiful temperament, and near the end of its training. With Amy prepared, we set off. As they walked at an even pace, I suggested, "Amy, jump up and down and scream loudly!"

Marvellous! Her scream pierced all of our ears, yet the dog remained unfazed. He waited until she was calm and for the trainer's command to walk again. It was humbling to witness. En route, Dale answered Neil's questions. We reached a busy road. Immediately, the dog stopped, stood glued to the kerb. I couldn't resist. "Amy, run away and pull as strongly as you can."

Oh boy! She pulled that dog lead like she was in a tug of war, but to no avail. The dog remained anchored, and *she* succumbed.

For the rest of the walk, Neil and Dale discussed an excellent Irish programme strategy. On the adult's lead there was a sign which read: "Please Ask Child to Pat Me." This is an unconventional tactic. Generally, a working dog should not be disturbed when it's with a client. Neil explained parents had reported that their child remained calm and enjoyed people admiring and stroking their dog. Dale and I recalled parallel situations with Henry: "It made me feel good when people admired him, and would talk to me about him."

Our weekend was memorable. I learned so much, and we even managed to have some social time with Neil and his family. On our way back, we needed to pick up the boys. They had had a whale of a time, but something else happened. On sighting Dale, Henry greeted him as if he hadn't seen him for three years, instead of just three days! Happily, he jumped into the boot. However, Thomas was a different story. He had become far too comfortable with hotel life. Indeed, he'd fallen in love with a guest Spaniel. He was so besotted that he refused to leave! I had to drag him into the car, with his tail between his legs.

A few weeks later, Dale and I visited Dogs for the Disabled (DFD) in Banbury, who had started a pilot scheme with three families using the Canadian model. Jamie was working, so he couldn't be with us. Maybe we both knew that wasn't the whole truth, but it was as much as I could take on at that point. *Focus*, I told myself. *Focus*. I looked ahead. I needed to share my work with interested charities; the wider the knowledge, the better the chance of success. We spent a lovely day, which mirrored our Irish visit. While Dale had time with a trainer, working with a dog for a physically disabled client, I had a chat with the fundraising manager. Deep in conversation, I had to interrupt to "take a moment". Dale was outside and caught my eye, and I simply had to watch. He was sitting in an electric wheelchair, with a beautiful and dedicated "carer" called Hal by his side. I stood, gobsmacked, as Hal pulled off Dale's jacket; picked up his mobile phone, then walked beside the chair, anticipating the next time he would need help. Hal was a gorgeous golden retriever, who did his breed and peers proud. Dale was using a training clicker to reinforce when a task was done well. It was more than a moment.

The trainer commented that Dale had a natural aptitude for using the clicker, a skill many find difficult. The CEO invited him back for a week's work experience. He seized the chance!

At Easter, Dale returned to DFD, staying nearby with his aunt and uncle. He blossomed under the staff, who made him feel comfortable and welcomed. The trainer he spent most time with sent us gorgeous pictures of him working, including a special one: Dale in a wheelchair, with Hal by his side. He learned how to groom the dogs properly, clean the kennel areas, look for health problems and best of all, he was involved with training the dogs.

The staff were well aware that Dale, as a child, had been as severely affected as the children they were now seeing. That way, the week worked for everyone. When he returned home he bought some clickers to fine-tune Henry's tricks. He had such a natural aptitude for dog training.

After all our amazing tuppence coloureds, we were back to penny plain in no time, and it was fine! Before the end of term, Dale had to complete a written assignment, "Understanding and Managing Children's Behaviour". The topics were insightful, and I got that irony! He had to describe types of bullying, and the discriminatory behaviour people with disabilities (particularly those with ASD!) face. I couldn't help but wonder when the tutors marked his work, did they notice anything? I'll never know. However, the tutors could see Dale was progressing, and this was acknowledged in his June 2008 external assessment. As ever, his attendance and timekeeping were *Highly Satisfactory*. As was his relationship with the children and staff. What was more important was that all other areas of his practice were *Satisfactory*. Now, he was achieving the standard expected for an HNC student, despite the lack of support and adjustments. He passed with flying colours.

At last all his coursework was back on track. He entered the summer break in great spirits, ready for a few weeks of happy adventure.

# 8

## Different Places

It was a dream of a summer, and the A-Team embarked on their personal rite of passage. Enjoying rock music was one thing, but that first festival beckoned – T in the Park! Dale and Ryan were nominated project managers, and once again, the plus side of autism kicked in and their adventure was super organised, military-style. Firstly, the concert website was combed to meet all their needs. They carried their Autism Alert Cards and used their transport concessions, allowing them a significantly bigger lager budget. They selected the quieter camping area, with plenty of room for those essential, pre-ordered crates of Tennent's. Lockers were booked. Dale was pleased to discover he could get his daily shower, despite having to queue two hours for the privilege, and skim £5 off his alcohol allowance. Every penny was counted. Each boy took responsibility for buying one piece of decent equipment, because they planned this to become the prototype for an annual beano. As I watched him humph that bulging rucksack full of junk food, I mused that I'd never seen Scout camp leading to this!

Thankfully, the sun was with them. I watched the main acts myself, but there were no fields or tents for me! In the evening, on my own, red wine in hand, I enjoyed the television coverage from the deep comfort of my sofa. Cameras scaled the audience. Though the crowd, which looked like tin-jammed sardines, did give me a bit of worry, I was so proud. Dale and his friends were really amongst that lively, squashing throng.

On his return, the rucksack contents pretty much walked through the door before he did! The guys had had a fantastic time, and the free floor show of merry revellers had been every bit as good as the staged events. The outrageous fancy dress gear, the mankinis, the banter – okay, lads, no more! That's quite enough for any mum to hear!

Meanwhile, back indoors, both Dale and Amy were hooked on reality television: *The Apprentice*, *Big Brother*, and particularly *I'm a Celebrity . . . Get Me Out of Here!* I was astonished. The entertainment was, after all, largely at the cost of the contributors. But both of them were remarkably astute at working out the behaviours and predicting who would be voted in or out. If only I'd been a gambling woman . . .

They were thriving. However, that October a terrible incident occurred, reminding us all that no matter how high-functioning a person with ASD may be, they are still vulnerable. An eighteen-year-old friend of Dale's with Asperger's syndrome was walking home one afternoon. He glanced at a man, drunk in a van. The man acknowledged him. "What are you looking at?"

He replied, "You."

The drunk leapt from the van and punched him repeatedly in the face. The lad had to be rushed to hospital with extensive bruising and swelling. Doctors feared that his cheekbone was fractured. He was in a state of shock. Thankfully, there was no lasting physical damage, but the psychological harm was devastating. He explained to the local paper, "I've lost my confidence. I just don't want to go out."[1]

Dale and his friends were sickened and rallied round to support their friend for weeks. Steadily, they accompanied him outdoors to help him overcome his fears. What a painful reminder of their situation. Dale's reaction was sharp. He had to stay safe . . . so he took up a martial art! Once again a friend was on hand – a karate instructor! It worked on so many levels: helping improve his balance and co-ordination, and the repetitive, precise movements increased his spatial and self-awareness. He graduated quickly, acquiring many coloured belts. At the time of writing, he is a green belt. Perhaps, more importantly, the discipline it instilled and the sense of safety he gained gave him courage. He made new friends, his self-esteem soared and his stress-levels dropped.

In November, Dale's nursery assessment report was equally impressive. He received two *Satisfactory* and six *Highly Satisfactory* grades for his practitioner skills. At last, we began to believe that he would achieve what many had thought unachievable. It felt wonderful! Better and better, staff at Barnardo's nominated him for the *Sunday Mail Young Scot Awards*. He didn't receive an award, but it didn't matter. It was enough to know how highly Barnardo's valued him. He received a certificate from the awards panel, stating that his nomination was deserved and his contribution was "outstanding".

With Christmas approaching, I began to relax. What a relief! Life was settled and straightforward again. For once, the festive season could be a peaceful, happy time. I should have known better! In mid-December, my cousin Veronica phoned from Dublin. My uncle Peter had died suddenly. He was the last of my mother's siblings. I had been close to Peter all my life. He visited my mum's for holidays, so he understood our family well. So instead of preparing for Christmas, Dale and I were in Ireland. The day of the funeral was cold, the pavements slippery with ice and the air thick with frosty breath. Dale looked very much the man of the family in his new suit. The night before, in accordance with Irish family and Catholic tradition, he attended family prayers at Peter's side, by the open coffin. Until then, Henry's was the only lifeless body he had seen.

I told him how good he looked, how pleased I was that he wore Grandad George's gold watch. That watch was very special, having belonged to my dad's great-grandfather. Dad gave it to Dale a year before he succumbed to Alzheimer's. My son understood how precious it was and wore it at times of importance or stress. It helped him feel better, rather like Henry's collar, tucked under his pillow, did.

It was bittersweet to witness my son getting to know his near-aged cousin Gemma as if for the first time. Throughout the difficult years, so much time had passed during which I had little contact with my sisters. For the first time in a decade I really felt part of my wonderful family, all pulling together, helping each other in times of crisis. Saying my goodbyes, I vowed to keep in touch more. How could I know that soon a close family member would need my help?

Once home, I was desperate to see Amy, aware my emotions were churning. I was really happy to be working to improve the lives of those affeced by autism. But by doing so, I still had to sustain a secure income working as a community staff nurse and accept I was trapped in a loveless marriage. Since I wrote Dale's story in 2006 the fractures in my relationship seemed to emerge all at once, but they happened throughout my married life. I had adapted to coping with a magnitude of stress. Juggling everything became a normal part of my life, but I couldn't deny the fractures were now reaching breaking point ... and so was I.

Since Amy's diagnosis I had needed low-dose anti-depressants to help me sleep at night, because I suffered with episodes of insomnia. As the stress and marital problems escalated, so did the dose of my medication, to help me cope.

Once again, back in Scotland, festivities took a back seat. Peter's death and seeing my family had deeply affected me. I reflected. That weekend was a wake-up call. The years of fighting and caring for the kids had taken its toll. What had happened to the best years of my life? I reached in my handbag before I turned the key in the lock. I took out the bottle, half empty, and rattled a capsule into my mouth. No water. Right there on the cold step, I threw back another. Nuala's little helpers, I joked in my head. Anti-depressants. Well, I bloody well deserved them. I needed extra chemical support to face Jamie and return to an environment which for years had caused me anguish and despair.

To compound matters, the welcome home was not all that I had hoped. Nothing like. The house was a bombsite. Presumably, I was expected to return and restore order. Oh, yes, and work over Christmas too. Meltdown. Like so often before, Jamie and I erupted. This time, however, it was so bad that Dale had to intervene.

"Mum, Dad, enough of this terrible rowing! Think about Amy hearing this!"

He was right. I hated my kids witnessing the constant arguments. Doubtless, Jamie felt it too.

So, it took having some decent time out, yes, even for a family funeral, to really recognise the flaws in my relationship. It was nothing new; but wrapped up in the children's needs, I hadn't seen it. Dimly, I'd made out that something had changed with Henry's passing, but how could I know what it was, or indeed, that I would have to call on him again?

Just when I needed it most, Dale gave me my best ever Christmas present. It was a copy of his end of placement report, dated 17 December 2008. He had excellent attendance, was "always on time" (actually, most of the time, he was early). He formed excellent relationships with the children, had effective observational skills to take them on to their next steps. He listened actively, accepted advice willingly and was an effective team member with initiative. Very professional in his approach, he was keen to learn. In all nine categories of practice, he was deemed Highly Satisfactory. Now, all he needed was to pass his Graded Unit. I couldn't have been more proud. Mentally and physically exhausted though I was, my incredible son was worth it all.

In New Year 2009, with the incredible support of Sandra and his tutor Gwen, Dale passed that Graded Unit. Whilst the grade was a C, we didn't care. He had done it! In March, he received his letter confirming that he was an HNC Early Years Education and Childcare Worker, despite not a single penny of his £3,897 SAAS award having been spent. Everyone was thrilled! Thankfully, at that point, the future was unknown. We just couldn't see the barriers still ahead.

# 9

## *Different Faces*

Yes, he had passed that course, and Dale had most certainly earned a little time off, but very soon, he applied to go on the supply list for the college nursery. I helped him with paperwork, ensuring the interview panel had access to his DDA adjustments. Billy Docherty, Dale's Prospects employment support worker, had compiled them, so they were spot on. Prospects' role was clarified, and advisory notes about the necessary implementation of interview modifications were included. Something struck me. Billy's adjustments were universal, generic and suitable to be applied across stages and ages. If only everyone was aware of these basic strategies, how much better the world could be. So here they are:

> Say Dale's name, look at him, so he knows you are talking to him.
> One person, one question at a time.
> Give him six seconds to process.
> Say what you mean, and mean what you say.
> No abstract questions; closed rather than open ones.

While he waited for the outcome, Dale placed his name on the local authority supply list. He understood supply meant short notice in unknown nurseries. Unfortunately, in March 2009, like today, there were no suitable vacancies and countless qualified childcare workers waiting for work. Ideally, he needed part-time work or a nursery with school hours. Finding suitable employment is challenging enough for anyone in a deep economic recession. He would be competing with many experienced practitioners, and even teachers chasing childcare posts, the scarcity of work was so grim. We held onto the positive reasons why he chose childcare, and the fact that his CV was now impressive, with all those years of Barnardo's experience.

He had no alternative but to enter the welfare state minefield and the land of Jobcentre Plus. Unlike many of his peers, he had the good luck to be allocated a Disability Employment Adviser (DEA) to help him navigate the system. Fortunately, the DEA had known Dale as a child. He showed him where to go, and who to see about signing on for Job Seekers Allowance (JSA). Unfortunately, the DEA couldn't be with Dale all the time and the other staff weren't trained in autism.

Once more, he came home stressed and anxious. He handed me applications for jobs he had been told were "compulsory". One was a full-time position, based twenty miles away, from 7.45 in the morning to 6.15 in the evening – for the minimum wage. Another was also twenty miles away, inaccessible by public transport and with disastrously long hours.

We were despairing. Then, a couple of weeks later, he returned with the perfect vacancy, albeit a temporary one. Twenty-one hours a week, just fifteen miles down the coast road, a familiar bus ride away in Largs. He phoned Prospects. The next day they called, asking to speak to me first. The caller had been twenty-eight when he had been diagnosed with Asperger's syndrome; I knew him well. His voice was unusually hesitant. He'd spoken to the nursery head and had tried to explain Dale's autism, and how Prospects could support him and their staff. Before he was able to make his points, the Head assumed it was a hoax call! Prospects' advice was that as the Head appeared so unsupportive, his application was already doomed. Sadly, we had to agree; maintaining Dale's confidence was crucial. I tried to be diplomatic when I explained the situation. He was saddened, but he understood.

Something heartening was about to pop through the letterbox, however. Autism Scotland, the biannual NAS newsletter, had a cover showing a painting donated by the artist Peter Howson for the Auction for Autism. Other prestigious Scottish artists with a spectrum connection were also donating. The money raised would go to Prospects.

"Mum, do you think someone would buy my portrait of Henry?"

That portrait took pride of place in our hall. Tucked in the frame was a card, signed by the *After Thomas* cast: Keeley Hawes, Ben Miles, Sheila Hancock, Duncan Preston and young Andrew, who had played Dale. While I treasured it, I had taken several copies, and his gesture was fitting. What support Prospects had given him! Then I remembered another special piece he had drawn when he was eleven for the Project Ability exhibition at GOMA, as part of the Artism Europe Exhibition in summer 2000. This was a large pastel portrait of a friend's cat. Viewing it, many were struck by the array of colours, and how he had captured the texture of the cat's thick, fluffy coat. The eyes stared out and its posture suggested it was ready to pounce from the frame. Having caught the essence, he proudly named his work "Furry Cat". Not only that, but I had a copy! I retrieved it from the attic and our beloved Henry's wall space was filled.

The auction was held at Glasgow's grand Mitchell Library. The auctioneer opened, bidding was slow and because of the recession, sums raised were unusually low. Bidding for "Henry" began. My heart raced. An NAS supporter paid £300! Next was "Furry Cat". Surprisingly, a bidding war broke out between two people. The new owner paid £150. She was a cat lover who taught autistic children. Dale was moderately autistic when he drew the cat, so he hadn't signed his work, as it might have caused him confusion, "spoiling" his picture. He simply wouldn't have understood the concept. Times had changed. I fought back tears when the new owner handed Dale a pen. Boldly, he signed his name across the back of the frame, ten years after its creation!

The phone remained silent for supply work, but there wasn't time to dwell on that, as Dale and I had a prestigious event coming up. Another gift from Henry. I was to be guest speaker at the Sheriff of Chester's annual fundraiser, where the public joined him to enjoy a hearty breakfast, all for a £15 donation. Coincidentally, the Sheriff owned a beautiful chocolate Labrador called Henry and had been touched when he read our story. The proceeds were being donated to Hinderton School in Ellesmere Port, whose thirty-two pupils were at the moderate to severe end of the spectrum.

On arrival at Chester Station, I was pleasantly shocked! We received a civic welcome. The Sheriff donned his robes and chains, and a red carpet led us to the formal car. The friendship and hospitality we received made us feel like VIPs. That evening, the Sheriff and a close friend joined us for a lovely meal. Throughout the night, his empathy and understanding was affecting, and he shed many a tear over Dale's shared tales.

The next morning we went to the Guild Hall breakfast. We sat at the centre table with the distinguished guests. Dale took it all in his stride, as many approached him to talk and to shake his hand. What an ambassador for autism!

Meanwhile, I pinned up pictures of Dale growing up with Henry and Amy. I had a talk to give. I could hardly eat, but once I'd started my presentation, I delivered with confidence. I had the audience in stitches as I waved a cuddly dog (I always seemed to have a pack with me now!). They asked challenging questions, and I replied to them all. At the end, I presented a framed copy of Henry to the Head of Hinderton School. Hodder and Stoughton arranged a book signing, so we were all able to talk informally.

Later, the Sheriff, with the "freedom" of that beautiful, historic city, took us on a morning tour. In the afternoon, we visited Hinderton School, to be met by Julie, the school office manager whose son has autism. We got on immediately! The school had NAS accreditation, indicating it provided a high standard of condition-specific education. The Head showed us round. There were five classes, defined by colours – blue, yellow, orange, green and purple – helping pupils identify their age and stage. Every purpose-designed classroom included a quiet room. Activities and lessons were similar to those at St Anthony's and Struan School (Scottish Autism's provision) and there was a 1:2 staff/pupil ratio. Ideal.

The relaxed atmosphere permeated the whole building. Artwork displays were restrained and there were awards charts and PECS for each pupil on show.[1] PECS is short for a 'Picture Exchange Communication System', which is commonly used to help children with communication difficulties express their needs via pictures. For example, a glass of juice is shown to indicate they want a drink. The same method is used for other basic activities of their lives.

The Head explained the school's ethos was child-centred, with sensory integration to the fore. Each child had an individualised sensory profile, drawn up by an occupational therapist. Finally, we were shown a small room littered with old mats on the floor. Really, it was unfit for anything. If the breakfast raised enough, the Head hoped it could be an Acqualia Room. Such rooms provide quiet, calming sensory stimuli and a positive environment, using soft-coloured lava and bubble lamps. There are fibre-optic lights which change colour when touched. The children lie on mats with reassuring auditory stimuli, like waves or whale noises. Pleasant, subdued olfactory experiences may be added. The room gives those with acute anxiety time out and emotional respite, promoting recovery and minimising the possibility of their distress escalating. This would be a vital resource for one-to-one therapies.

The Sheriff had another engagement, so we bade him a fond farewell and thanked him for everything as we went on to attend the school's weekly assembly. Two weeks before, I'd sent a picture of Dale with Henry and me, so the children would be unfazed. Although Henry's portrait would be hung in the school's reception, Dale suggested getting thirty-two A4 copies made. He signed every one, so each child could have a memento. The Head suggested he give each child their picture individually, rather like a prize-giving.

The assembly hall was set up before the children entered. We sat beside the interactive whiteboard so the children could see us. The chairs were arranged in a semi-circle, in natural light, and soft music played as the classes filtered in. The majority sat as any would, while others displayed autistic behaviour – hand-flapping, rocking or verbal tics; a few wore ear defenders. One child entered last, cautiously holding his teacher's hand. The pair sat apart, beside the open door. I couldn't help but notice how few girls there were. Statistically, four boys to every girl are affected. While the noise was somewhat different from the "average" assembly, when the music stopped, the head teacher stepped up.

"Children, good afternoon!"

The staff and majority of pupils replied. He displayed our pictures on the whiteboard, reminding them that we were here to see them. After he had dealt with the usual school business, he introduced me. My heart sank. I was caught, unaware and unprepared. I took a deep breath, grabbed the bag containing the cuddly pack and began: "Children, I think your school is really good!"

I told them that, like Dale, I liked dogs. I also liked their blue school jumpers. Then I produced the toy! To their delight, I pointed out its blue collar. "Does anyone know what a dog needs?"

Immediately, hands spiked the air. I chose one excited little boy, who shouted, "Dinner!"

I gave him a Makaton thumbs up. "Yes, dinner. Well done!"

Producing the metal bowl from the sack, I then worked through all the equipment, telling them I was giving their school the pack. I left them to name the "dog" and put their school badge into the key ring fob, letting everyone know it was Hinderton's. The Head then explained that Dale also had a gift. One by one, each child came forward to receive their picture. Dale leaned forward to be at their eye-level. With a quiet, calm voice, he said, "Hello Tony, I hope you like my picture."

Everything progressed beautifully. I was so proud.

At the close of the assembly, the Head asked if anyone wanted to ask anything. Hands flew up.

"What was good about having a dog?"

Again, my son surpassed himself. He looked at the boy, repeated the question, so everyone knew what was being asked, and said, "I got Henry when he was a puppy. He made me happy, like a friend, and we grew up together."

The assembly finished with the children singing for us "Going to the Pet Shop".

As the purple class filtered by, one little boy left his group and approached Dale confidently. "Can I get another copy for my mum?"

Dale told him it was a good and kind question, and directed him to the Head, who reinforced that it was a good idea, and promised him a photocopy. What a school! Sadly, not all children are as fortunate as these pupils. It was a privilege for us to witness at Hinderton, condition-specific education at its best.[2]

A couple of weeks later the Sheriff called, with news. The Acqualia Room funding target had been reached! "Ripples from your visit are still going on. I hear your presentation was emotionally electric."

I thought it couldn't get much better. Then, the postman arrived with a card: "*To Nuala and Dale, thank you for the picture of Henry. I am buying a frame for it, to put onto my bedroom wall. From Tony, Year 4 Purple Class.*"

Soon afterwards, it was followed by an email from Julie: "Our pupils are very fond of the dog [. . .] he often disappears to various areas of the school leaving his basket empty [. . .] Staff have asked me to enquire as to the supplier of the dog to see if we could perhaps purchase another!"

Henry had truly made his mark in Ellesmere Port! Once again, I had that tingle, that sensation that something was happening, and part of my life, at least, was going somewhere very interesting indeed. "Career" wasn't the word, at least not yet. Time would tell on that. Maybe "vocation" said it better. I couldn't be certain, but I did know I was being taken on this walk into a new future . . . and I liked it, very much.

Back in Inverclyde, while Dale waited for supply, he continued with his Barnardo's drama group and helped out at their Easter Holiday activity group. I carried on working two night shifts a week as a community staff nurse. Holding down my job with the pressures of family life was no one's idea of an easy ride, but I loved it. The extra money gave us a good lifestyle, but more importantly, it meant I wasn't just a mum. I had some other kind of identity and a separate social life. But I had to admit, I was beginning to feel burnt out.

Community Nursing had merged with social work, so my responsibilities had increased, but I had coped – just. I felt I had no alternative but to keep working, despite my soaring stress levels. Now, however rewarding, holding down my job became one straw too many. For the first time in my career, I went off on long-term sick leave.

Thankfully things were good with Dale. At last! The phone call he had been waiting on! He was to start work, covering a full-time post with a preschool group until the end of term . . . immediately! Excitedly, he asked me to accompany him into town to help him buy new clothes for the job. Whilst I was pleased, I was intrigued. He had, after all, been purchasing his own clothes for two years. We started in Marks and Spencer's, a great favourite of Dale's. Browsing through the polo shirts, he announced, "Mum, I want five different colours. Will you help me choose?"

"Five, Dale? That's a lot. Why?"

I was astounded by his reply. As staff would be aware of his autism, he wanted to prove his professionalism by wearing a different coloured shirt each day. Not only would it be clear that his hygiene standards were high, but the children would learn colours and sequencing. However, his next words left me saddened: "Mum, I've learned that because people know I have autism, I have to prove how much I have beat it, so people don't see me with autism all the time."

I reassured him. The scenario was unfair, but his thinking realistic. He bought green, sky blue, red, black and royal blue shirts and some chinos. He was ready to start. A couple of days later, I had an unsettling thought. Would I work, unprotected? What cover did he have, in today's world? I advised him to join a union. Hopefully he would never need it, but having studied the workings of trade unions at school, he agreed. Far better to be safe than sorry.

On his first day, he was back into his routine, arriving fifteen minutes early, wearing the colour of the day. Generally, he didn't finish until 4.30 p.m. or later, but he fitted in well. I was pleased; he could relax at home. He kept up the same pace of social life and, faithfully, he continued karate every Wednesday. I was worried how he could keep on his Barnardo's group on Thursdays, because it started at 6.30 p.m. He was hardly home before he was heading out the door again. He didn't mind . . . but I did!

I was concerned that he might overload himself. The fragile state of my own health was proof of the risks, and that was without my having autism. So, I picked him up for his drama after work. We grabbed two large cappuccinos and muffins to go, and had an hour's chat before the group started.

Everyone was delighted to see Dale working, especially me. I knew he was managing the workload, paperwork and all the responsibilities that being full-time in a busy nursery brought. He had to prepare his group of children for starting primary. Staff were supportive and he flourished. Parents thought highly of him, especially those with children going through the assessment process for ASD. They would talk with him, comforted, seeing how far he had come.

One day he came home from work and I couldn't ignore his upbeat manner. "Dale, what's the cause of your good mood?"

"Mum, I can't tell you because of confidentiality."

Hmmm! I advised him that if he didn't give names, he could describe a situation, using words like "parent" or "speech therapist". He could even change a person's gender. Pausing, he began, "Mum, remember the head teacher at Highlanders' Language Unit, who helped me a lot when I was first diagnosed?"

"Yes . . . Irene."

"Today, I was working with a group of children. Irene was in the nursery and I was to carry on as normal with the group, while she observed one of them. Afterwards, she spoke to me, and said I was a natural 'teacher' with the children, and I had done a really good activity with them. It just meant a lot to me, coming from her."

I was delighted for him and couldn't help but wonder how Irene must have felt knowing, if it hadn't been for her determination and her belief in him back in February 1991, neither would have met again eighteen years on. He continued to thrive, as did his charges. At the end of term, he was captured in a super picture, standing proudly with his class; all were wearing their specially made mortarboards. Very much part of the team, he joined the staff for their end of term lunch.

All was well, and the difficult journey was now worth every painful step. His dream was a reality. His only barrier was finding a suitable permanent job with manageable hours. But hey! His career had begun at last!

# 10

## Colours of Autism

"The longer a child with autism goes without help, the harder they are to reach."[1]

Sometimes, I wished I could have thrown it all up in the air, pitched a tent and blasted my ears out at T in the Park. I could have rolled in mud, danced, anything . . . anything but this. There was my hand, back in my bag, back in the bathroom medicine chest. I had a bottle of pills at hand, inside and out. Again. I could find them with my eyes closed. Again. Again. Thank God Dr Grose was so vigilant. I was a wreck. I suppose not working helped to some extent, but the hoped-for respite was constantly undermined by guilt. Not earning was harrowing, and Jamie was stressed too as he tried to adapt. Royalties from *Henry* helped salve my conscience, but not quite enough. Somehow I got by, and I could just about imagine that I even enjoyed the normality of having time to run the household. In truth, supporting two kids with autism and being on tap for others going through their own spectrum crises more than filled my days. I don't know whose time I was on. Certainly it wasn't mine. Yet, there was one call I needed to make.

I hadn't spoken to my cousin Laura for ages. Her daughter, Katy, had just turned two. As they lived in the Highlands, our contact was sporadic. At last, I picked up that phone.

"Oh, Nuala. Good to hear from you . . . I was actually going to call you."

Something in me knew that, already.

I first met Katy when she was only three months old. A family baby! What a lovely excuse for a visit, to have a weekend break, and hey, even throw in an outing! We booked into a hotel, to give Laura space and make the most of our own wee family holiday. She was isolated and needed a break, so I offered to take the baby out for the day, when we visited the Loch Ness Monster Exhibition. Amy was seven, and it had been a quarter of a century since my midwifery days, but it was fun to have a wee one in tow again. For once, the weather was beautiful, and the gardens bustled with families. Katy loved the car ride; we hardly noticed we had a baby on board. She sat wide-eyed, staring ahead, but blankly, and there was never a whimper, nor hardly a muscle twitched in that seventy-five-minute journey. There was no air conditioning, and though I tried to offer her a drink, she was so content and, despite the heat, she ignored my attempts.

On arrival, I popped Katy in her buggy. Though wide awake, she transferred easily. We joined a large, bubbly tour group and tailed into a dark room, projected all around with loch pictures. It was like being in the middle of the water. The story began, and my heart sank.

There were roars and simulated monster screeches, there was thunder and lightning. The sound effects were at the legal maxima and the tension palpable as we waited for Nessie. Amy was terrified! I couldn't see or hear Katy and I became desperate to bale out. I had no wish to return a traumatised infant to her mother! Moments later, the sound faded to an eerie silence and the lights returned us to daylight. Thank God! Katy had fallen asleep. Indeed, she slept deeply throughout and we were able to see the entire exhibition, uninterrupted. Yet that noise could have wakened the dead.

Outdoors at last, in still-fantastic weather. While Katy slept, we lunched alfresco. In the midst of a bedlam of hilarity and playing kids, Amy joined in a game of chase, and Dale headed for a stroll while I saw to Katy. After all, she hadn't eaten or drunk for five hours, and with the long car journey back ahead, I wasn't willing to leave her any longer. I picked her up gently, but I needed to stimulate her to waken. I tickled her feet, removed her cardigan, and then and only then she gave a big hello yawn and stretched as long as her tiny body allowed.

Thankfully, Katy wasn't the least upset by her awakening. I changed her nappy so she could enjoy her overdue bottle. Bizarrely, she wasn't interested in it. I had plenty midwifery experience, encouraging legions of reluctant feeders, but this one was adamant. Jamie drove us back to the hotel so I could take her to the quiet cool of our room. I was determined to return with a happy baby. At last, she fed. As she did, I had a terrible sense of déjà-vu.

Her beautiful brown eyes stared right through me, taking me back to a haunted place, with my own Dale as a baby. I couldn't deny my thoughts: for the third time in my life, I was cradling an infant in my family … another ticking bomb. For me, it wasn't a matter of if Katy's autism would explode, just when.

On our return, Laura was eager to know how we had managed. Naturally, I assured her, all was well. This wasn't the time to worry my cousin. She would have a sore path ahead, waiting and watching, but the mother and nurse in me knew. It would have been cruelly irresponsible to mention anything then. There is a time for recognition and acceptance. It cannot be imposed.

Two years on, that time had come. Laura talked to me of her suspicions. As she was voicing the word "autism", I told her of my own concerns. She had read my book, and reread it, just before my call. She understood the enormity of her thinking, but was grateful to have help. Katy's few words were termed echolalic by the health visitor and, perplexed, Laura Googled what that meant. Echolalic, yes, echoing words, repeating them instead of answering. "Are you cold, Katy?" batted back with the uncomprehending reply, "Are you cold, Katy?" again and again. It was all too familiar. Every reference was to autism; indeed, all Katy's emerging traits fitted that very template.

The wee one displayed similar behaviours to Dale, but one feature worried me particularly. In order to cope with a hostile environment, deal with body awareness problems (proprioception), difficulties with spatial awareness and all round sensory chaos, Katy, like so many others, had begun to tiptoe walk. Both my children had done this, and Dale's pattern was so ingrained that it required years of intervention. Yet, this chilled me, because it was the most extreme I had known.

Katy's autism was consuming her days; she had no peers to play with, and because Laura and her husband worked long and anti-social hours, she enjoyed no significant intervention. Nothing could break into her autistic world. She adapted, moving everywhere, indoors and out, like a ballerina, on her tiptoes. A dance teacher once explained that no child was allowed to perform a pointe until they were six, as it can seriously damage the Achilles tendon, and the ankle muscles. Katy was just two.

Worse, she walked backwards! Laura was exasperated, tried everything, but even shod, she still reverse-manoeuvred, on her toes. Early intervention would help. Many children benefit from occupational health and physiotherapy. Even so, for some, despite all the measures, the contracture of the Achilles tendon needs more radical treatment. Indeed, unaddressed, mobility will be reduced in the long term. Surgery, and surprisingly perhaps, even medically supervised Botox injections, have been used to try to help sufferers regain a normal walking posture. Not a rosy outlook. Fortunately, it wasn't all bad news.

Katy had shown a preference for the colour red, in tune with her obsession – Mickey Mouse's shorts! The time had come. I urged Laura to seek an immediate referral to an Educational Psychologist, to begin the journey to an early diagnosis.

I assured Laura, that with early intervention, Katy would improve. I would help her negotiate the system to ensure her child would receive that all-important, condition-specific education. My present was in the post the very next day. Like the cuddly pack, it was no ordinary gift. In *A Friend Like Henry*, Dale described how *Thomas the Tank Engine* characters' and Henry's facial expressions were easier for him to understand than human faces. He was not alone. Recent work with children with ASD aged four to eight has enabled the development of an autism-specific DVD, *The Transporters*. The eight toy vehicles have human faces, individual personalities and functions. Storylines are simple and teach fifteen basic emotions. Research shows that ASD children using *Transporters* can catch up with their non-autistic peers in their understanding of facial expressions and emotions. I knew it could help Katy when I read a parent's review: "After only watching three or so episodes, my son knew the names of every character [ ... ] 'Look, Daddy's happy' [ ... ] It's a bit like someone has flicked a switch in his head."[2] I hoped that my gift of *The Transporters* would help Katy as the research has shown.

With the summer ahead and my programme in good shape, I just needed to find a family! Okay, I needed funding to really make things complete, but despite that – yes, despite that – this was moving and taking real shape. I lived it, I dreamed it. I spent hours on the computer, or with sheets of paper at my kitchen table, working, modifying it, changing it. I wish someone had funded me. I really wished that, but it didn't stop me. This was the dog on my shoulder ... and it wasn't going away! So, in the absence of funds, where was the family, or more importantly, the right family? While many had contacted me, none were in the position to pilot the work. Just as I was about to give up, Jim Taylor emailed, asking if he could pass my number to a mum and teacher called Beth. She was interested in getting a dog for her nine-year-old severely autistic son, Keir. A few days later, my phone rang.

As we talked, we clicked. I asked why she wanted to explore getting a dog. She was desperate. Despite all her best attempts, avenue after avenue was being blocked. She needed to make a change and was prepared to look at something that the conventional paths didn't offer. Perhaps, her personal final straw came when an involved professional, who should have known better, described her son as showing no progress. Oddly, with such a damning comment, the professional was unable to offer any stalemate-breaking suggestions. No one should be treated like that, parent or child. Fortunately, Beth was not prepared to accept that callow remark. Nor was I.

Keir participated in many activities, but being an only child, he needed company. Beth knew meaningful interaction would improve his life quality. His dog experience was with a family friend's Dalmatian and he showed an interest. Clearly, a puppy was inappropriate, and not any dog would do. Keir needed a dog with the same qualities and maturity as an assistance dog, the qualities Henry had had. I reassured Beth her call was timely; my programme was ready. We talked for ages. We agreed to try out Keir with my system; it would do no harm. All going well, I would help Beth source a suitable dog. But first we needed to be certain that Keir would benefit from having a dog at all.

I went through my checklist to tailor Keir's resources to his autism and his intellectual level. While his autism was severe, he had a small vocabulary, and though some phrases were echolalic, more usually, they were in context. Keir's sweet voice had different pitches and tones, and it was difficult for an adult to tune in, so it was easy to miss the extent to which he was already communicating.

Now that I had a sense of this, I asked Beth if he had a colour preference. She confirmed that though he was not wild about any colour, he had a way of gravitating towards a certain, bright Percy green! That answered my next question! Children with ASD can adopt more than one obsession at a time and replace one obsession with another, so we agreed to include the ever-useful Thomas and his cohorts in our plans. Beth was far from oblivious to her son's autism, recognising in detail how it affected him, but significantly, every day she valued that endearing, cheeky personality. Keir was Keir, not an autistic boy, but a lad with autism. That's a distinction well worth making.

He didn't look at adults' faces when verbalising, and additionally, he used PECS so his comprehension was variable but encouraging.

Beth hoped a dog might help reduce his ritualistic behaviours, which dominated his life (and the family's!) daily, especially outdoors.

A few days later I sent the initial, Red Stage folder to familiarise Keir with a dog's needs. The colouring-in pictures showed a dog wearing a green collar with matching lead. Beth photocopied them and sent them to Keir's wonderful teacher, who shared the activities with him and his peers. Keir's parents knew how to "dogify" him with DVDs and books, a happy process.

Six weeks later it was Yellow Stage time, preparing Keir for a visit from Dale, Henry and me. Being strangers, I sent through a social story with pictures of us, explaining we would be visiting. To help Keir understand our visit was imminent, I sent through Henry's furry duck. This allowed him to play with his parents, by throwing it. He was taught it belonged to Henry. Keir would give Henry his duck on arrival.

We set off with Henry, in all his finery. His green collar had a picture of Dale in the key ring fob, to remind Keir that Henry belonged to Dale. The harness had "Keir's" green lead in a loop handle and I put on a little Thomas on the other hook. Such was the enormity of what we were trying to achieve that Keir's teacher gave up her Saturday to be there.

When we arrived, Dale let Henry run around and explore his new environment. Keir was clearly excited meeting Henry, and gave little attention to the new humans. When Henry stood still, Keir smiled. He grabbed his bright green lead. Then Beth remembered, "Keir, go fetch Henry's duck."

He ran into the kitchen, retrieved the duck, which Henry obligingly wedged in his mouth and excitedly carried to the lounge. Keir followed Henry throughout, often trying to interact, even though the dog never stood still! Because there was enough space and the duck was safe to throw, I let Keir hear and see the command: Henry, fetch! Henry returned, and dropped his toy at my feet for another go. The third time, Keir took the duck and copied, despite having difficulty mastering the throw. Several little throws later, I noticed he was waiting for the dog's attention, ensuring he "sat" before he was prepared to throw. He gave no verbal command, but shrieked with laughter, watching the fetch and return. Both had mastered the game.

Throughout, Keir showed little curiosity about us, but his Henry-fixation continued into the garden. They ran around together and he held his lead tightly. I demonstrated "sit", and Beth noticed thereafter that Keir repeated the word to Henry. He was intrigued that the dog obeyed him. Several times, he pushed the patient Henry's back-end down, but quickly he learned that he had to command and Henry was to comply.

It was thrilling to see another child learn through a dog as Dale had, seventeen years earlier. Communication works! Keir was comfortable communicating with the dog because Henry gave him no verbal or social pressure. We witnessed how children with autism are able to understand and begin to verbalise using a dog because of the consistent, non-threatening sharing the animal allows. The dog enables the child to engage and interact without the human's social baggage. There are no complex facial expressions or language to bombard and intimidate. I was beginning to recognise the piece of the jigsaw I had sensed was missing since Dale's childhood.

What was the dog doing right that we neuro-typicals were not?

Keir was so comfortable, connecting and interacting with Henry. Several times he attempted to sit astride the dog's back. Henry stayed in the "down" position, unfazed and tolerant. A bond had been created. Although Keir's eye contact was initially fleeting, his teacher noticed as the game progressed that with Henry it improved. He looked directly at his face. The social timing was correct for Henry alone. History was repeating itself.

Keir had a great interest in "his" lead, so much so that he tried to remove it, repeating, "I want it . . . I want it."

This was a definite request. Dale obliged by removing the lead and Keir showed him his approval, displaying a big beam while he wrapped the entire lead around his right wrist.

As anticipated, Henry made a large deposit in the middle of the garden. Thankfully I had covered the dog's toileting needs in the resources! Keir accepted the novelty, while Dale did the needful.

The only negative response we observed was when an excited Henry let out an almighty bark. Clearly, that bothered Keir, but with reassurance he accepted that Henry was his "friend" and calmly played on.

As I had done once with Dale, all interaction for Keir was directed initially through Henry. We didn't force him, and allowed his rituals to emerge. He had to know that what we were doing was on his terms; like all good practice, it was child-centred. Soon, Keir could be diverted to what we wanted, through Henry. This approach had worked well with Dale, and the autism assistance dog charities have found similar patterns.

Bit by bit, Keir seemed to grasp that Henry was barking with excitement, a kind of dog-speak, and this very aurally sensitive boy began to tolerate the sound. Things were going well, the weather was favourable, and so we tried a walk. Dale used his black lead attached to Henry's collar, so he was in control, while Keir held his, which was unhooked to full length. Clearly, he wanted it that way.

Keir's teacher commented on how much she liked my approaches. The Red Stage resources complemented his schoolwork. Although things were working out, we assumed nothing. Beth showed Keir the PECS park symbol. That entailed a left turn, but he was heading right, in the direction of his beach walk. We changed communication tack and set off to the shore.

Dale remained on Henry's right, Keir on his left, so he was shielded from traffic. I had used this safety barrier strategy years before with Dale. If Dale bolted, I intended to give Henry the "down, stay" command to let me catch my boy. Thankfully it was never needed, because Dale stayed with Henry throughout. When he was ten he told me he felt safer with Henry at the traffic side, and he never wanted to leave his dog when they were out. Henry made our outings more fun, and more secure.

Dale believed he was in charge because he had his own blue lead. At twelve, six years on, he had become sufficiently confident to take Henry for small familiar walks.

As we strolled, Keir's gait was bouncy and happy. He jumped, climbed on walls, emitted the odd scream and enjoyed using his lead as a lasso. Henry didn't bat an ear lobe. En route, Keir stripped leaves from bushes to scatter confetti-like and collected gravel to pattern on the ground. We let him be, have his rituals, as we could quite easily move him on with Henry as a prompt. Whenever Keir abandoned Henry, leaving his lead on the ground, the dog was commanded to sit and stay; we all stayed until Beth reminded him, "Keir, look . . . Henry is waiting for you." After a few minutes, Keir returned, picked up his lead and walked.

Approaching the kerb Dale said, "Keir, we stop, we stay. No cars, we go."

Just before the beach, Keir entered a familiar walled grassy area, a regular sticking point on family walks. Again, Beth used Henry. "Keir, look . . . Henry is waiting for you. He wants to go to the beach."

Minutes later he returned, and off we went. Next, Beth warned me of a potential problem. Keir liked to slip behind some lampposts, and his favourite was about to appear.

"Now, this will be interesting."

Keir had a tight hold of Henry's lead. Never scared to take a risk, I said, "Let's see what happens."

Keir's lamppost! He stopped. We stood, silent; Henry sat; and Dale remained anchored. Keir made his move. Gleefully, he squeezed between the lamppost and the dyke, his precious lead clutched, firm in his right hand. We braced ourselves for his first meltdown. He paused calmly, looked at the lead in his right hand, and then effortlessly swapped the lead from right to left, as if he had done the manoeuvre many times before. We suffered a collective jaw drop, and then walked on!

This may seem trifling to those unfamiliar with autism. Our trepidation was significant, because differentiating right from left is a significant barrier for many on the spectrum. It was for my own children. It is not unusual to see children wearing their shoes on the wrong feet, and it can take years for some to work that out. It never ceases to amaze me how complex and interesting those affected with ASD can be. Daniel Tammet, an adult with Savant syndrome and Asperger's, can memorise long numerical sequences, learn a foreign language in a week, yet he was hindered hugely by his right/left confusion as a child.[3]

Keir was determined to keep Henry very much under his charge. This was momentous and we couldn't help but feel a quiet optimism. At the beach, he laughed raucously and showed great delight as Henry played with seaweed and dangled it from his mouth. Frequently, Keir alone had control, and Beth and I commented how natural and comfortable he looked with a dog in tow, running along the shore. At times, his autism was invisible. Keir loved seeing Henry in the water and while his autism re-emerged on the beach, as he lined up shells and pebbles, his determination to interact with Henry never faltered.

Returning homewards, we came to a busy road. The traffic was so bad, as we waited, Keir decided that Henry needed a rest, and pushed down his rear. Henry sat. When Henry sat, Keir copied him and sat with his legs crossed as if they were going to be there for some time! A quick-witted Dale had Henry stand and Keir copied. As we walked swiftly, Keir started pulling in the direction of a familiar sweet shop. This time, though, he was obviously upset and frustrated when Beth refused. As I had done so often with Dale, I tried to use Henry as a diversionary tactic.

"Keir, look, Henry says 'No!' He doesn't want to go to the sweet shop. Henry says 'No!'"

Beth stuck firmly by her decision, and we found the strategy a boon! There were many curious looks from the public. Henry was looking somewhat different from your average dog. However, these were further de-stressing qualities as people seemed to appreciate that the dog was there for a reason. Some stopped to pat him and acknowledge Keir, too, which let us see at first hand the rightness of the Irish Autism Assistance Dog policy "Please Ask Child to Pat Me." Autism, so much an "invisible" disability, had become visible in exactly the right way.

Before Henry, I felt I had to ignore stares or justify Dale's behaviour, which was a major source of distress and an added layer to the challenge of being out. Once again, having Henry present in all his kit seemed to change public perceptions and encouraged some people to engage. Handsome Henry was a magnet.

Back home, Keir was able to hand feed him treats, and help me with his dinner (he did attempt to taste a piece!). Three hours into our experiment, Keir had definitely earned some time out.

Before leaving I produced a sack containing the cuddly pack, which was tied with a green bow and a plain gift tag: "To Keir, with Love from Henry." He didn't show much interest, but that didn't matter. It was for long-term use while we sourced his dog. I tried to catch his attention by revealing the contents, one by one, ending with the toy dog, complete with the same lead and collar as Henry . . . but this time the fob held a picture of Keir, with his beautiful smile.

As we prepared to leave, we agreed that the green lead should go with Henry. His mum and I did have to gently prise the lead from him, which, although he found a little upsetting, he accepted. To divert and soothe him, we prompted him to ensure Henry got back his duck. He did his job with great pride.

We waved off a very happy and accepting little boy. The entire visit was about five hours, and it was very encouraging for Dale and me to witness the effects Henry and our preparations had had on Keir. We were thrilled by the response from the parents and the school. What more could we have asked from that day? That four-legged specialist had opened out all sorts of change and progression in one wee blonde chap that a highly trained human had been unable, or unwilling, to do.

[ 113 ]

A couple of days later, Beth rang me to say she wanted me to go ahead and source a suitable dog. I was delighted, but now we had to overcome another major obstacle. What breed of dog? Where would it come from, and when?

As the saying goes, you wait for a bus then three arrive at once, and so it was with parents. A family near me had a five-year-old severely autistic, non-verbal son, Jack, and a non-affected ten-year-old daughter.

I sent the Red Stage resources and arranged a Henry visit eight weeks later. Again, the school co-operated and the duck arrived in time. This time Henry's collar and lead were yellow. I attached a little Bob the Builder figure to the second hook because Jack once named "Bob" on seeing the TV character. Indeed, perhaps the yellow came from the builder's hat. Jack had no obsessions, but Bob had possibilities!

At first, Jack clung to his mum. It was a glorious day, and once in the garden his sister produced Henry's duck. Just like Keir, Jack launched into the game. The eye contact, the game . . . he was totally focused on Henry. The yellow lead didn't seem to hold much appeal until I removed it. Then he grabbed it! Sitting side by side at the table, I encouraged Jack to feed Henry some treats. We managed a useful rhythm of turn taking. So much learning.

In the shade, a smiling Jack sat astride an accepting Henry. I gave him the cuddly pack, and in keeping with the inclusive family spirit of the programme, his sister received a canine-themed book. Jack was mildly curious about the toy, but more interested in the toothbrush and metal food bowl. I found a teaspoon and started to hit the bowl, singing, "Beat the drum . . . beat the drum." He copied, using the toothbrush. While his mum and I chatted, suddenly we heard a musical echo from the loveliest little voice. Jack was echoing, "Beat the drum . . . beat the drum."

That night, Jack took his play dog to bed, and when his parents wished him good night, he replied, "Nigh, nigh", not once, but twice! That was a first. Day by day, Jack's Bob obsession blossomed, and he and his toy had to be forcibly unclipped for school! When their son offered biscuits to his new "pet", the first, precious shoots of imaginative play were sprouting.

The family were determined to find a dog for Jack, and had contacts with the gun dog field. Fully trained, mature dogs. Perfect! Whilst pursuing their own dog plans, they gave me a contact for Hugh, another gun dog owner in Ayrshire. He was rehoming a three-year-old fully trained yellow Labrador called Ellie. I phoned, explained what we were trying to achieve, and within a week we went to meet her.

Hugh let me see his impeccable kennels. Unlike the other gun dogs, Ellie had been domesticated and was used to children. The minute we met her, humans and dogs alike, we were welcomed by a tail-wagging, attention-hungry golden friend. I patted her and fussed – what a gentle soul, what a trusting, angelic face. Yet, Hugh needed to move her on; she was far more interested in staying at her keeper's side than fetching pheasants! As he put it, "Thon dog's too posh to be a working dog!" Indeed, Ellie needed a family. Her vet would later describe her as a very bright dog who had successfully manoeuvred her career change! And why not!

She walked to heel without a lead, would stop at kerbs on command, not moving an inch until commanded to do so. She seemed to tick all the boxes, but I needed to give Ellie the ultimate test ... Amy! I asked her to go over, make a noisy fuss, play, touch her tail, and have fun. She sprang into action, and Ellie passed with flying colours. She lay on the ground while Amy rubbed her tummy, hooting with laughter, to the thuds of her tail. I was certain this was the ideal dog for Keir, and called Beth.

The next hurdle was to get Ellie from Ayrshire to Tayside. We broke it down into two stages, for both Ellie's and Keir's sakes. I sent a picture of her so Beth could adapt the Yellow resources. It was time to show Keir his dog.

Our wonderful vet Nigel checked Ellie over, and that dog sure settled on the couple of days we shared!

She clung to me as if she was transferring the bond she had had with Hugh. Naturally, she had anxious times, particularly at night, so I let her sleep beside me. Jamie was demoted to the spare room. I never slept a wink. She slept like a baby! There was one final test I needed to perform. I was confident Ellie's temperament training was superb, but I needed reassurance. Call the in-house guinea pig!

The weather was amazing. I dressed Ellie as she would be for Keir. On went her green collar, his picture in the fob, her harness with the green lead, and Dale took control, as usual, using a black lead. I attached a little Thomas to the second hook, giving her the full experience. Off we set, and I stayed well behind. Her pace was perfect and she accepted her different walking method and attire. I took my cue: "Amy, jump up and down, and scream."

Both girls did me proud! Ellie looked from Dale to Amy, and it was time to walk on. Our test wasn't over.

"Amy, now just lie on the ground and don't move."

Again Ellie stopped, and stayed, looked at Amy for a clue, as if something was not right, but she knew Dale was in charge. She waited for his command. It was wonderful to see all three together and I knew that I had found Keir his special dog. Exams over. Time for Ellie to meet her master.

We all set off on the long drive. Dale was going to stay with me to help settle Ellie, while Jamie and Amy were off for an afternoon at the park and shops and then a special lunch. That journey was fraught with excitement, tinged with anxiety about my first dog placement. I desperately hoped Ellie could help improve Keir's quality of life and that she would adjust to her new home and master. Minutes from our destination, Dale cut through my concerns: "Mum, stop the car! We need to get Ellie ready."

I was so caught up in the moment I'd forgotten. All those years of teaching him not to butt in! Just as well he did! We were only metres away.

Panic over, and suitably attired, I decided that Dale should walk Ellie towards the house. I phoned to let them know we were near. Beth and Keir were waiting at the door. He was glued to his Mum's side when he saw Dale and Ellie approach, walking like a couple of professionals. He froze, completely overwhelmed.

His response was more than we could have hoped for. Ellie was definitely "his dog". He needed time, so while he played and relaxed in the garden, I looked over and saw Ellie with Beth, who was kneeling down to greet her. Ellie's two front paws rested on Beth's shoulders, her tail wagging furiously like a propeller. She looked ready to take off! Ellie was giving Beth her unconditional love, greeting her new mum, and it was lovely to witness. She would be good for the whole family; after all, there was more than autism in the household.

After we were revived with refreshments and while the sun still shone, we cajoled Keir into taking his dog to the park. Dale took control with the black lead, while Keir took "his" lead, attached to the harness but unhooked to full length. As Dale tried to move them through the garden gate Keir stopped, turned and looked his dog straight in the eye. He gave a clear, perfect command: "Sit." Dutifully, Ellie obeyed. They reached the park in record time, and the new master smiled approvingly throughout. I felt relieved. Ellie would lead the way to a happier future for him, and most important of all was Keir now had . . . a friend like Ellie.

Now, effectively, Keir had entered the Green Stage of the programme. His parents and school would use Ellie, and his liking for dogs, as an educational motivator and tool. I gave Beth a new *Heaven* book (appropriately vandalised!) as a resource for the Blue Stage. She would know when the time was right to teach her son about Ellie getting old and the concept of letting her go.

As we waved off Beth, her husband and a very happy little boy holding his special dog, we knew that we had all been on quite a journey. We didn't know it at the time, but the future held still more, probably another world first. All that was to come.

[ 117 ]

As we drove home, someone was readying herself to visit the next family.

"Nuala, what colour is the next kid's autism?"

"Amy, it is your favourite. Red."

"Good, Nuala, that's right!"

In the months that followed, Beth kept me up to date with how boy and dog were progressing. The news was wonderful. Keir was walking with Ellie with his lead on her collar, with his parents close by. He was encouraged to groom his dog. He fed her, filled her water bowl, celebrated her Christmases and did so many of the things that Dale had done for Henry. Beth overheard Keir telling Ellie that he loved her, and seeing Ellie after she was spayed, he empathised, "Poor Ellie." While his autism remained severe, these moments opened up hope. Soon, the family couldn't imagine life without Ellie.

Helping others helped Dale and I carry on and gave us hope when our lives were at a very low ebb; our futures remained desperately uncertain. Perhaps the only certain thing was that book had made a difference. Continually inspired by Henry, Dale and I visited eight more children to pilot the programme's transitional stage. All to a lesser or greater degree showed me that my programme worked. We saw a full spectrum of colours – blue, red, green, yellow, orange. One child's colour was purple and pink (and especially pleasing in stripes!). At last I understood how to use the dog to create the best chance of success for the child, where before we neuro-typicals were getting it wrong!

I received a phone call from a psychologist, seeking advice on dog phobia. The problem was challenging and I was pleased to help, although I had never considered addressing dog phobia for a child with autism, let alone an adult. The psychologist was working with the parent of Matthew, a teenager with severe autism. Matthew's life was compromised because of his fear of dogs running up to him outside. Together, they were working intensively to desensitise him and give him coping strategies.

We spoke for two hours. I offered ideas and sent programme resources, including a DVD of assistance dogs helping children and other positive images. Matthew was taught basic dog commands so he could have some control. The big cuddly dog helped him address sensory issues and alleviate his worst fears. For nine arduous months, he slowly learned to adjust, coping with all types of situations and all things dog. I remarked to the psychologist that if this worked, then by extension all sorts of other ASD fears could be overcome too. All the same, I never expected this email from Matthew's mum: "Matthew has overcome his phobia of dogs. We spent less than a year working with PAT (Pets As Therapy)[4] dogs with great success. It has made such a huge difference to his life, ability to learn, etc. We now even have a puppy of our own at home, a Westie. Unbelievable and fantastic."

Absolutely! I was delighted to hear of Matthew's success, but my reality was that in order to continue my work I would need to find purpose-trained dogs like Ellie and juggle a career, and as for what this escalating happening in my working life might become . . . It was brilliant, and burgeoning.

What was I thinking? Amy was still young. She needed me. Dale needed me. When does a son stop needing his mum? When does she stop needing him? Then there were the dogs, the house, the garden . . . there was Jamie. Somewhere there was Jamie. I didn't want to think about where he was in all this. Thinking just wasn't working. Focus. Focus!

I opened my bag. I popped yet another pill. Take two, just in case.

Nuala, Nuala, get a grip. But how, exactly? What was I meant to grip? Something was ready to snap. Yet Dale and I were going to need the strength of every sinew and every bone we had in order to survive the months ahead.

# 11

# Highs and Lows

Struan School and the Gardner family go back a long way. It was, after all, Jim Taylor who first moved things for us, making sure Dale had that all-important diagnosis when he was still tiny. We have been so supported by Scottish Autism and the National Autistic Society that when either of them asks something of us, we are only too happy to do it. In May, the Head of Struan, Janet Stirling, called. She asked if Dale would visit to talk to three senior pupils who were preparing to leave school. Of course, he was pleased to help. A few weeks later we headed there, with Henry in the boot and Dale's guitar and a framed portrait of Sir Henry sharing the back seat.

On arrival, Dale went off with Janet to meet the pupils. I sat with Jim in the dining area, drinking gallons of coffee, served with very good cake. I updated him on my work. I explained how the working dog world was training dogs for autistic children, how this was growing internationally, and with promising results. I also gave him Henry's portrait, which he decided to hang on the dining room wall. Anyone familiar with that beautiful school building will know that's a prime spot, so dear Henry is seen by visitors and pupils alike, every day. Jim was delighted to meet up with Dale again and observe how much he had progressed.

It seemed such a long time since Jim had first met the preschool Dale, when he was completely gripped by his autism with those horrifically frustrating tantrums as his sole means of communication. My son had been four on our first trip there. I had been so desperate to help him. And desperate for help. At the time, I really wanted him to attend Struan. He caused havoc, screamed and lay under the dining table, where everyone simply ignored him until he calmed down. That day so long ago, Jamie and I joined eight severely autistic pupils, accompanied by staff, for their morning break. Their ages ranged significantly. One or two had some spoken language, but most were non-verbal. However, all were impeccably behaved and polite. Bizarrely, the snack time resembled a charming Victorian tea party! It progressed at a sedate pace, with a quite decorous atmosphere and very proper etiquette. A plate of prepared fruit was held at eye-level and passed around to encourage eye contact. "Anna, would you like a piece of fruit?"

Anna took a piece, then passed it at the same height. "Stuart, would you like some fruit?"

It was insightful to witness these pupils, who were being taught virtually twenty-four/seven. Every daily activity was an opportunity for communication or social education. I had been aware of this strategy already, but at that time, Dale's autism was so challenging that alone or even with Jamie I couldn't begin to approach the resourcefulness and stamina that the team at Struan had. However, that visit changed forever how I worked with Dale. It had given me the key, but it would take Henry to unlock him.

So, twenty-two years later, Jim and I were able to sit, swilling in coffee. Independently, Dale was with pupils whose early childhood had been every bit as hard as his own had been. Struan had given them the chances he had been given, and now it was his time to tell them that adult life was there for the taking.

Before we left, the pupils went to the car to meet Henry. We let him out to exercise. The seniors were fine young men and our visit was a great success.

In the months that followed, these same young people spoke at the Scottish Parliament to plead with MSPs to invest in autism, and I followed on directly after their appeal. Firstly, though, I had to apologise for Dale's absence, because the evening coincided with an Alice Cooper concert, so naturally, Alice had won! Jokes aside, I appealed to the politicians: "The young men you have met this evening are the minority, because they have been fortunate to receive condition-specific education at its best. If this government invests in autism now, it will save millions ... and adults of the future like them will be the majority."

I still carry that hope.

With the summer break upon us, Dale and his friends returned to T in the Park and had a brilliant time. Ryan had recently passed his driving test, which encouraged Dale to learn too. Yet again, an acquaintance who had known him since childhood was a driving instructor, and he took him under his wing. Thorough as ever, he bought a *Learning the Highway Code* DVD, and very quickly, he got the hang of how to handle the car safely. So much so that his instructor noted that because he followed instructions precisely and adhered totally to the Code, he was the safest and most trustworthy client he had ever taught!

Driving lessons filled Dale's time well, and it was wonderful to see his life settle down. Meanwhile, my own life was anything but normal. I remained off work, and the Bed-a-thon continued to decimate any chance I had of a decent night's sleep. Certainly, Amy was now well installed in the study and things were better than they had been. Better, but anything but fine. In an attempt to reinforce her new routine and increase the hope of success, I sought the help of her ASD specialist paediatrician. I was aware of an unlicensed drug commonly used for children on the spectrum with sleep problems, Melatonin. Melatonin is a sleep hormone, which normally increases at night. It is, of course, not really a drug, as it is produced naturally by the body. The doctor felt, as I did, that it might help Amy establish a new sleep routine, so it was well worth a try. There are various starting doses, the full dose being kept in reserve, as a last resort.

To make sure I had covered all options, I did more research into sleeping disorders with autistic children. I came across a successful tactic: using a "snuggle sac". This was a furry but snug sleeping bag, which gave a feeling of security to the children using it. Dr Temple Grandin, who has autism, has written extensively on how sensory issues adversely affect those with ASD.[1] Her work details how controlled, tight pressure works to address the imbalanced tactile need. As a veterinary inventor, she has created a squeeze machine for herself, based on a device she had earlier designed for cattle. Unquestionably, it has helped reduce her acute anxiety levels and alleviate her feelings of insecurity.

"I have been talking and writing about sensory problems for over twenty years, and am still perplexed by many people who do not acknowledge sensory issues and the pain and discomfort they can cause."

– Dr Temple Grandin, *The Way I See It*

The "snuggle sac" and weighted blankets have proved successful for many children, giving similar feelings to those Dr Grandin experienced with her machine. I found a sac (a horse one, of course!) and put it on Amy's bed. On the first night, I gave her the minimum dose of Melatonin, sat at the door of her room, vigilant and silent, until she slept. A successful week later, I thought the problem was solved. Not a chance! Steadily, as the nights passed, the old Bed-a-thon routine crept back. Nothing had changed. I had to ask. When she explained why she still woke up, I thought the Bed-a-thon was with me for keeps: "Nuala, I like my sleeping room, but I still miss you too much!"

Wow! How could I find a sensory replacement for me? I could understand how she missed stroking my hair, and her dad's, because she had done that since babyhood. Seemingly, she received the same calming effect from our hair as she had gained when flicking her "Golden Pillow's" ears. How could I provide her with all the other positive sensory stimuli I gave her – my smell, my clothes, my whole physical being? A few days later, a mad idea came to me. There was a risk it wouldn't work; it was somewhat unconventional. But like so many times in the past, I felt it was worth a try. Sometimes we all need to take a risk. Especially when the stakes are so high. I needed to make a mini me!

I paid £30 for a two-foot tall, lifelike doll, complete with long, dark brown hair. Together, we cut the doll's glorious tresses until they resembled my own short style. Poor "me" had had a bad hair day, but Amy loved the result. Then I found a pair of doll's jeans to fit "me" and a T-shirt, (with a horse on the front!). Finally, I let her spray "me" all over with my best perfume. Subtle this was not! Well, the first night "we" slept together was a complete success. For months thereafter, with her Melatonin at maximum dose, Amy and her "Nuala Doll", slept until dawn. Having two Nualas in the house offered us some extra opportunities for fun. Some days, to divert her from the computer, or just to indulge her a bit, I used my effigy as a prompt: "Amy Gardner, will you please go and change my clothes, I've been wearing the same knickers for weeks – they'll be stinking."

While the Bed-a-thon wasn't completely cured, it was more manageable, and just in time. Our lives were about to be shaken to the core.

In August 2009 we headed to Fife to support a friend, Gillian Naysmith, who was holding a fundraising day for the NAS at one of the local churches. She had asked me to speak at the event, and parents were attending to meet me. However, like most mornings, with the entire household to rally round and try to get the time for me to look and feel the best I could, it was too much to ask. Jamie had his schedule to get us there on time, which he stuck to.

As I tried to take a few minutes to ready myself he reminded me, "We need to leave now or we will be late." Aware of the time, in desperation I asked him to ensure Amy was ready. Minutes later, with the pressure mounting, I seized my bag and coat to find Jamie with Amy in the hall. He grabbed Amy's brush from the hall table and started to brush her hair.

"What are you doing?" I asked. "Amy can brush her own hair."

"I was only making a start. We need to go now, we're late."

I wearily responded, "If it's speed you want, the worst thing you could do is give Amy more pressure by telling her to hurry."

There are so many pressures being a mother of a child with autism, and the strain it puts on a relationship is immense. It is vital when working with children with autism that all involved must have the same approach. If one person undoes the chain, the child gets confused and frustrated as a result. More annoying for the child and "teacher" is that the skill has to be retaught from the beginning. All my married life I resigned myself to the fact that addressing the majority of the children's autism and giving them discipline was mainly my job as their mother. Jamie was able to opt out because he worked with computers, reminding me, "I'm not a teacher." I had no alternative but to learn on the job all the different skills I had acquired throughout the years. It was a hard, lonely, frustrating and mentally exhausting never-ending workload.

We arrived as the event was getting busy. Inside I felt numb with stress with the resulting domestic in the car that took up most of the journey. I took a deep breath, to get on with the job in hand: to ensure Amy had some fun.

I had taken along a cuddly pack, and Dale was to be signing A4 copies of Henry's portrait for a donation to the cause. Adding some interest, we dressed Henry as an "autism dog", with a green collar with a recent picture of Dale in the key ring fob. Henry's harness had a green lead in a loop, and I added a model Henry train on the second hook to complete the package!

There was a superb turnout. We set up a table for Dale, with Henry by his side, near the front entrance to the hall. That dog was such a draw. Firstly, it was unusual for a dog to be in a church at all, and secondly, his attire was somewhat different and just a little eye-catching! Within minutes, I was on call to act like a celebrity's security guard!

A mum passed, holding a beautiful little girl by the hand. The child looked about seven. She stood mesmerised, seeing Henry and observing people fuss over him. Slowly, she approached, saying nothing, and then she began to touch him. She patted him, and then gently ran her hands up and down his back, enjoying the whole sensation. She moved on to fingering his face, whilst looking deeply into his eyes. By the way her mother supervised her, I sensed that she had autism. Henry, of course, didn't bat an eye during his examination. All was going well, until her mum tried to move her on. She jumped up and down with anxiety and excitement, screaming, "My dog, my dog, my dog!"

She became so upset that Dale had to intervene. He knelt beside Henry, moved his collar round and showed her his picture tag. "I'm Dale, and this is my dog . . . Look, Dale's dog."

She studied the picture tag. Wonderfully and almost instantly, she calmed down, gave Henry a pat, and then wandered off happily with her mum. She returned several times thereafter, just to pat and touch Henry, fully accepting that he belonged to Dale. I was relieved that I had taken the time to put that picture on his collar. One little "adjustment" was all that was needed to prevent a tantrum for one little girl.

That day, many autistic children gave Henry a good once over. Some had a tug at his tail, intrigued I think, that it was definitely attached! Others were drawn straight away to his train and green lead.

A four-year-old non-verbal boy was totally captivated by the cuddly pack, so I helped him play with it. He clearly loved the big toy, complete with Dale's picture on the collar, and so he was able to accept it too was staying with his master. He laughed loudly when I pretended it was barking. I grabbed the brush, showed him how to use it and gave it to him. "Ross, brush Cuddly?"

He copied my actions, and was amused when I put the toy's head in the metal bowl and "it" made loud munching noises. If it had been another time and place, I could have sat with that lad for ages. I truly enjoyed building on the interaction, lengthening his fleeting eye contact and developing imaginative play with him. He was just so responsive.

His parents were delighted to see their son's potential with the right educational motivation. Anyone could have understood that fact, watching those children that day. Dale took good memories home too.

After the school term started, he was recalled to work in the college nursery. By now he had acquired a good level of practical experience. Not only that, his CV was terrific. One morning while he was at work, the phone rang. The caller was his DEA (Disability Employment Adviser) at Jobcentre Plus, to inform him that a part-time job-share (17.5 hours) was available at the college nursery. A permanent position! It was a chance in a million and perfect for him! The hours were manageable and therefore virtually stress free. Job sharing would allow him to work with his group, with the added support of an experienced childcare worker. He applied immediately.

With Prospects on board, the interview panel was well aware of the adjustments he needed. He was informed that, "The interview should last for approximately forty-five minutes." We felt quietly optimistic, knowing that he would get an impeccable reference from Barnardo's. As well as being on the panel, the Head of the College Nursery was another referee. Prospects had him well prepared; he even felt ready to attend on his own, knowing that he had already been doing that very job on a full-time basis, if only for a short time.

On the day of the interview, he looked so professional and confident in his suit. On his wrist was his Grandad George's watch. He left in plenty of time. His dad was driving him, so he was not under any extra pressure. I enjoyed my shower and was just settling down to a leisurely breakfast when, to my utter amazement, Dale and his dad arrived home. What was going on? Jamie explained: "I was sitting waiting in the car, reading the newspaper, and he was back within fifteen minutes. His interview only lasted ten minutes."

What was going on? Dale's adjustments alone should have taken time to implement. Something wasn't right, whether he was successful or not!

As we waited for the post to arrive, for the rest of the week he continued to work. Returning home on the Friday, I met Dale in the hall. Something was wrong. He avoided looking at me; his eyes blinked furiously as he struggled to get out the words. "Mum, while I was in the office, the head told me a girl got the job because she gave lots of feedback at the interview, but they are happy to have me on supply."

He made his way up to his room. I stood absorbing his words and became absolutely enraged. How could an interview of ten minutes have given him any chance? On that basis, how can anyone with autism be given a fair chance to find work?

"I don't think that applying normally for jobs works because on all of their adverts [. . .] you must have strong communication skills."
(Source: Paula, NAS. Don't Write Me Off campaign.)

The more I thought about Dale's situation, the angrier I became. Why did he have to find out about the job from his DEA? Why had no staff at the college mentioned the position to him? It was the perfect post for someone like him, particularly given his disability. If that wasn't bad enough, ten days after the interview, the letter confirming the bad news fueled our outrage: "You have not been successful, as other candidates have come closer to the specification for the role."

I got in touch with Prospects, who were upset that Dale hadn't had a fair chance at his interview.

Dale plummeted. All the autistic tics returned; his eyes were sunken and dark and blinking constantly. His voice became hesitant, and that cough returned. He was simply wrecked. Yet, he did something that I don't think anyone else would have chosen to do in his shoes: he continued to work in that same nursery until the new girl started.

"Mum, where's the picture the college sent me of my graduation class? It reminds me that I did do well, and achieved a lot for the kids."

We were determined to obtain answers, so we met with Billy Docherty. Yet again, we had to compile a long, strong letter to the college principal: "If Dale was not the most suitable candidate, why was he constantly being relied upon to cover shifts at short notice? What is your policy on informing job candidates whether or not their application has been successful?" Dale had, after all, been told in front of an office assistant and the deputy head. Afterwards, he had to carry on regardless and complete his shift.

"Why did a forty-five minute interview process last no longer than ten minutes?"

We requested copies of both the interview notes and the questions set. Further, we made the point that the permanent post would have been better for Dale because of his autism, rather than working at short notice in erratic and unpredictable patterns. While we awaited a reply, Billy sought advice from the Equality & Human Rights Commission. Just a few months after Dale had joined Unison, a public service union. We also requested their advice.

In order to maintain his self-esteem and to increase his opportunities to secure a permanent job, assisted by Prospects and with help from his DEA, Dale agreed to start a work preparation programme. It commenced in November at Cairn Curran, a local private nursery. He attended, voluntarily, every Tuesday and Thursday and worked in the same way as any other member of staff. Some weeks he worked at both Cairn Curran and at the college nursery. Truly, he was in demand.

When the new girl started at the college nursery, he found himself back in the maze of Jobcentre Plus, as Cairn Curran was unpaid work. He coped with incredible fortitude and was not to be crushed. He had to attend a back-to-work session in order to keep his Job Seekers' Allowance (JSA). This meant: "You must make suitable efforts to find a job and put yourself in the best position to get offers of work."

I appreciate that the welfare system is complex and has to meet many situations. However, what Dale had to put up with was stressful in the extreme, and ultimately confusing. No wonder many of his peers give up. It took me months to decipher the system to try to support my son. Matters were doubly complicated because he worked on supply. With help from his DEA, I devised a checklist to help keep him right. It was necessary because the process was so perplexing. Without that safeguard, he could have lost money or even been fraudulent, inadvertently.

As he claimed JSA, he was permitted to earn £100 a week, but only if he worked sixteen hours or less. When Dale declared this work, he had to ensure a B7 form was filled in, to allow his JSA levels to be adjusted. The B7 was to ensure he wasn't called for "back-to-work interviews" if he was actually working on that day. If he was free, supply or no supply, he had to attend. That was just the beginning of an administrative labyrinth. Working more than sixteen hours? Sign off within twenty-four hours (assuming someone was there to answer the phone). Sign a book! Return it to Jobcentre Plus! Have your P45 at the ready, take parts to your employer for tax purposes ... and then there was the tax situation to be addressed! Is it any surprise that people give up? Is it any revelation at all that someone with autism would let go? Dale would never have been able to manage the system, and nor would I, without the guidance of his DEA. At least there was good news elsewhere.

At the end of his work experience he received a glowing report: "Both Prospects and Dale's host employer feel that Dale has demonstrated the knowledge, skills and personal qualities necessary for employment in early years support." He enjoyed working at Cairn Curran so much that he continued there, on a voluntary basis, after his work experience had ended. He wanted to maintain his skills whilst seeking permanent employment. It was encouraging for me to hear from the Head: "Dale is amazing with the children. They all adore him. I just wish I could offer him a job, but there's no sign of any hours becoming available."

Eight weeks later, we were to receive a reply from the college. Had we wanted to challenge Dale's situation at an employment tribunal, it would already have been too late, as cases have to be submitted within three months of an incident. We had thought seriously about doing that, but in truth Dale was too stressed, and it was already detrimental to his health. The reply to our letter was inadequate and unhelpful. The requested copies of the interview notes and questions never materialised. Why not?

We decided to support him in his plan to move on, so he resigned from the college supply list, to focus on Cairn Curran and local authority supply work. There was another arduous road ahead, and we didn't have the luxury of spare time to dwell on the past. No matter. It was Dale's future that mattered most.

## 12

## *Open and Closed Doors*

Any barriers obstructing Dale's career path certainly didn't get in the way of his flourishing social life. This was a mercy, as that particular rollercoaster kept him sane. Whether it kept me sane or not is another matter entirely. God knows my mental health was under enough of an onslaught, but there are things that Dale, like any young man, needed to do, and I don't begrudge him a moment of it!

From one of his more surprising shenanigans I have a mental snapshot of Dale that I would have never believed possible. A close friend from his karate club was marrying a Columbian girl. At the groom's request, close friends and family were to wear full Highland dress. The kilt and Dale had history, and none of it was good. In his Scouting days I used to be so jealous of the other families at those special events – prize-givings and parades – because he refused to wear the company kilt. Despite having the perfect height and stature for it, he avoided any contact with plaid. He told me he hated kilts; they were just like skirts, and the coarse woolly texture of the tartan was a sensory disaster zone. For years, I pleaded with him to wear one, for me, just once so I could capture a picture of him, but his reply never changed. "Mum, I wouldn't be caught dead in a kilt . . . so get over it!"

I was resigned to never seeing him in Highland dress, even if he had a Nobel Prize to collect.

Yet this time, because he was so pleased to be invited and he knew the Columbian men were to be wearing kilts, surprise of surprises, he submitted. He was prepared to wear the dreaded garment out of respect for his friend. It was recognised as such a significant gesture that the groom even thanked him during his speech. Everyone applauded. He wore that kilt the whole night and wasn't the least bit bothered. Doubtless, a snifter of alcohol helped him cope, but before he got too drunk, I captured him perfectly in a real picture, knowing it would definitely be a one-off!

Every parent worries about their children when they become adults, particularly when they discover the social scene and alcohol. Now that Dale had adapted to social drinking, I was concerned how it would affect his personality. At his grandfather's eightieth birthday, in a luxurious hotel, alcohol in general and champagne in particular flowed. I decided not to touch a single drop because I needed to see how Dale was affected by drinking. On arrival, he was reserved, and wasn't wildly tempted by the champagne, but he did help himself to a bottle of lager. He sat alone with his grandfather while everyone else mingled. Four bottles of lager later, we were all summoned to the dining room. My beady eye was on him. I could see he was relaxed, comfortably out of his shell, as he sat beside his uncle, conversing and making jokes. During the meal, the supply of champagne continued, as if the bottles were bottomless. Dale's appreciation of quality began to show! I noted his glass was replenished quite a few times. After the meal, we retired to a private room for coffee and mints, and for the first time in four years I witnessed my son somewhat the worse for drink!

Everyone in the room commented as they saw him socialise confidently with his family, some of whom he had never met before. When he cornered his uncle, I was able to have a good idea of the type of drunk my son was going to make. With relief, and a little amusement, I saw Dale with his arm around that same uncle's shoulders, telling him what a superb relative he was whilst simultaneously teasing him, in keeping with the general merriment. Similarly, with a couple of other family members, he spoke openly about their good points and regaled them with tales of how much he liked them. Thankfully, he was the jolly, friendly variety of drunk. Whew! Anyone who finds it odd that I would stand by, fizzy water in hand, and analyse my son's reaction to alcohol simply doesn't understand autism. Unquestionably, he was going to go out, drink – indeed, have too much to drink – when I wasn't there. I needed to know he would be okay. He would be fine.

Now he was twenty-two and he joined his dad and his dad's mates for the occasional night out. I was pleased that they were getting on so well. No doubt they had an easier time together without me in the mix. Jamie and I were getting tetchier by the minute in each other's company. But the guys were good together, and I held onto that. Even some of Dale's favourite music was from Jamie's era.

On one memorable Saturday, a Queen tribute band was playing at the local theatre. Post concert, there was a certain unwritten rule stating that some Gourock bar had to be drunk dry. The usual suspects were present: John and Kenny, who together had entertained Dale and made him laugh since his childhood days. Then George joined them. He, in turn, as both an ambulance mechanic and the one-time owner of an old Ford Zodiac, had once helped my son live out his youthful transport obsession. The alcohol supply was generous, and the comic duo started to have their fun. George was wearing a stylish silk shirt, which was a bit dapper in the context of an evening in a not so salubrious pub. Metaphorically, at least, the shirt was shredded.

George rallied, "You're forgetting. I'm back on the market and I'm off to the Cafe Continental after this. I've got to look the part."

John nudged in a reminder. "Make sure you stick to your price range, now!"

Price range? This wasn't literal enough, and Dale needed an explanation. The unconventional lesson that followed was only possible because both the student and teachers were intoxicated. They reassured Dale that he was a great-looking guy, with a fun-loving, good personality. One day, he'd meet a smashing girl.

When dad and son eventually rolled home, my quiet place on the sofa was book-ended by inebriated and vociferous males, keen to entertain me with tales of the night's adventures. Before too long, Jamie headed for the stairs, but Dale decided I hadn't yet been bored to death. He had all the time in the world.

In classic drunk style, firstly, he had to prove to me he wasn't really too drunk. He got up and tried to demonstrate walking in a straight line. Of course, he failed, which prompted the itemising of how little he actually had had to drink. With an imperceptible shake of the head, it fell to me to humour him, in time-honoured fashion. Eventually, though, he explained what was really nagging him through the beer fuddle. Kenny and John had spent an age advising him how to steer the "market". Suffice to say, I got the impression they hadn't done so very badly in their efforts ... God knows how! Unorthodox as it was, that drunken discussion boosted his confidence and gave him some kind of framework for whatever, and whoever, was out there – when he was ready.

January 2010 was so cold. It snowed heavily, and Dale's chance of finding a job seemed every bit as bleak. One day I noticed his mood was low, and I asked if he was all right.

"Mum, I'm okay, but I'm fed up. I just want to work. I hate this."

I tried to advise him, reminding him it was only the seventh day of the New Year and things would pick up. He was so unhappy that I grabbed my laptop and began surfing. Just as I was on the verge of giving up, I stumbled upon a new vacancy twenty-five miles from Gourock, with a five-minute walk from the train station to the nursery. Superb! We called Prospects and Billy, in turn, spent ages on the phone to the nursery's Head, who was keen to support Dale's application. I offered her a copy of my book by way of bridging any potential understanding gap. All was going well ...

And then I learned that the vacancy had been removed from circulation following seventy applications for the post. Amongst those seventy applicants there were even unemployed teachers. On 25 February, despite a foot of snow on the pavements, Dale attended an interview.

When the letter arrived, with a certain dread, I put it on top of his laptop to give him his privacy. Only five minutes later he appeared. "Mum, read this! It's looking quite good."

He was one of the three final candidates who were to attend a second interview. They were to work with the children, and then the successful person would be appointed.

On the morning of the practical trial, he wore a blue polo shirt, because he had noticed that the staff there wore that same colour and style. He told me that he wanted to blend in so that the children would feel more comfortable with a stranger in their midst. Again, his ability to see things from the child's perspective is a unique quality, gifted by his autism. When he came home, I was bursting to know.

"Dale, how did it go?"

"Good, Mum. The morning went really fast. I felt comfortable with the staff and children. I put Henry's collar in my bag, just for a wee bit of luck, and it really helped me feel confident."

Two weeks later, the letter arrived. I stuck to my routine, placing it on his laptop. He met me in the kitchen, handed me the letter, and put the kettle on.

"Mum, I feel like giving up. I'm only good for voluntary work because of my autism."

My heart sank as I read: "Unfortunately, due to your lack of experience since qualifying, [we are] offering the position to another, more experienced candidate. We thought you were brilliant with the children."

I had to take heart, even if at that point Dale could not. It was hardly a bog-standard rejection letter. The Head had even contacted Prospects to ask if they could secure a year's salary so she could offer him that length of experience, but, alas, no funding was available.

"Due to financial constraints [. . .] we are unable to employ two new people."

However, Dale could work voluntarily. From his point of view, that was all there was for him, and I struggled to highlight any positive aspects of the letter.

"Mum, the job advert said nothing about securing funding for wages. Autism changed the situation for me, didn't it?"

I managed to convince him that his work with Barnardo's and Cairn Curran was the best way forward, but I felt his pain and frustration. It would take a long time for me to be able to help my son see that things were tough out there for everyone, and being one of the final three from a pool that size was incredible. Where getting a job is concerned, even second place just doesn't cut it. Far from his autism going against him, I could see that that head teacher had really seen potential in Dale and had gone out on a limb, even using his autism advantageously to try to secure funding for a second post. She had been ingenious, and brave on his behalf. It was just so hard for him to understand that, holding yet another bloody rejection letter.

Then, just when we needed it most, our wonderful Sir came to the rescue again. I was aware of the great effect Dale and Henry's story had had internationally, because of all the uplifting emails and Facebook messages. This one came from Italy. Giovanna, whose ten-year-old son had autism, contacted me. She was another of those mother warriors, and in company with several other parents, she had formed a non-profit-making charity, Cancellautismo (www.cancellautismo. org). Having read my book and seen *After Thomas*, she sensed that my experiences paralleled her own. Ever resourceful, she wanted to do something special to raise awareness of the condition in her own country. Could I help her obtain permission from Hartswood films to transfer some scenes from the film onto her charity's website? Of course I could! The scenes would have Italian voice-overs and would show different aspects of autism.

Later on, she sent me the link, and it was superb to see Henry making a difference somewhere else. I began to wonder if he needed some extra names in view of his international standing . . . Enrico, Henri, Enzo!

At last, at the end of February the local authority phoned to ask Dale to cover a full-time position ten miles away, in the east end of Greenock, at Gibshill Children's Centre. Within the first week he had settled in as if life had been kind. He had to get a bus in order to catch a train, to ensure he arrived that necessary fifteen minutes early. While a few of the staff were aware of who Dale was, the Head, Isobel, decided not to disclose his autism. She hoped that staff would get to know him first, as a person and as a practitioner. He was pleased with that approach, which seemed right in light of his recent history. Indeed, that strategy proved really successful. Dale was respected and liked by all the staff, and more importantly, by the children! If proof was needed, two encounters, the first a chance-in-a-million meeting, were about to verify it.

My mother-in-law was having a medical investigation, requiring a day-patient admission to hospital. The male nurse in charge of her case asked if she was by any chance related to a certain Dale Gardner. When she said that she was, the nurse smiled. "My daughter attends Gibshill and adores Dale. When she comes home, all she talks about is Dale, Dale, Dale. He's her hero!"

Also around this time I went to a local support group to see old friends and catch up on any latest research or advances in autism. As the session ended, a mother called Louise approached me, asking, "Are you Dale Gardner's mum?" After I confirmed that I was, she said, "Please give my regards to Dale. He was so good with my son Luke."

Louise explained that Luke has severe autism and is non-verbal. He went to Gibshill, and when she would drop him off there, Dale would help him with his coat and shoes. Every time Luke attended, he calmly went with Dale.

Louise was really touched because Luke's autism was delicate, he needed to feel comfortable to gain trust with others. Through Luke's non-verbal communication he gestured a real liking and affinity with Dale, as if he sensed his autism was safe, secure and understood in Dale's hands. When he attended nursery, Luke went happily off to his room with Dale, hand in hand.

At that time Louise didn't know Dale had autism, although she had heard other parents comment, "Dale is wonderful with the children." She learned from Isobel who Dale was because Isobel advised her to read his story. Louise was truly pleased with Dale. He gave her hope knowing they were together, a child with his "teacher", but because of their autism they were and always will be connected.

Of all placements to date, Dale felt most comfortable and, significantly, most part of the Gibshill team. Isobel and her staff supported and respected him. Despite the long hours, he took on all the responsibilities the position required, attending Parents' Nights and in-service days.

Now that he had a regular income, he used it to really focus on learning to drive. His quality of life soared and it was superb to see him getting on so well. Suddenly, he was buying new clothes, and he could afford to attend some big concerts, bands like Coldplay and Green Day. Better still, he proved he wasn't a miser after all, and bought his sister and me birthday presents and even wee impromptu gifts, without needing any prompts.

He continued to play in his own band, but on nights out with the crew, he hated wearing his glasses because it affected his confidence. Now that he was earning, I suggested that he might want to look into having laser eye surgery. I went with him to the appointment in order to ask the in-depth questions – and, yes, I was hoping that one day I'd be able to afford the same treatment for myself! His karate practice meant that it was advisable for him to have both eyes lasered at the same time. In fact, he needed the advanced procedure that was performed on astronauts, which was the safest but also the most expensive. Unfortunately, that would kill off all his savings but the outcome of the surgery would be worth it. Having done the research, I drove him to the clinic to support him. He was slightly nervous, but the staff were excellent and he went through the whole process without a hitch.

Ever the nurse, I took responsibility at home for administering his eye drops. We both knew that infection was the big risk. He returned to Gibshill a couple of days later and for that whole week, every single lunchtime, I drove up to apply his drops.

Staff members were impressed that he was brave enough to have the procedure performed on both eyes. Certainly they couldn't miss what he'd done, especially when he wore his sunglasses to reduce the glare when working outdoors. Such was his gangster-like style with the shades that his dad and I referred to him as "Mr Green" from *Reservoir Dogs*. When he ditched his sunglasses, fully recovered, the change in his demeanour and confidence was impressive. The results were excellent. Now he could virtually see around corners, which even improved his already competent driving.

While he was settled at Gibshill, despite its demanding requirements, the Jobcentre Plus policy had to be followed. It was imperative that Dale secured suitable employment in view of his autism, but because he hadn't worked for eighteen weeks prior to starting at Gibshill, he had to apply for any local jobs in childcare or he would lose his JSA. The voluntary hours at Cairn Curran counted for nothing. The theory was that supply work could end at any time. Fair enough; it could! What wasn't fair, however, was the mounting pressure that put on Dale. All the efforts he continued to make to secure employment were ignored.

At the time, Dale was still registered with Duncan Currie and the local authority supply lists, while simultaneously working at Cairn Curran. He received notification from his DEA of vacancies available for sessional childcare workers within a charity-run provision, which also ran an autism-specific play day every week. I drove him to that interview and waited. Encouragingly, he was given a copy of the interview questions – but at the end of the interview! I hid my frustration and made sure I didn't voice to Dale that he really should have had those questions a few days before. I buttoned my lip on my opinion that that would have made a real difference to his chances of success. At no point did I even say, "And that would just have been in line with DDA demands!" I kept my own counsel – just! Why, though? Why?

I saw it coming: "Unfortunately, you have not been successful on this occasion." No reason was given. Yes, we could have requested written feedback but by now neither of us had it in us. Anyway, what was the point? We knew employers could justify their stance, as Dale didn't have enough experience, particularly knowing the abundance of unemployed practitioners who were available. So we moved on. Still, it rankled. Dale would have been an asset to the position, especially in view of the ASD play day. He would have ticked inclusion, equality and fulfilled their legal requirement to employ a person with a disability. But for some reason, once again his name wasn't on the job offer.

With this last despairing message, Dale concluded that his best chance of finding employment was by upgrading his existing qualification to a diploma. He reckoned that by the time he graduated the economic climate might have improved, even if disability discrimination hadn't! Frustratingly, Duncan Currie College ran the diploma course but with his history there too recent and too painful, this was not an option. Another college, thirty-five miles and two train journeys away, was a better bet. I sat with him while meticulously he completed the online application. On 12 February 2010, Dale was relieved to receive the written confirmation: "You will be contacted shortly to attend an interview/information session."

With a contingency plan now in place, Dale felt more able to soldier on, gaining experience and earning a living at Gibshill. Thankfully, he was needed right until the end of term, but before he could take a breath and relax, Jobcentre policy required that he apply for another position: "This post is temporary until the end of June 2010." What was the point of Dale applying when he had work at Gibshill until the end of the school term? Regardless, he still had to submit an application form for a vacancy he didn't need or want.

For once, the recession and avalanche of applications for childcare workers seeking any employment worked in his favour: "After careful consideration, we will not be progressing your application."

Thank God!

Just as well, because in 1991 when we drove to the support group in Glasgow, a momentous event was already beckoning. It was a day no parent would miss for the world. College Graduation. The day we thought we'd never see. Yet, we chose to miss it. Could you blame us?

A few weeks later, it angered me to read in the local newspaper, the words of the DCC Principal: "Graduation marks an exciting new chapter in each of our students' lives. Everything we do at DCC is aimed to help our students reach their full potential, and it is inspiring that so many individuals come to us for that opportunity."

Dale hadn't heard any more news regarding his nomination for the Adult Learner of the Year Award. A member of staff had tried a few times to contact him, but he was busy working at Gibshill and didn't manage to return the call. He emailed an explanation of his situation, but after a few failed attempts to talk, the nomination for the award simply disappeared.

Despite these setbacks, his success at Gibshill helped him maintain his self-esteem, and Sir Henry provided a welcome boost to his confidence. Out of the blue, a teacher from a Primary 2 class in Richmond School, Skegness, contacted him, having read my book. Her class was doing a project, writing uplifting canine stories on how guide dogs and similarly trained animals can help people. She explained to her class about autism and how special Henry had been for Dale. The children's stories were being put into a book to sell for Guide Dogs for the Blind. She asked if he could draw a dog portrait as an illustration to a special tale.

With Beth's permission, he drew a lovely picture of Ellie and I sent a short story called "A Green Day", about Ellie and Keir's special friendship. It was lovely to receive that teacher's response: "We all loved it so much. In fact, there were many tears shed. I was able to show the children exactly what I have been telling them about – how eyes make a picture come alive – and they all agreed. Dale's drawing did just that."

By May, Dale was becoming anxious. He hadn't received any notification regarding an interview for the diploma course. I phoned the college, intending to alleviate his concerns, and I spoke to a course tutor. Well, I was extremely relieved that I had been the one to make that call. When I explained that Dale had heard nothing since the confirmation of his application, she sounded surprised.

"That's strange, because they are interviewing students for that course just now."

My heart sank. I explained that his interview must have been missed or overlooked. The tutor advised it may have been because he had a "C" pass for his Graded Unit, and the course entry required an A or B. I couldn't understand that, because this requirement was not on the website or indicated anywhere on the form. If that was the case, why had he been informed, in writing, that he would be contacted for an interview? The tutor advised me about other options. She was sympathetic, but there was no denying the outcome. Diddly squat, once again!

For Dale's sake, I waited for the official, written confirmation. It arrived on 1 June. It enraged me more when the college patronised him further: "You may also wish to contact our partners, SDS/Careers Scotland, Jobcentre Plus, Routes to Work, to discuss education, training and employment opportunities."

When I told him, his response wasn't at all what I had expected. Unsettlingly, he accepted the news calmly, passively, and somehow he just got on with things, as if nothing at all had happened. With the long summer break ahead, he applied to work in local authority summer play schemes and was placed on their reserve list.

His time at Gibshill was ending. Certainly, he had mixed feelings, because for the first time since qualifying he had enjoyed the "normality" of employment, and with real job satisfaction. That was what he had grafted for, for five long years. On the last day, he came home laden with cards and presents from parents, children and staff. Isobel's words were particularly poignant: "Hope to see you back someday. Thank you for all your hard work. The children just loved you."

To ensure he kept his place for voluntary work at Cairn Curran, he wrote to the Head to let her know what his situation was, and if possible, he would return there. He headed off on his annual jaunt to T in the Park, and had his now customary great time. Just as well, because he came home to more hassle. Now he was signing on for benefits, the vicious cycle of being bombarded with the insistence on applying for impossible positions was once more under way.

Somehow he found the emotional strength to forge ahead. In order to improve his CV, he attended a day course on Food Hygiene and passed that, then he did a Fire Awareness course, enabling him to be the Fire Awareness staff member in any environment. His morale was low, and when Billy suggested that he join Prospects' Social Group, which had adults in similar situations to his own, it seemed a brilliant idea. The group helped members support each other, with the extra advantage of some informal socialising, heading to the cinema or meeting up afterwards for a meal. It helped maintain Dale's self-respect, as he came to realise increasingly that he wasn't alone. That was a two-edged sword, of course. Their plight was every bit as bad as his.

No matter! After all the setbacks he had endured, Dale wasn't about to be defeated. A special time lay ahead. Thirteen years after the death of his beloved Granny Madge, he was preparing to connect with her again.

# 13

## *The Chauffeur*

Granny Madge was always special, and the greatest of her gifts to her grandson was his very first word. Mum was one of seven siblings who had been brought up in a modest two-bedroom cottage in the village of Chapelizod, which is now part of greater Dublin. The enormous back yard housed the miniature zoo and a closet toilet for the entire household. Four menfolk slept in one room and the women in the other. Granny and Grandpa were in a bed recess in the lounge, hidden by a curtain, and that lounge was the hub of their home. Central to that was the great cast iron range, which heated the whole house, gave all the hot water and bubbled up huge, comforting pots of thick Irish stew.

Over a hundred years later, that cottage remains. The yard is gone, and only a few metres from the back door there is an ugly big wall, all grey cracks and concrete. Behind that, there are rows of new estate houses, all thrown up where the yard and the acres of fields used to be where there were once horses, donkeys and sheep. Today the cottage is virtually derelict, and it has been like that almost since Uncle Peter's demise. My family lost the back yard, and some of the land, because the lease had expired after a hundred years of tenancy. Thankfully, my cousin Veronica now owns the cottage and it has recently been listed. She intends to restore it to its one-time glory. If my treasured Irish roots are earthed anywhere, it must be there. That wee cottage is a hoard of memories.

A very precious part of that memory hoard is my dear old Uncle Tommy, who was my mum's brother. Now I know that like so many of his generation, Tommy had undiagnosed, classical autism. My Aunt

Eva had been his main carer, but all the family over in Ireland simply accepted Tommy's difference. He rarely spoke and gave little eye contact, but he managed to hold down a labouring job on the railways and he appreciated a pint of good Guinness at the pub every night. He had his routine, and in over forty-five years, he was never off sick, nor was he ever late for work. Working was perhaps the easy bit for him. Retirement and the loss of his purposeful routine came hard. Perhaps it comes hard for a lot of folk, but Tommy wasn't just anybody.

Somehow, a few months later, he managed to develop a new routine; sleeping a little later, walking to the shop for his paper and feeding the stray cats in the field behind his house. He'd have a wee nap, and then nip to the local for a refreshing pint of two of the black stuff. He was always abed by eleven. That was working out fine, but alas, he'd developed another habit: a sinister, hacking cough. Eva fretted him into giving up his beloved Woodbines, and plied him with wholesome food, the all-curing boiled country eggs and other remedies and a raft of advice, most of which he ignored. He never complained, but his cough worsened. The doctor was summoned at last, but in truth, it was far too late. Advanced lung cancer was diagnosed.

When Tommy was admitted to hospital it was the first time in his life he had been near one. The doctors were shocked at his poor physical state. Near death, Tommy was put on a morphine infusion because the doctors deduced he was in severe pain. His deterioration was rapid. A scan revealed extensive cancers throughout his body.

The family was ever faithful and vigilant, knowing the bewildering strangeness of it all for him. As he lay there, staring up at the ceiling as if examining the paintwork, he remarked to my cousin Veronica, "Did you ever see a cricket up close?"

"No," she replied, "I don't believe I did. I think I just heard them. They are very noisy little creatures."

Then, as if it was the most ordinary thing in the world, he continued, "Well, I did, and they are very odd-looking fellas altogether. They look exactly like creatures from outer space."

And that, as my cousin recalls, was the essence, the innocence and ordinariness of Tommy, even in his final days. There were those moments of absolute joy and devastating pain, in equal measure. Such was the gentleness of this incredible and, yes, this odd oul soul.

The doctors told Eva they couldn't understand how Tommy had tolerated such excruciating pain for so long. And no one knew just how long. I understood. There it was again, that sensory processing problem, and no means of communicating his agony. Unlike Dale, he had no charging trains, nor did he have access to Amy's galloping horses of pain.

Mum and I felt a great relief when Tommy died peacefully a couple of days later. Distance meant I never had the chance to know my uncle as well as I would have liked, but I adored him. There's an extra-special bond, surviving now, in the shape of my children. May they never suffer as he did. Bless you, Uncle Tommy.

Dale was back in my country of memories, not looking back, however. He was most certainly looking forward! Before Amy's new school term started, Dale had a rather special twenty-first birthday present to spend. Veronica's husband, Anthony, is a driving instructor, so she had invited her honorary nephew to stay for a long weekend, when he would receive intensive driving lessons, on the house! This was a superb gift, but I was unsure how he would receive it. The one-time tiny village of Chapelizod had been developed almost on a par with Benidorm, and he knew that the roads and streets of Dublin would challenge Stirling Moss. Dale, however, was delighted and couldn't wait to get started. I was thrilled that he had this opportunity, yet it was tinged with a certain sadness that he would be driving in those same streets that his granny had wandered so freely as a child.

When he returned from Dublin, he told me he had driven past the cottage several times and each time he thought of Granny Madge. The street signs and traffic were chaotic, and one of his more alarming moments at the wheel occurred when a horse and cart waited beside him at traffic lights. It all paid off. The hours of driving through Dublin bolstered his confidence, changing his driving forever.

Back in Inverclyde, as he'd done in previous summers, he helped out at the Barnardo's play scheme, and he knew how much the children benefited. Amy, meanwhile, continued to thrive at Moorfoot, settling effortlessly into Primary 6, with all her friends by her side. Dale was recalled to cover at Gibshill, but there was a small, practical problem.

While his driving had improved, he struggled to pass the theory test, having failed at two attempts. Such was his frustration that I asked him to show me the mock test DVD he had been using to prepare. The questions were in multiple-choice format, with four possible answers. At the end of the test, the correct answers flashed up, but there was no means of storing them to support revision. I've been driving for more years than I'm prepared to say, but when I sat with him and we did that test together, we both failed spectacularly! I found the choices quite confusing, and I felt the frustration for Dale and others who have conditions like dyslexia. Perhaps it needs a format which obliterates the wrong answers, a bit like the popular *Who Wants to Be a Millionaire?* game show. I phoned and spoke to one of the assistants who supervised the test, highlighting Dale's difficulties. I explained the issues around information overload. Indeed, she agreed, the test format was far from ideal for candidates like Dale, but unfortunately it was the only one available. She did, however, reassure me that the organisation was looking into a more accessible system, but that would take time. He needed it now.

In order to help Dale overcome this, I typed out the questions he got wrong and printed them out so he could revise them without the attendant information overload of the multiple-choice setup. He built up a long list and, bit by bit, he improved his score until he managed more passes than fails. He applied to resit the test.

Dale's time at Gibshill ended at the October break. Isobel arranged for him to do some voluntary work with them in order to maintain his skills. He'd enjoyed his time at Cairn Curran, but he also wanted to increase his chance of work in the local authority sector. Covering all bases, he wrote to the Head of Cairn Curran, thanking her for his time with them and letting her know how much he had enjoyed the experience. He requested that his CV be kept on file, in order that he could be contacted in the event of any future vacancies.

Usually at that holiday, he would do some voluntary work for Barnardo's if he was needed, but this time he wanted to try something different. Dale and I had continued to develop our friendship with Gillian Naysmith. Her own young son has autism, and she got in touch after reading my book. She was then the co-ordinator of a new UK charity, founded by the author Rupert Issacson. Named after his book,[1] the Horse Boy Camps provide autism-specific equestrian therapy for the child and their family. Rupert's book tells how a chance encounter with a horse broke through to his own severely autistic son, in a similar way to how Henry had come through for Dale. Rupert was deeply impressed by Dale when he met him.

Gillian was running a four-day Horse Boy Camp at Newtonmore in Inverness-shire. After Dale had spoken with her, he decided to help out at the camp, knowing how much horses had helped his own sister. Preparing to attend, he tapped into his HNC skills and worked hard to bring different play activities to suit all the children at the camp. Inclusion for those with autism and those without was a strong underlying principle. By necessity, children and families would have to wait for their turn on the horses; there was plenty of free time and fun to be had for all. Physical and aesthetic play opportunities abounded for the child with autism and their siblings, together.

Days before, I was handed a shopping list: crayons, glitter, glue, stickers and the like, and the all-important play dough ingredients. There would be multi-coloured dough, glittery dough, scented dough. Dale planned to make a mountain of the stuff, having already found it to be a real winner with all. When I took Amy to her Sunday riding lesson, we set up a collection box for old horseshoes, and he ended up with dozens of them. I helped him wash them and get them into a safe condition, ready for the children to paint and decorate. Keeping with the equestrian theme, he downloaded and printed images of different types of horses, which he would use for colouring-in exercises to help the children learn they were about to be involved with real horses.

The day he set off, his bag weighed a ton. Thankfully, Gillian was collecting him from the station. She hadn't told any of the families who Dale was, nor had she disclosed his autism; the staff knew, so they could support him if required. Just as Isobel had done at Gibshill, Gillian wanted parents to get to know him firstly as a person, because it was entirely possible that they wouldn't even notice his autism.

As a volunteer, he helped the families and children in any way he could. When an autistic child was on a horse, Dale and another supported them, walking alongside, in order to stabilise the child and make them feel safer. He played with the children, and the resources he had brought were a big success. The children with autism connected more with the horses through them, just as my canine resources had supported that connection with dogs. He fully involved himself with all the chores – yes, even the mucking out! In the evening, most of the children settled, including those with autism, and this allowed the parents some time to relax and have a drink while Dale entertained them with his guitar. He enjoyed the evening down time with both the parents and the staff. He played games and even had a few wee drams, brought by a parent or two, because he was off duty. Although he had worked hard and had had a brilliant time, when he returned he informed me, "Mum, it was good helping the parents and kids, but horses are not my thing. I think I will stick with dogs. I'm glad I've done it."

I didn't tell him, but later in the week I was desperate to hear from the "horse's mouth" how he had got on! I called Gillian, and I was pleased that I did. She had a good tale to tell. During the camp, a popular big Clydesdale horse, who was universally adored by the children, took ill with severe colic. The vet was called. The children were so worried, and

Dale encouraged them to colour in pictures from his resources. They decorated the sick animal's stable with them, to help it get better.

I had a story to share too. A mother of a six-year-old on the spectrum who had been to the camp emailed me through Facebook. She explained, "Dale was a marvellous help to us and our son." She had been telling Gillian about a book she was reading. Unbeknown to her, it was my book. Then Gillian told her she had, in fact, already met Dale. Hearing this she was totally blown away! "No! That can't be Dale! I hadn't realised he had autism." As her tears welled up, she wrote how she had found him such a fine young man, and the experience had truly touched her. She felt inspired "even more in our quest to help our son reach his full potential".

The holiday period over, Dale entered the scenario he had worked for five years trying to avoid. He retreated to his room, with only his laptop and the boys to fill his day. His monotony was interrupted with just the weekly degradation of signing on. Walking the boys around our estate was as good as it got. For the sake of his sanity and to keep his skills sharp, he continued to volunteer at Barnardo's drama group. Life was pretty stagnant for both of us. There was one interesting glimmer: his third attempt at his driving theory test. On the big day, he set off feeling more confident, agreeing he would phone me only if he passed. An hour later, the phone rang. When I heard his voice, I expected happy news but didn't expect his particularly nuanced delivery.

"Mum, I passed! Did it by a ba' hair, but I don't care, as long as I passed."

Well, I was delighted, of course! Whilst the terminology might not have been my own, it certainly was his, and the kind of bantering tones he and his friends used. Not for the faint-hearted! Hearing this, Amy ran into the computer room. In a nanosecond she returned with an A4 bespoke congratulations card for Dale, complete with blue sports car, adorned with "L" and "P" signs, and the message: "Well, done! You have passed your driving test theory."

I thought to myself, Well done to you, too, Amy. Little Miss Bill Gates in the making!

Mostly, however, there was more of the duff stuff than thrills to be had. Some days, to break the boredom, we went out for lunch, or drove to the beach at Lunderston Bay. The boys could get a dip and a long walk, which helped us all. Around this time, Beth contacted me to ask if I would meet Keir's additional support needs assistant (ASNA), Blair Cochrane. Blair had read my book and wanted my thoughts on a project he was developing, called DATA (Dog Agility Therapy Autism).[2] Blair knew Keir and Ellie well, and wanted to explore if he could help improve Keir's quality of life, working with him and his dog. Again young Keir was to be a guinea pig, and if the results were good, it would be rolled out for others.

I was aware of YouTube footage of a teenage boy with Asperger's whose life was transformed by a service dog.[3] The story was being reported because a whole new social world had been opened for him when he participated with his pet in dog agility. I understood the therapeutic benefit dog agility could have for an older child on the higher end of the spectrum, but Blair wanted to do so much more. If he could help severely affected younger children access dog agility, it would take them into a world that I believe had never been entered before.

After we talked on the phone, I couldn't wait to meet him. His knowledge of autism was on a par with my own. Blair had the added experience of being an expert dog trainer. He was so successful that he'd even competed in dog agility at Crufts. We met soon afterwards and talked for ages. Just as it had been earlier with Alberto and Jane, we knew immediately that we were on the same page with our thoughts. Blair understood that transitional care was paramount, and though his resources to help the child connect with DATA were different from the ones I had used, they were equally appropriate to the task in hand. We discussed ideas over lunch, but truthfully, Blair just needed me as a second opinion. Undoubtedly, he was on the right track with his project.

This was revolutionary stuff! He was hoping to create a therapeutic programme, which would reduce the sensory chaos children with ASD experience. As luck would have it, the new agility equipment he had ordered was bright green! It was meant to be. Keir was to have a really positive start.

Before he left us, Blair gave Amy an invitation, one I imagined would be mission impossible. "Amy would you like to try DATA with Thomas?"

"Yes, please, then he will be my DATA dog."

While I was pleased for Amy and Blair, I was sceptical. Let's face it: when did that Thomas ever do anything sensible? Nonetheless, I knew that it pays to have an open mind, and I have never been scared to take a risk. If the worst really came to the worst, what harm could it do? I couldn't wait to find out, and so I began preparatory work with Amy. She watched dog agility clips on YouTube, and Blair's resources helped her to learn names for the equipment – the A-frame, the seesaw, jumps and weaving poles.

A few weeks later, on a bitterly cold day, we arrived at Blair's with an embarrassingly tubby Thomas in tow. I confessed. The bold boy had managed a couple of successful forays and had gorged himself on chocolate and biscuits, left out by yours truly by accident. Down to business! I was the camerawoman, and at Blair's command, I stood back to let him take control. That, I must admit, felt odd!

With Thomas on a normal lead, Amy said, "Thomas, this is your dog park. It's time to play."

Immediately, Thomas sussed that she was in charge. If he did something right, he was rewarded with a tiny treat. That made his day. He managed a few little jumps, and then it was time for the big A-frame. With a bit of a heave-ho to Thomas's ample back end from Blair, within minutes he had tackled and completed it. I was astounded, and he must have been just as delighted – that tail wag was in overdrive! What a thrill for Amy. She quickly picked up how to change her tone of voice and place herself correctly to help him complete the course. What a blisteringly brilliant first sessional round! Amy was hooked. On the way home, she confirmed that, as only she could. "Nuala, when I take Thomas to do agility at Crufts, I will need to give him a bath first!"

There was so much more to come from DATA, and it seems right to hand over this part of the story to Blair to tell in his own words:

Blair: The thought of combining what I knew about dogs and autism had been going through my head for some time. There were so many situations I wanted to explore, so much learning potential untapped. I had no doubt. I had known Beth and Keir for some time. After a chance conversation with her about the possibility of starting to teach Keir and Ellie the basics of agility, I was introduced to Nuala. Beth lent me the book, and I admit that I raced through it in a couple of days. It whetted my appetite to meet this woman! She had had such a successful time with a dog, and I understood that completely; my own dogs are my constant companions. After meeting Nuala, DATA (Dog Agility Therapy Autism) was born.

As this was a completely new venture for me, I decided to start at a very basic level with Keir. Firstly, I introduced him to line drawings of a dog similar to his own. The images showed her in the "sit", "down" and "stand" positions. This was to allow Keir to colour the drawings whilst, simultaneously, I subtly reinforced the command by repeating the name of the posture. After six weeks of this learning, I decided that I should introduce Keir and Ellie to the equipment. I have to be honest; this part of the process did not go very well initially, as Keir thought the equipment was for his own use! He proceeded to run along the dog walk and climb on the seesaw. Needless to say, this was gently but firmly discouraged. Once he had settled, I used a jump, with the pole positioned on the floor, to introduce a very basic cause and effect lesson. When Keir said, "Over," Ellie duly went over the pole. We used the same concept for a tunnel and also for the weave poles, positioned on a wide setting. Extremely quickly, Ellie picked up that if she did as she was told she would be rewarded with a snack. Funny that! As most people know, there are not too many things that Labrador Retrievers won't do for food!

After a few weeks of doing jumps and tunnels, I decided that they would attempt the A-frame. This is a rather large piece of equipment; the dog has to climb from one side, right over the top and come down the other. It's pretty steep and, indeed, seen from the side it does look like the letter A. Perhaps that sounds very straightforward, but it is quite a challenge for the novice. However, there are contact points on each side. Ellie was lifted onto the frame and allowed to walk down; the next time she was lifted further up until, bit by bit, she was managing the whole obstacle without any human intervention. I used that same process for the dog walk, which is a narrow plank with a ramped start and finish. This also has contact points at each end. Ellie took to this one extremely easily.

The next obstacle to teach was a seesaw. That's a very difficult device for dogs, as it moves, so I thought it would be best if Keir helped Ellie onto this. He pushed the seesaw down whilst saying the command "Push" to help her. That was a huge challenge, but once again, we achieved it, just as I had planned.

Once I had taught all the pieces of equipment, it was time to start to put them together. That's all very well in a straight line, but how do you get the handler and dog to turn? In this case I simply said, "Keir, left" and he turned to the left! This had to be a fluke! Not believing what had just happened, I tried again, saying, "Right!" and, lo and behold, he turned to the right with Ellie. Throughout all those many weeks of lessons I had been following Keir, but now I wanted to introduce greater independence. I purchased footstep shapes for him to follow and we started putting a small course together. This was working brilliantly until the bright Ellie sussed that I was the food carrier! She just would not go with Keir, knowing which pockets stored the treats. Back to the drawing board! I tried a ball and a short lead ... and hey presto, off went Ellie with Keir to do the course without me. I cannot tell you how proud I felt.

If only all of life went with such beauty! In November, once more Dale and I had caved in to our grim routine. I desperately wanted my health to improve so I could plan for my future. Future? What the hell was that? My medication wasn't hitting the spot. Even the increased dosage. I rattled. I wished I could stop digging that wee brown bottle out of the cupboard, or out my bag. I wished. I wished. Well, I could bloody well keep wishing. It wasn't happening. Tomorrow. I'd find time to fix it tomorrow. Think about it. Think about me. Tomorrow. But in the meantime, I'd need that second pill. Tomorrow. I'd sort it.

In truth, all Dale needed was a job. Then, out of the blue, from Jobcentre Plus he was given just a little hope. A temporary vacancy of ten hours a week was available in an environment Dale had known forever, Highlanders School – the very place he had attended immediately post diagnosis! He was there until he was six years old.

No parent forgets the day that a professional informs them that their child has autism. Our own day was on Wednesday, 27 February 1991. Before meeting the educational psychologist in the school, I had been given that word, autism, from a friend in nursing. Still, I needed that formal diagnosis, and I believed I was prepared to receive it ... I was so wrong! There I was, getting Dale ready in his new jumper I had chosen especially for the day, and yet, deep down I was praying it wasn't autism. Could it just be something else, something less scary? We drove to the school, and Dale, for once, was passive. Jamie and I took a hand each, and led him through the big storm doors of that Victorian building. After the meeting, we passed those doors again. Oh, Dale! He was still the same child, still my gorgeous wee boy, but from that day, officially, I had a different child from the one I thought I had! I was heartbroken, but bloody determined.

Nineteen years later, here I was, driving him to Highlanders for his interview, and he was wearing his good suit for the umpteenth time. I wished him well, waited in the car, and watched him disappear through those same storm doors, keeping my memories to myself. I hoped that fate would be kind to him, but it delivered him yet another blow. Oh yes, he impressed the interview panel. However, they offered the post to a candidate with more experience.

November was a depressingly dreary month, and not just because of the climate. Now that he had passed his theory exam, Dale's driving instructor advised him that he was ready to sit the practical test. On the day of his test, the weather was horrendous, all torrential rain and winds. As he set off, we stuck to our agreed phone rule. According to the television, there was already flooding in the west, and worsening storm conditions were imminent. It seemed likely that his test would be cancelled. I began tidying up to take my mind off the wind, the wet, and that test. A couple of hours later, I sat down with a cup of tea, and saw Dale coming up the stairs of the house. I continued to drink my tea, determined to keep things low-key as he loped into the lounge.

"Mum, have you seen the weather? It's mad out there."

I couldn't disagree, and I reassured him that it was just as well his test had been called off. Then came the bombshell . . .

"Mum, I had to sit my test anyway and . . . I passed!"

I ran up to him, unsure whether to hug him or to hit him! I went for the hug, being just so thrilled that something had gone right at last for him, against all the odds. Delighted though I was, I was also frustrated, as he wasn't in permanent employment, and the chances of him being able to afford a car were non-existent. I knew he felt that too.

A couple of weeks later, as we lunched out, he shared his annoyance of not being able to get out and drive. I decided to overrule a decision Jamie had made earlier, on the basis that the insurance would be too high. Arriving home, I immediately phoned our car insurance broker and had Dale's name added to our policy. He was chuffed to bits! It was expensive, especially at a time when our income was tight, but he deserved it. He offered to put petrol in the car, paying with his own money. With Dale mobile again, I got myself ready to collect Amy from school, when something interesting occurred to me: I now had a live-in chauffeur!

"Dale, here's the car keys. Go and get Amy from school."

"Are you sure, Mum?"

"Yes, you're legally allowed to drive. There's no time like the present to get going!"

Off he went. I loved watching him driving away. Okay, I admit that I twitched the curtains with a wee bit of apprehension, but where would my kids be today if I hadn't been a risk taker? Thereafter Dale would drive anywhere, any time, whenever I asked; if I needed milk from the shop, or I wanted him to collect his Dad from work – whatever! The new freedom was wonderful for both of us. He especially liked driving the boys to Lunderston Bay, particularly without his mother around!

A few weeks later, he came home from a jaunt with the boys to Battery Park. Immediately, I knew something was wrong. Reluctantly, he explained that he had reversed too far when parking and had hit an iron drainpipe. He had broken an indicator light. He assured me that the pipe was unscathed and no other car was damaged, but he was too worried to tell his dad. As he hadn't long had that full licence I didn't want anything to lower his confidence. Without wanting to jinx anything, Dale's driving ever since has been without incident. He's a terrific driver. Some things you just have to do quietly.

Between us, we went to the garage and we stumped up, somehow. Maybe it wasn't just for Dale's sake that I didn't tell Jamie the whole story that night. He was fine about it later, but I didn't have the stomach for yet another battle. There were too many already. I was tired, so tired of it all. It wasn't just him. It was both of us. I hated what we were becoming when we were together.

# 14

## Enough Is Enough

November 2010 brought some of the coldest days any of us could remember. The weather was crazy, and it played havoc with our routines. It was so bad that often we had to start for school early and work late. That took some explaining, to Amy in particular. Snow fell, and stayed, and with it came that cruel, sharp white light. Locking the door for just a moment of privacy, there it was, streaming into the bathroom and showing my face up in the mirror. Suffice to say, that light was taking no prisoners! I shook my head and wearily unscrewed the lid of the moisturiser.

"Nuala! Nuala!"

With two fingers, I scooped up what I can only call a dob of cream and began to rub.

"Nuala! Where's my bag? I need it. Nuala!"

"Amy, ask your dad. I'll be down in a minute."

I rubbed quickly, and looked. It didn't seem to be doing a lot, this not inexpensive cream. In fairness, how much time was I really spending on my appearance? The last five years in particular had been a rollercoaster – Amy, Dale, and then Jamie. There hadn't been a lot of time for nourishing me.

"Nuala! Where's my bag? Dad doesn't know where it is. Nuala!"

"Mum!"

My forefinger moved the cream towards my eyes. Oh God, whose eyes were these? Not mine, surely!

"Mum! Can you come and check my folder? Mum?"

"Dale, I'm coming. Just give me a moment! Please!"

"Nuala!"

Aye, Nuala! Who was she when she was at home? I'd begun to forget. Where was the girl who danced all night, glass in hand, burned the candle at both ends, and sometimes in the middle too, and still came up with the big lipsticked smile? Where was Nuala? And when did she last find time to paint on the lippy? I stuck the moisturiser back in the cupboard, with the lid half on. I took a couple of tablets from the bottle next to it, cupped my shaking hand under the tap, and swigged it all back in a oner.

"Mum!"

"Nuala!"

"Will you get on with it? I've cleared the car and we need to get going. Sometime this year. NUALA!"

Jamie now too. Would it ever stop? I held my face in both hands and my worn gold band caught the light. Even my wedding ring looked done in. Maybe there was something in that. Where had these past five years left our marriage? In truth? Breaking point.

"Nuala!"

"MUM!"

"For God's sake, Nuala, will you get down here?"

A bark.

Hell's teeth. Even the dog was joining in now. I unlocked the door, leaving the unused cosmetics in the cabinet – again – and picked my way downstairs, passing the wires, and increasingly the wireless. Whatever they were. The sixteen remote controls. All that technology. All that STUFF! His stuff. Stuff I'd never understood, never wanted, and really didn't want to begin to understand. HIS STUFF. Everywhere! Squeezing out the space. Squeezing out me. Nuala. Whoever she was. Nuala, the idiot who didn't "get" computers. That Nuala. The Nuala who, however, did get the sensory overload that Amy and Dale got. In spades. The Nuala who knew the overload that can overwhelm anyone with autism. That Nuala Gardner.

Bags, folders and family sorted, for this time at least, Jamie, Amy and

I bundled into the car. My shoulder ached. My back throbbed. My eyes nipped. When did I last find time to get to a GP? The optician? Go to a spa? Hahaha! There wasn't time in this life to allow myself health issues. Make no mistake, being the mum in a family with autism doesn't need a fit woman. It needs a fully blown bionic one. Sooner or later, we all find out that not one of us is made that way. We find out that maybe, after all, we're only human. It's scary when all the systems crash.

I sat in the back seat of the car. In fact, I was in the back seat in so many other ways. My health remained fragile and I was still off sick. Consequently, of course, I was earning far less. There wasn't a moment when that wasn't an issue for me. Not one moment.

Jamie drove on, in silence, and it was a very uncomfortable one. At least, for now, we weren't carping. I'd tried to keep that from the kids. No doubt so had he, but did we manage? No, I don't think we did. As I say, all too human.

As Amy got out at the school gates, my husband said his first words of the journey: "You have a good day today."

*Who was he talking to?* I thought. I thought aloud.

"Amy, of course!" he said.

There it was in a nutshell. How was Amy meant to know he was talking to her? Day after day of my starting every chat with "Amy" or "Dale" seemed to mean nothing to him. All that work, all that research – nothing! Did anything I say to him mean anything? Where was our shared territory, our consistency of approach? We were on two very different planets. Parents with divergent views and strategies are bad news for any child; parents like that with a child or children on the spectrum are unmitigated disasters. I flared!

"I thought she'd heard me!"

He didn't get it. Didn't get it. He didn't get me, for that matter.

I wish I could say that Amy missed all this, but I can't. I apologised, promising I would never let it happen again, knowing similar promises had been broken already. The strain was unbearable.

Later, Amy and I needed to talk this one through. We found time that afternoon. In the midst of our shared calm and my explanation, she interrupted. "Nuala, are you and Dad getting a divorce?"

I was devastated. It wasn't the right time. Somehow, I reassured her that her dad and I were having problems. There was more: "I'm sad. You're not a nurse, and Nuala no longer plays with me."

My daughter was right. I barely got through each day. I was neglecting her, and most days she was left to play alone. Around this time, she became quite obsessed with her Nuala doll. She insisted I help change its clothes many times throughout the day and she slept with it every night. I realise now that in her own way Amy was taking care of me via that doll. The real Nuala wasn't in her life as much as she needed.

Once, I was shaking with anxiety, and she noticed. "Nuala, would you like a massage to make you feel better?"

I used to massage her, but that day our roles were reversed. She gave me such a good massage that I fell asleep for a couple of hours and wakened feeling much better.

Today there was to be no massage, and certainly no sleep. We chatted more, and explored her worries – and mine. Talk over, Amy went upstairs and collected her horses, content, for a while anyway.

I was pleased that we'd managed this together. Alone in the kitchen, I needed a cup of tea. My own state wasn't going to be fixed in a hurry. Lifting the kettle, I noticed, and not for the first time, the tremor in my hands. My right one was especially affected, to the point that I could barely write. To try to get around the problem, I used the same pens that Dale and Amy used, ones with broad plastic tripod grips. It was really frustrating, but it was insightful too. Making such a simple adjustment allowed me to write legibly again. I hoped that, in time, my acute nervous state would settle . . . whenever the truckload of pressure fell off me. I wasn't sleeping or eating well and, certainly, I was depressed. I began to have panic attacks.

Some nights I lay awake and thought I was heading for a mental breakdown. Thank God for Dr Roddy Grose, my GP! That man, and my four-legged canine friend, saved me from self-destruction. Before my health crashed, I rarely saw my doctor, but suddenly, I was never away from him – ongoing sick lines, changes in medication, anti-depressants, sleeping pills, or Valium for panic attacks. Dr Grose always had time to listen, and he is the reason I survived those years of illness with no lasting mental trauma. I knew, for my health's sake, that I was unable to continue to hold down the job I had loved for twelve years. There was so much at stake, so much that I still cannot bear to look at. Something had to give. But before I realised that and sought out Dr Grose's life-saving help, I hit rock bottom.

Our financial situation was not good. Jamie couldn't cope with me being off on long-term sick leave, and eventually the pressure I felt to get back to my nursing job was so bad that I tried to return to work but barely managed three night shifts I was so ill. To cope with this added burden, I did something as a nurse that I should have known better. I wasn't sleeping or eating, and the panic attacks blighted me virtually on a daily basis now. To try and get some mental respite from everything, I started to swallow my prescribed medication like sweets to get through the day, while desperate for my mind to shut down, especially at night.

As the weeks passed and I popped pills at random, my mood swings changed drastically. I would become euphoric until I crashed into the deepest and darkest depression I have ever known. I was unaware of the severe side effects of overdosing until I ended up feeling acutely suicidal. I was toxic with the pills and emotionally empty. My mood was so low. Soon, I reached zero function.

It will haunt me forever, the image of me sitting, with my friend Lorraine by my side, with the risk of me being admitted to the local psychiatric unit looming over me. Thankfully, though, under Dr Grose's care and with Jamie and Lorraine's help, I didn't need to be hospitalised. I came through the darkest part of my life and was determined to change things for the better, and for Amy and Dale's sakes.

Now, I can see an ironic twist of fate. It took all this to give me the wake-up call I needed. I made a life-changing decision. For the first time in twenty-five years, I put my own health and future well-being first. I had to. How else could I continue to fight to ensure Amy had the same life chances that Dale now enjoyed?

My friends saw the changes in me, and worried. Amy had already asked about divorce. She wasn't the only one with that word in her head. Yet, where was my way out? Way back in the days when Dale's autism had tested me to the limit, I relied on Jamie's support. He had helped me through some dark times, but the constant arguing and strain of our relationship made this situation now unliveable. Deep down I knew the day would come when I would decide to get out. But how? And when? Would I ever have the physical and emotional strength to leave? Where would I stay? We needed a garden. My head was birling. Years of fighting for both my children had left very little over for me. Who was that woman in the mirror? Nuala?

Once again, Amy came to my rescue in the most unlikely way. Back to the Bed-a-thon! While she had settled better in her own single bed, which we had moved into the office that was next to our bedroom, the problem was still not sorted completely. As often as not, who ended up in our bed? No prizes for guessing! One morning, casually, she opined: "Nuala, I like your big bed. Mine is too skinny. I'm scared I'm going to fall out. I like your red room and wardrobes. Red makes me feel good and it helps me sleep good too!"

When I chose the red, glossy furniture for our bedroom, with wallpaper and curtains in matching tones, it never occurred that I was creating an Amy-perfect haven. I should have known – she liked red. But the complexity of autism can so cloud our judgements. And memories! Throughout Dale's childhood, he slept in a double bed, allowing room for us to settle him and most of his toys, including his pedal bike!

That night, we let Amy sleep in our room. I slept in hers, and Jamie took the office. Safe with her Nuala doll, Amy slept soundly all night, and stayed put. It was the same every night thereafter, without the Melatonin. We only took a decade to solve the Bed-a-thon! Not only that, but a change in living arrangements was introduced to my children, in the kindest possible way. The first step towards the biggest change they would have to make.

With the sleeping arrangements sorted, on 7 December I asked Jamie for a divorce. He agreed, knowing it was best for all of us. We went through the motions of Christmas together. Christmas has never been the family time for us that we might have hoped. Plenty of families with autism will empathise with that. But December 2010 was easily the worst Christmas I had ever known, and it had nothing to do with autism. In fact, Amy's excitement motivated me to get through it for Dale, as well as for the boys.

For the first time in my life, that festive season my weight fell off. I was miserable. It was all too easy to go without food. Yet something odd was happening when I caught sight of myself in the mirror. I knew years of comfort eating had taken their toll. It had been so long since I could remember being any size under 18. I had given up on myself, my appearance. Yet as I now checked my reflection in the mirror again, I couldn't ignore this change that had come over me. The weight loss was actually working wonders. I even felt better! I might even begin to recognise that woman. *Is that you, Nuala?*

Something clicked! I never do anything by halves. In the weeks following, I spent a significant proportion of Sir Henry's book royalties. It was time to reclaim something of the real Nuala. I needed to find someone who wasn't always a wife or a mum or a campaigner for causes. A Nuala I'd almost forgotten. Me. There was much nurturing and cosseting to be done. I had a good twenty-five years to catch up on!

My accidental weight loss gained me entry to shops I'd scurried past for years. I loved those tailored, figure-hugging business suits ... *Well, hello, Nuala in the changing room mirror. You wear them well!* Now I needed to ditch the flatties. I imagined Cinderella smiling at me when my feet fitted those foxy stilettos like the proverbial glove! Within weeks, my wardrobe doubled. Anyone seeing it would probably conclude that I was some sort of manager in a major organisation. Now at presentations and similar public speaking events, I looked and felt the part. My confidence soared with my new-found height! I treated myself to laser eye surgery and began again to recognise and love the Nuala I saw in the mirror.

Outside the shops, my old friend Jan nearly walked right past me. "My God! Nuala! What's happened? I barely recognised you. You look fantastic – better than you did years ago!"

Ho hum! I explained that I was seeking a divorce, and why.

"Never mind! You'll meet someone who appreciates you. You're a great catch."

Laughingly, I replied, "Oh yeah, all the men'll be queuing up for a middle-aged bird with two massive daft dogs and a live-in interrogator!"

How we hooted! Still, Jan left me with something else. "Nuala, promise me you won't become that downtrodden person ever again."

I was sure on that one! "Don't worry, Jan. She's never coming back!"

On the way home, I had my ears pierced. Gorgeous earrings suddenly had my name all over them, and those nails I'd bitten to the quick for years? They were growing! I had them manicured the very next week and treated myself to all the colours of polish my newly sharp eyesight could take . . . and no, they weren't going to sit unused in any cupboard! Jan wasn't the only one to comment on the new me. All my friends complimented me, and it felt great, but there was one particular voice which was extra special, Amy's. "Nuala, your nails are nice. Well done! You're a very good girl."

Thereafter, Amy and I would share "girly night" manicure sessions. After our pampering session, all four of us – me, the Nuala doll, Amy and the cuddly retriever toy she called Thomas – would end the evening dancing to the latest disco music until my breath ran out. Amy would insist I danced with "mini me" and she would partner the big cuddly golden retriever toy she called Thomas. Sometimes the real Thomas joined in too, unable to resist an opportunity for madness. Our particular favourite song was Alexis Jordan's "Happiness". I taught Amy some disco moves and she, in return, taught me some street dancing techniques she had been learning in an after-school class.

Happiness! As the song repeated the word regularly, I felt better than I had in years, and I knew that "Team Amynual", as Amy now called us, would work together just fine. I couldn't wait. Thanks to Henry's gift, my health was improving, slowly.

I know Dale, and especially Amy, will never forget the terrible scenes they witnessed when I was at my lowest. Children bury hurt deep in their minds, but they never forget. Amy confirmed that for me. We were cuddling together, enjoying breakfast in her "new" bedroom, with Thomas and Henry beside us, mooching for crumbs. It was a new and pleasant routine for Team Amynual, and all seemed to be so easy and relaxed.

"Nuala, have you fallen out of love with Dad?"

I took a risk and went along with her calm, inquisitive mood. "Amy, thank you for asking such a good question."

"You're welcome, Nuala. What's the answer?"

"Yes, darling, I have fallen out of love with your dad. It's been for a long time now."

"That's all right, Nuala. That happens and people get divorced. Are you doing that?"

"Yes I am. And Amy, don't you worry, because we have been practising living as Team Amynual with Thomas, your DATA dog, and it has been good. That is why I sleep in your bedroom upstairs and your dad sleeps in the office. When I find Team Amynual a new home, we will be all right."

She agreed. I thought we had come to the end of that, for now at any rate. Wrong!

"Nuala, I like you better since you took off your mood ring. You are happy now, and your tone of voice is always nice now."

"Amy, what do you mean? What mood ring?"

"I mean your mood wedding ring. You took it off at Christmas."

I needed to brace myself. The Interrogator was on a roll.

"I like the new Nuala best. She's nice and skinny, looks beautiful, and she has gorgeous lips."

"Amy, that's so kind of you to say that."

There was no stopping her.

"The old Nuala had hair like a hedgehog, shouted and was upset too much and was crying a lot. You have improved. Your hair's lovely and the shouting and crying has stopped."

What can I add to that?

That morning, we talked openly, at her level, about the future. I reminded her of some basic rules I'd recently taught her about how to maintain a good relationship with someone that you love. The first rule covered mutual respect: never knowingly hurting a loved one. I thought we'd covered everything. Wrong again!

"Nuala, we need to change the old Nuala doll to the new Nuala."

"Amy, you are so right. We will do that today."

So, with the help of some permanent felt-tipped markers, the old Nuala doll was upgraded, made-up. She gained a new wardrobe and some smashing dangly earrings. We were both ready to face the world again! Personally, the revamped doll put me in mind of Chuckie from the horror movie, but she hit the spot with Amy. "Nuala, I love the two new Nualas!"

I was relieved. Even so, my weird effigy did freak me out!

She was only ten and I was completely overwhelmed by her. Dale, by contrast around that age, couldn't bear me changing my hairstyle or experimenting with the colours or types of clothes I wore. I had to wean him onto acceptance of any new looks I managed. However, in my old-life situation, it wasn't often an issue!

Such was Amy's relief that life was getting better that a couple of days later she emailed me from her new, state-of-the-art iPod: "Hello Nuala, do you like the cake I found for you?"

I scrolled down. I was stunned, but couldn't stop laughing. Even for Amy this was a topper. She had surfed the net and sourced a picture of a divorce cake! It resembled a traditional wedding cake, with ornate icing and a bride, standing in the middle in all her glory. But the groom was missing. He was clinging to the edge of the cake, as if he was dangling from a cliff top! I thanked her. "Amy, I love my divorce cake! You made a great choice for me."

Not many months later, I looked in that bathroom mirror again. I liked what I saw, and felt. My hands jangled with pretty bangles, but they weren't shaking. As for my "mood ring", I'd no idea where I'd put that, and that felt brilliant.

I mouthed at my own reflection, with smiling lips, in what I must say was a very fine, audacious red. "Hi, Nuala! Welcome back, girl!"

No matter what I was to face in the future, I was going with Liz Taylor: "Put on some lipstick, pour myself a drink and pull myself together!"

And just before I opened the door, I couldn't resist turning. "And see that auld dame, that other Nuala. No way is she ever coming back!"

# 15

# *The Last Straw*

No, that trachled woman was never coming back, but if I had thought I'd fixed everything with a new wardrobe and a fresh outlook, I would have been naïve, and dangerously wrong. No divorce comes easily, for any of the parties involved. Perhaps it's a bit like crying at a funeral, when you don't only shed tears for the one just gone, you find yourself remembering every funeral, everyone you've ever lost. So in the ending of a marriage, there are tears for things long past and ripples from other times. Things are exposed, even when you suppose them hidden or lost. Meanwhile, life doesn't stop because a marriage happens to be finishing.

Early in 2011, my worries were mounting about Dale: he was again in limbo and without supply work. When he needed it most, real hope came as a new private nursery opened with eleven vacancies for HNC childcare workers. With the help of his DEA and The Trust Employability Services he applied, despite the intensity of the recruitment process. His CV earned him a place from sixty applications for around twenty places overall. Dale attended the nursery's open day, as usual suited and booted – well, he needed the boots, as we were knee-deep in snow once again.

After the event, his DEA phoned the Trust staff to get feedback on his performance. He'd made a real impression on the nursery managers. The Trust staff gave him a mock interview, and his four years of employability training with Prospects had paid off. His interview skills were excellent. This time, Dale was relieved to hear, he was to get advance notice of the panel's questions. As the interview was only a couple of days away, I phoned his DEA, anxious that the questions hadn't yet arrived. My heart sank when she told me, "They are generic questions. It wouldn't help to have them ahead of the day."

My blood started boiling. If the questions wouldn't help, then why not supply them anyway? It was, after all, my son's right. Infuriatingly, there was no time to challenge the situation, and he had no choice but to attend, unprepared. Yet when he came home, he was relaxed. It had gone every bit as well as his mock one. However, his next words floored me. "Mum, one of the panel told me I had done well to get to this stage."

The gravity of that was lost on him, but not on me. I already knew what the outcome was: "We regret to inform you on this occasion you have been unsuccessful."

Again, no reason.

Outraged, and with Dale's permission, I phoned his DEA. She had obtained feedback from the nursery managers. What I was to learn horrified me. There was just one question that confused Dale to the extent that he struggled to answer, and no wonder! If he was left alone with the children and two kids had a fight, what would he do? Dale's answer was ambiguous and confusing, because, to him, a fight would be what he'd expect to see in a boxing ring. Secondly, he had understood the word "alone" quite literally, that is, that there would be no other staff available in the building to help him. Following on from this, the nursery wanted "More detailed information on Dale's capacity to do the job ... [and that] the children were safe in Dale's hands because of the nature of the job." Discovering this was devastating because many a time he would tell me that the children's safety was his priority at all times, and he would do whatever it would take to keep them safe.

Such was the gravity of the nursery managers' concerns that they had sought advice from Isobel at Gibshill on his performance in a workplace. Not surprisingly, she felt able to reassure them. She had, after all, given him a reference. The quick-witted DEA saw an opportunity to salvage something. She asked the nursery managers if they would consider a work placement for Dale affording them the opportunity to see for themselves how he worked.

This would entail him doing the job for four weeks while staying on JSA. His placement would be supported and monitored by the DEA or by another agency. If it went well, the position would be made permanent. As the nursery hadn't opened, this couldn't happen immediately, but certainly the DEA would be in contact and something could be arranged. This gave us all a little faith, but we still had huge concerns about him working in an environment with such a poor understanding of autism.

However, there was one more point which needed to be addressed. At the end of his rejection letter, the Employability Services invited him to utilise their expertise, including CV, application and interview workshops, to enhance his employability. This was deeply distressing for Dale, and added unnecessary insult to the already painful injury. Prospects had, after all, spent four years training him in all aspects of employability. Billy Docherty contacted the Trust, recognising that maintaining Dale's increasingly fragile self-esteem was of paramount importance. Sadly, that chance for him to try a work placement disappeared. Strangely, it didn't even reappear when a second nursery opened within easy commuting distance from home.

Somehow, he carried on. Barnardo's provided him with training in Makaton sign language, and despite all the obstacles, all the setbacks, he still beefed up that CV, still grasped the belief that one day, he was going to get that job. But when?

In February a familiar voice called on the phone. Moorfoot School wanted him to cover a full-time nursery position! The receiver was hardly replaced but Dale was on his way there! It was quite a challenge. The preschool provision was fully integrated into the Primary setting. It had one class of thirty in the morning and another of the same number after lunch. The pressure was on. His life revolved around work, and not just in work. At home, he was planning play activities and taking children's profiles home to complete. He was often stressed and exhausted. Despite this, I was hearing great things on the grapevine. The staff were delighted to have him on board. A young teacher made a point of telling him how impressed he was by his performance. He taught Amy and had read my book, so he was under no illusions about the extent of my son's achievement. This meant a lot to Dale. Even other parents I knew at the school who were looking out for my son witnessed him in action and reported back to me. It was all good.

There was only one problem in need of urgent attention. We had another, smaller mole on the premises!

"Hello, Dale! Dale! What are you having for dinner today?"

Amy was having a ball. Her brother wasn't. "Mum, we need to call an emergency family meeting to explain to Amy that when she sees me at school she has to call me Mr Gardner. She's even got her friends calling me Dale!"

So Amy learned to call her brother Mr Gardner, and would even send him formally addressed emails, knowing she had got the last word. Eventually, Dale ignored her and the fun, at last, wore off.

With Dale settled at Moorfoot, I felt a lot stronger, so I made That Appointment. The one with the solicitor. Jill Carrick came highly recommended. Emotionally, I still had an age to go, but my confidence was rising daily, and thankfully, even the tremor had gone. My decision was made, and the relief I felt at that office door was palpable. Being my son's mother, I arrived there early! If I had any nerves, they soon dissipated. Jill was about my own age, and her greeting was both professional and warm. I sat down, and she opened the meeting. "How are you feeling about things? Is this a separation, or have you decided to divorce your husband?"

I replied with conviction. "Thank you, I am certain that I want a divorce. I wish I had had the courage to do this years ago."

"Why is that?"

Why was that? Soothed by her kindness, the words tumbled out. Thoughts and explanations, reasons I hadn't even really formulated before. In that stranger's office, I bared my soul until my voice cracked. The nerves crept back.

"It's all right. Take your time."

I did take my time. I took all my time to explain things twenty-five years and more in the making. I described how I had kept going for the children's sakes, especially given their autism. How were they to cope with a divorce? My terror in the face of it all.

"So, what's changed?"

"Both of them have improved so much. I know they will be able to cope now."

Jill had seen so many mothers who had struggled on in marriages. The autism in mine added an extra ingredient to a mix we both knew to be already unpalatable.

"It must have been so hard."

"Oh, yes."

Jill gave me the time and space to say more than I had ever intended to say in a legal appointment. It was more than professional courtesy, and it enabled me to unravel a great many knotted threads for the very first time. I will always be grateful to her. When at last she did interject, it was to let me know she empathised, and that she was there to help me and my family move on. She explained that the best way forward was to sell our home. It was impossible for me to keep it. It was too big, with too many bad memories. Anyway, I needed a fresh start. I wanted to keep things amicable for Dale's well-being and especially for Amy's; she was so young.

When I left Jill's office, it was a beautiful day. The sun was high in a cornflower sky and there was a brisk wind. I returned to the car, ready to head for the shore and unleash the waiting boys on their much-needed walk. Doubtless, they'd chance a bracing swim in the Clyde. I needed the walk too. The swim I could forgo. I felt great. I'd turned the corner, taken the first legal step. I was on my way . . . then I put my key in the ignition. What had I said? What had I done? Why was I spilling out my past . . . to someone I'd never even met before?

Once that distant past is unblocked there's just no damming up the torrent. Old times, good times, bad times, times with Jamie, and times before Jamie. I gripped the wheel, sobbed and sobbed, still parked – in full view – in that busy street. I wept as if I'd never stop. I sunk my face in the wheel. Sometimes I think I'd have stayed in that car; I'd be there yet. Oh, I'd have filled it with tears and stayed there, stuck, a permanent fixture in the gutter. But I was saved from that by twin cries cutting through my own.

The boys! I'd completely forgotten them. I pulled myself together and took my red-eyed, puffy-faced self and two very desperate dogs to the beach. I reckon I was as needy of the time and space as they were.

There were harrowing weeks to follow. More weight fell off. There was loss, there was grief, regret about what I might be losing, regret about what I had lost, even before my marriage. I began to wonder if I should have married in the first place. Or at any rate, should I have married him? Had Jamie ever been The One? Was I ever right for him? So many fears, so many doubts. I managed to dissect my life and fillet out any shred of my own self-worth. I was a complete failure. A failed wife, a failed woman!

I salvaged one thing in all the darkness: I was a good mother.

Eventually, one almost sunny day, I managed to drag myself back into town. There it was, in that boutique window: the dress of dresses! Even in my downed state, I swear, that dress was winking at me! *Come on in. Try me on!* I obeyed!

The shop was quiet and the assistant greeted me immediately. It was my old friend Susan, whom I hadn't seen in years! We went back ages, through the challenging times with Dale. As ever, she looked great – being a former beautician – and she complimented me on my look. "Back to your old self," as she put it. Once I'd started explaining, I told her everything. Nuala, the disaster with men.

"Nuala, your emotions are all over the place. You're grieving. You've been living in an autistic bubble for twenty-three years and you deserve to be happy now! You are not a failure. You've just not met the right one, and it's not too late!"

I so needed to hear that.

That evening, as I reflected on her words, I realised something huge. Autism and disability puts a huge strain on a family. Marriages crack up under the strain all the time. The really weird thing was that, for us, autism was the glue that held our marriage together. Our children were the best things to ever happen to our relationship. That strongest love of all kept us together as a couple, way beyond our own partnership. I don't think Jamie would dispute that either.

I dug out old files, letters, cards and photo albums from the bottom of the wardrobe. I looked back into the dark stuff, looked at things I'd buried for years, and I sat on my bed and wept. Suddenly, I remembered Amy, downstairs on her own. I dried my eyes quickly and returned the folder to its grave, where it belonged. She was playing contentedly with her iPod, so I sat across from her, pretending to watch TV.

"Nuala! Is your eyes all right? What's wrong with your eyes? I'm worried about your eyes."

"Amy, come over to me. I want a big hug. That will help my eyes get better and help me."

As I hugged her I couldn't help but acknowledge, through my heartbreak, that I was the luckiest woman alive, having such wonderful children. It is no mean feat for a child with autism to be able to interpret the signs of distress, or indeed any emotion, skills we neuro-typicals take for granted. Amy had starred again, or so I thought until a few weeks later when she completely astounded me once again by asking, "Nuala, is Madaleine still missing?"

Now this may seem like simply another question, but for Amy to display this particular emotion – empathy – that was astounding. She had not been prompted by any news show and had no other reason to ask this, but simply from her own observations she thought to say it.

This demonstrated her awareness of other events and a true ability to empathise, an emotion that is very difficult for people with autism to display. I was completely blown away.

Hearing this, and having finished processing my emotional tidal wave, I sat her down and explained that, sadly, the little girl she had asked about was still missing. Amy nodded in understanding.

Back to a few weeks before, presented with a big hug from my daughter, I also thought of her brother. How would he cope? I was to find out a week later.

I was passing Dale's bedroom when he called out, "Mum, are you all right? I'm worried about you. Are you upset about divorcing Dad?"

I was astounded by his remark, because I thought I was just fine, outwardly at least. I went into his room.

"Mum, I'm really worried about your health. The weight you have lost has happened too quickly. Please, Mum, tell me what's wrong. Have you got cancer?"

Shocked, I said, "Dale. Oh no! It's not anything like that. I will explain but you have to promise me you will keep what I tell you private, just between us."

"Mum, I understand. You can trust me. Remember, I have to keep my work with the children confidential."

I went to my wardrobe and exhumed my bombshell – a couple of wedding pictures of myself, not with Jamie but with Alex, who had been my first husband. My first marriage. My first divorce. Before I let Dale see them, I had to explain, had to share how much of a failure I felt. I had to share my past.

"Jesus Christ, Mum! You were married. Alex was your husband?"

I let him see two pictures. The moment he saw them, he became subdued, but relieved. Finally, he understood what was really going on with me. His next words floored me. "Mum, these pictures are really beautiful. You made a nice couple."

[ 177 ]

"Dale, my emotions have been in turmoil. It's been twenty-five years. It wasn't meant to be, life is like that, but thank you for understanding. That means so much to me."

Now I was composed. I asked if he wouldn't mind telling me how he felt about the future, about living with his sister and me.

He had his own bombshell. "Mum, I'm sorry, but I want to live with my dad."

I felt as if he had stabbed me in the heart. Then I did what I have always done when conversing with anyone with autism. I paused for six seconds to process what I had heard. Then I replied. "Dale, that's absolutely, one hundred per cent fine. I respect and understand your decision."

He went on to explain. "Mum, I love you very much, and I know all you have done for me to get me the life I have now, but you need to let me go. I'm twenty-two, an adult. Let me make my own mistakes in life and be the independent person you made me."

Yes, I felt sad, but I couldn't have felt more proud. Dale was absolutely right. I had given up so much in my own life, in the hope that one day I would hear these very words. Dale's day had come. With the decision made there was one important issue. I had no option but to split up the boys. I explained to him that Henry would obviously be with him, but for me, and especially Amy's sake, we needed Thomas every bit as much. I couldn't imagine living without a golden retriever in my life, even if it was Thomas! I'd never cope!

Before I left his room, I said, "Dale, I'm going to let you go with all my love, and remember I will always be there for you. If you need me, for anything, promise me you will come to me."

"Thanks, Mum. I know that."

He stood up and gave me a big, manly hug.

"Mum, you will get through all this, but it will take time. I will help you any time as well."

I left him to continue watching his DVD, and shut his bedroom door.

With a heavy heart and a sense of relief, I had said a loving goodbye to my wee Dale and Henry that night.

There wasn't much sleep to come when I did find my pillow. That's not strictly true. I never did find my own pillow that night. Wreck of a woman that I was – after a decade-long puzzle to solve the Bed-a-thon, after only a few weeks of successful nights – yes, this wreck of a woman crawled right in beside her daughter, in her daughter's own bed! Hands up, I admit it: the perfect lesson in what not to do. I crawled in, trying to lie still. My mind wasn't managing. It was churning.

There was so much loss. My marriage, my nursing career, and now this. Sure, there was the canine education programme, but none of that was secure, it was only in its infancy. In its infancy? That was a joke. It still felt unborn, with no money, no dogs – no nothing to advance my ideas! All the avenues I'd gone down – the emails, the letters, the phone calls – all very interesting, but funding? No. Nothing. All my work and shared thoughts offered to other dog charities in the UK was for nothing. I was at my lowest ebb. What else was there left for me to fail at? Hell, by undoing my good work on the Bed-a-thon this very night, I was failing at the one thing I did do well. Was I really now failing as a mum too? Was it possible? While I was sure I was doing the right thing in leaving my marriage, the future began to terrify me just as much as my unhappy past had. Where was I going?

Suddenly, I heard the sweetest little voice. "Nuala, do you want me to hug you, to see if that helps you?"

"Amy, thank you! Yes please, darling! You are so kind."

She hugged me tightly, and kissed me on my shoulder.

"Nuala, I love you. Do not worry. Team Amynual will be good."

What was coming next? I couldn't know, but face it I would! I had to think about creating a future for team Amynual, and the vandal! I would! And somewhere, unknown to us, a certain Sir Henry had his part to play too.

# 16

## Moving On

"We need another and a wiser and perhaps a more mystical concept of animals. Remote from universal nature, and living by complicated artifice, man in civilisation surveys the creature through the glass of his knowledge and sees thereby a feather magnified and the whole image in distortion. We patronise them for their incompleteness, for their tragic fate of having taken form so far below ourselves. And therein we err, and greatly err. For the animal shall not be measured by man. In a world older and more complete than ours they move finished and complete, gifted with extensions of the senses we have lost or never attained, living by voices we shall never hear. They are not brethren, they are not underlings; they are other nations, caught with ourselves in the net of life and time, fellow prisoners of the splendour and travail of the earth."

– Henry Beston, *The Outermost House*

At last, the Moorfoot school term had ended and Dale came home, spilling over with the now customary but still welcomed gifts and cards and good wishes. That summer wasn't the worst I had known. It brought us stability, despite the change in family dynamics. Dale and his friends opted out of T in the Park 2011 because the line-up wasn't to their liking. Instead, they upped their Glasgow social life. Amy was excited about starting Primary 6, and busy, attending play schemes and shared days out with Jamie and me. Maybe a little of the tension had begun to lift at home for her, knowing that her parents were going to go their separate ways. It's a myth to think staying together is always in the best interests of the children. Even planning the move was helping to stabilise Amy. All of us, if truth be known. Even Jamie was already beginning to move on. I could see it in him. Even if that paper was still between us, something was moving in the right direction. On that, at least, we could agree. That helped Amy, a lot. So she was settled, but life for Dale was less easy.

Again, he had no supply work. He continued working with Barnardo's and Prospects Social Group helped fill in some time, which maintained some sense of worth. However, the gap in the week was huge, and I witnessed scenes he had struggled to avoid for five years. He retreated, spending hours alone on his laptop. At least now he could drive, so he broke the monotony by taking the boys out. Nonetheless, time remained his enemy. Day after day, he searched for jobs, but there were none. Weeks became months. His only time out was signing on. This degrading routine – endlessly seeking employment, dependant on the welfare system – was grinding him down.

One morning there a loud knock on my bedroom door. Jamie handed me the phone.

"It's Alberto, calling from Spain."

It had been four years since I had seen Alberto. Refreshingly, he had lost none of his enthusiasm. He brought good news. His friend Beni wanted to translate my book into Spanish. Marvellous! That wasn't all. "Nuala, we have placed a few dogs with severely non-verbal autistic children, and it has gone well."

PAAT had used my book when training autism therapy dogs for a couple of families. There had been problems – but not with the dogs! Sometimes, the parents' knowledge and management of their children was inconsistent, and that hindered progress. PAAT wanted my help with the parental side of their programme. The transitional care before the dog's arrival was inadequate, and strategies on the use of dogs as educational facilitators were lacking. PAAT were exhausted. It would certainly help to have my book available to parents in Spanish. However, Alberto and Jane wanted to do much more, bringing my experience and theirs together to replicate lessons learned from Dale and Henry.

I felt alive again. My hopes soared!

It didn't matter who used my work. What was important was that it reached families! PAAT's aim was mine: to achieve the greatest independence possible for the child using the dog. Our programme would be unique. I was inspired.

Already they had achieved so much. In their programme, the children chose their "own" coloured dog lead, just as Dale had done. PAAT found that the children held onto these leads, and spontaneously walked beside their dogs. The adults had control of the dog with another lead. Just as I had found. This was momentous. If children are attached to their dogs it is difficult to undo that teaching. There was so much to discuss.

"Nuala, you must come to see us so we can make this work."

I couldn't wait! I could hand my programme to PAAT to be translated. They would encourage interested parents to read my book so when they used the resources and strategies, it would be meaningful.

"Nuala, what shall we call our programme?"

Simply, "Gardner & PAAT Canine Guide to Autism."

I explained about my pending divorce and my perilous health. Our phone call finished with Alberto organising a date for my visit.

Just when I thought things couldn't improve, I came across a vacancy in a newspaper. Cairn Curran Nursery! Dale had worked there voluntarily for seven months, and it needed a permanent, part-time HNC childcare worker. Janice, the nursery head, thought highly of Dale. Earlier, she had been unable to offer him employment, although she wished that she could. She had given him such a glowing report. He was on to the case immediately!

Seeing his enthusiasm return as he prepared for his interview was brilliant. How many times had he worn that suit now? I treated him to a morale booster: a silk tie and blue shirt. When the day arrived, he looked really professional.

"Mum, I feel good about this, because my voluntary work at Cairn Curran was in the hope that I might get a job there. Janice will be one of the staff interviewing me, so I have no worries."

He came home, relaxed.

"Mum, it was the best interview I have done. They will let me know in a letter in a week's time."

It was a long week, but when the letter arrived, I left it in his room. Minutes later, he came downstairs. Silently, he handed it to me, and put on the kettle. My heart sank. There was no offer.

That was it. No reason why, just the usual words of rejection.

I went to my bedroom, clutching the letter. If I felt hellish, how was Dale? I was beat. How could I help keep him going, bogged down as I was? There was that spectre again. Should I have let him be? Let that lonely, autistic world keep him? Would that have been kinder? How would this latest, most cruel rejection affect him? Despite his determination, he was reaching his limit. I went upstairs. He was in front of his laptop, drinking his tea, withdrawn.

"Dale, I'm so sorry. You deserved that job. I know you want time to think. I will talk to you soon. I love you, and will never give up on you!"

How could I help him maintain his self-respect? It was vital. If a person with autism loses that, the consequences can be dire, and can lead to regression. Unthinkable. As I had done many times before when lost and desperate, I emailed Jim Taylor for advice.

His response was not what I had expected, but as I read it, a light flicked on. "I guess that this is the next big barrier for those kids that we see making SO much progress. They are more ready for the world, but the world isn't ready for them. I remain in contact with a young man who left Struan School last year. Again, he is a very able young man but is struggling to make headway."

His words echoed what I knew from Prospects and elsewhere. Dale read Jim's email. It did make him feel a little better, but it opened up his feelings instantly. He didn't hold back!

"I've had enough! I've lost my passion for nursery work. I never want to do it ever again. Barnardo's is different. They treat me well, and I can give something back and use my skills, but Mum, there's more to me than autism!"

He had met Janice. They had taken on a more experienced candidate. She thought he should work with people with disabilities and autism. This enraged him. After all, he had five years of experience with Barnardo's. I let him use me as his emotional punchbag.

"What more do they want? I'm worthless, only useful for voluntary work!"

I put him right on that. By now his curriculum vitae was incredibly impressive – autism or no autism.

"Mum, I grafted for five years to work in my chosen career, but it's useless. Many treat me as if I'm stupid, stereotype me as being obsessive and incapable, because they know I have autism. No matter how much I have achieved or how successful I am, I have to prove and achieve more than my peers. I am as capable as anyone else, despite my autism."

I saw his choice in tatters. Who could blame him? Both Dale and Jim's words rang in my ears.

"It's useless."

But the world isn't ready for them.

"Dale, what if all you have been through isn't for nothing?"

"What do you mean, Mum? I'm going to try to get any job now. I've definitely had enough. I mean it."

I respected that. I sat down beside him and asked, "Will you allow me to tell your story again? Let people know the barriers and injustice you have faced as an adult."

"It's not just me. My friends and clients at Prospects have faced the same. I'm not that special."

My brave son agreed to let me tell his tale. The decision was precarious, but worthwhile. Not nearly enough has changed. Even in death, Henry had gifted us a future. We chose to unwrap it.

On 30 September 2011 I ended my career as a nurse, took my name off the register and put it all where it belonged, in the past. Dale continued his voluntary work at Barnardo's and became involved with The Shaw Trust, a local employment agency connected to Jobcentre Plus. At last he was on a new pathway and he had a chance!

While I began to work on the sequel to *Henry*, my progress was interrupted. Nothing ever works uninterrupted in real life, after all! Laura's daughter Katy remained in some kind of administratively-induced limbo. For the past two years, I had continued to visit the Highlands to back up my cousin in her fight to ensure that Katy received her entitlement – yet again, that essential, condition-specific education. In a fairer world, that would have happened automatically, but families with autism haven't discovered that just planet as yet. Letter after letter, meeting after meeting, a familiar, wearying course. But luckily, Laura was up for the journey! Many a day, I spent hours on the phone talking through problems, just trying to keep her sane. One by one, I passed on the tools of my well-honed trade to my cousin: how to obtain an early diagnosis, and when that isn't forthcoming, how to persevere in the face of an uncooperative system! After all, Katy was already four. She had made excellent progress. Her speech, her interaction with peers and even her diet had improved. That ballerina, tiptoe walking? It was hardly ever evident now and perhaps only really happened in times of acute anxiety. All these developments pointed my niece firmly in the direction of properly supported mainstream schooling.

Perhaps you're wondering: with such leaps, did Katy really need a diagnosis? Why label the child? Well, here's why. Without a formal diagnosis, support at primary school could not be guaranteed or adequately given. If her parents were to need respite (which they did already), how else could they access it? Their right to apply for benefits like DLA, The Family Fund[1] and Carer's Allowance would be curtailed. These benefits and supportive pathways are not luxuries, whatever any passing governments may think. Most immediately, without a diagnosis Katy would not be eligible for the ASD support services available at The Pines, Inverness' new NAS Autism Centre.

While in principle the diagnostic process has to be thorough, multi-disciplinary and not rushed, Katy's own problems had been identified within her first year of life. Add in my two children's situations, plus Uncle Tommy, and there was undeniable evidence of a strong family history. Further, it was obvious that Katy's ASD was global. What more could be offered?

Once again, I sat down at my table with notepaper and pen. I seemed to have been doing this on a regular basis since Dale's second birthday. My letter stated the case for Katy's need for a diagnosis, on the tactful suggestion that many children still slip through the net. That was not all. Before writing, I did something that I wished someone had done for me when Dale was a child, something which might have saved me two years of hell, and avoided a painful trip to England to secure his diagnosis.

Since the emergence of her daughter's problems, Laura had sent me copies of every letter and report she had received from the multi-disciplinary team. Only broken by needful tea breaks and the odd biscuit, I took my time, making it my business to be familiar with the notes. It was well worth it. I tracked forty-five signs, behaviours and traits matching those on the ICD 10 Diagnostic Criteria, thus qualifying Katy to have her diagnosis of autism. The most common ASD diagnostic tool is the WHO (World Health Organisation) ICD 10 6, which is used to determine the level of autism as a sliding scale (or continuum). A person diagnosed with severe autism, like Dale, can slide up the scale with a good education or can regress in times of crisis. That information is readily available on the Internet.[2]

I put all of this in the letter. Within weeks, Laura's daughter was diagnosed. The multi-disciplinary assessment became a formality. Thankfully, the doctor and staff present were all very professional and were truly sympathetic to the significance of her diagnosis. Katy did indeed go to a mainstream school, with support. Her dad summed it up, perfectly: "If only Katy had been diagnosed a year earlier. We would have got on the Early Bird Training then, because it really helped us to get through to her."[3]

For now at least, her future and that of her family had become a whole lot rosier.

I had a future to face too. Alberto had arranged an Easter visit to Zamora, which was timely. I was moving on. Although my confidence was still fragile, I prepared to talk to a letting agency. It felt like getting ready for an interview. So many private lets didn't allow pets, but I needed a home for Team Amynual, including Thomas. I viewed a tenement flat in the heart of Gourock. Although initially it looked depressing and unkempt, I saw potential. What beautiful Clyde views! More, it was on the ground floor, with easy access to the communal back garden. Thomas Heaven! It had two enormous bedrooms and many Victorian features. The owners were a lovely family who had immigrated to Australia. They allowed me to do up their flat to suit us, and even reimbursed me for doing so!

I made a transitional plan to help Amy adjust. Her bedroom furniture was painted, I made curtains, and I shopped until I flopped, to create all that was needed to make the flat home. In fairness, Jamie was supportive, and we split our possessions to furnish both homes. Maybe he wanted me out as quickly as possible! No, it was more than that. The decision had been made. It was almost the first thing we had agreed on for years. We both needed this move. The whole family needed it. Amy was part of all the preparations, visiting and helping. Dale pitched in too. Together, we painted the lounge walls and when I needed a chauffeur for the bigger items, Dale was on hand, thankfully! For the first time in thirty years, I had no car. I couldn't afford one. However, this was to have benefits for Amy.

She was a less independent, streetwise child than Dale had been at eleven, mostly because of where we lived and the preceding years' difficulties. Suddenly, we had Gourock Railway Station, buses and a taxi stand on our doorstep. Amy had much to gain, and Dale agreed. On the worst days, Dale could collect her from school, and he was happy to drive her to their dad's house. I never quite got over my pride when I waved off Dale, confident in the driving seat, Amy in the front passenger seat, and Henry sitting bolt upright in the boot, handsome as ever.

With life normalising – whatever normal may be – we settled into our new abode. I spent every hour I could writing. The one who had the most difficult transition was, of course, Thomas! In our new life, that dog and I became joined at the hip. He couldn't cope alone. Wherever I went, Thomas went. Even in the flat, he followed me from room to room, and he couldn't settle at night unless he slept beside me. Vainly, I attempted everything to alleviate his anxieties. I tried leaving him with a generously filled Kong. When I doubled up his walk with a trip to the newsagent or the Co-op, Thomas became something of a local celebrity, if an anti-social one.

Naturally, I had to tether him outside shops. However, within five seconds, he would strike up an ear-piercing bark, which would continue until I returned. It would only cease if a passerby consoled him. To this day, shop staff and locals know when I'm in town. No one is deaf to the wails of the Gourock Canine Town Crier.

Somehow I managed to shed him occasionally! In November I had a presentation to give which tested my confidence but was also good practice for my Spanish trip. Blair Cochrane had arranged for us to talk to staff at Kingspark School in Dundee. It was important to both of us to get it right. Kingspark was a large special school, with a significant number of pupils with autism. On the big day, we synchronised our presentations as if we had rehearsed. In fact, distance hadn't allowed that! Many of the staff were moved by my talk, and stunned by Blair's work. To this day, a framed copy of Henry's picture hangs by the school's reception area.

Blair had become such a good friend. As Easter 2012 approached, I decided to ask him to accompany me to Zamora. He would help support my still delicate confidence, and it would be advantageous for Alberto and Jane to hear another dog expert's perspective.

Waiting at Glasgow Airport, Blair teased me about my suitcase. "Typical woman! No doubt you've got the kitchen sink in there." Yet when our cases were weighed, Blair's was 4 kilos heavier! I always packed light. I used my laptop case as hand luggage, stuffing it with my purse and other essentials. However, it was a large suitcase. It contained a full cuddly pack with a big dog for PAAT, so that Spanish parents could see how to recreate one for themselves.

Alberto met us at Valladolid, and it was wonderful to have some sunshine back in my life. Beni came too, and we went over the launch of the Spanish book during the 150km drive to Alberto and Jane's beautiful home. From there, at Zamora's edge, the view of the wine-growing plains was breathtaking. Jane and I hugged each other, and Blair and I quickly adapted to the Spanish hola, kissing both cheeks. We were to have plenty practice!

PAAT had two visually impaired students. One was Alberto, a physiotherapist, who was being partnered with his first guide dog, a gorgeous golden retriever. The second student was Rocio, who lived in Madrid, 250km away. She was a petite, pretty young woman, with her third guide dog, a very friendly chocolate Labrador called Bruno. Unlike many visually impaired people who may have slight peripheral sight or be able to see light and vague shadows, Rocio had been born with a condition which left her in complete darkness. She was a translator, and such was her fluency in English that it was hard to discern that it was not her native tongue. She had been reading up on autism, and was hooked. I was delighted to be able to send her a copy of my talking book, because she would be working with me as my translator. We would become a close team.

We discussed parallels in autism and visual impairment, shared sensory and spatial awareness problems. As we talked, I knew in Rocio I had gained another Spanish friend. I looked forward to sharing a platform with her, and with Bruno.

Afterwards, we made our way to our hotel, where people invited by Alberto were waiting. Rocio, with Bruno in tow, came to translate, and Alberto came too, with his new guide dog. Jane and Alberto made inclusion for disability such a normal part of life. If only those involved earlier in Dale's adult life had had that same integrity. We had drinks in the bar, but despite the wonderful hospitality and the abundance of the local produce, I stuck to orange juice! How unNuala-like, but I was working! Everyone I met was so gracious. PAAT had wonderful supporters who were grateful that I had visited, supporting their work, but truly, the privilege and pleasure was all mine.

A parent, Marta, was coming from Madrid. Her nine-year-old son Jorge had severe autism. Marta supported PAAT and was a committed member of a new autism charity in Madrid, Fundación Quinta. Provision in Spain's largest city was so inadequate. How familiar. She was accompanied by a lovely gentleman, Joaquín, who worked tirelessly for the charity. His son Quinto was the same age as Dale, and had severe autism and was non-verbal. Fundación Quinta embraced the publishing of my book, which they hoped would help raise awareness of the mammoth task they had undertaken.

Marta hoped that Jorge could be a candidate for a canine experiment. Would he connect in the way Dale had with Henry? She worked tirelessly to address her son's autism. Alberto even described her as my Spanish alter ego, a fighter and mother warrior of autism! Apparently, she couldn't wait to meet me. I felt the same.

There was a tap on my shoulder. Marta! She was so attractive, and the strength just oozed from her. With her "*Hola*," Marta gave me not two kisses but three. We tried to talk using Makaton hand signs and other gestures, but it was futile. Rocio bridged the gap. When she heard how Dale was doing, Marta's mouth dropped open, pleasantly shocked by his progress.

It was time to eat and that meal was fit for royalty. Again, although Blair and I often didn't have a clue what was being said, the passion from everyone was uplifting! I sat beside a psychologist with very basic English (but a great deal more than my Spanish!).

"Nuala, you are a pioneer of how to work with *autisimo* children using dogs. Thank you for your work."

"*Gracias!*" I returned.

We exchanged a few remarks, but the language barrier made fluid conversation impossible. Alberto, Jane and Rocio were mindful, and kept updating Blair and me. Not only that, but without a second thought, Alberto ensured full inclusion for Rocio and Alberto, by reading out the menu in full. I learned to say Rocio's name when I needed her to translate, just as I would when addressing a child with autism. If only everyone in society had the same respect for disability as those grouped round that table!

After dinner, it was time for my presentation, and as Alberto and Blair set up I stood alone until Marta joined me. She put her arm around my shoulder, as if to say, *We cannot talk, but we need no words, as mothers we are connected.* I placed my hand on top of hers. *I understand.* I was a little nervous. I would be talking to Spanish professionals. Thanks to Alberto and Blair, it went well, although it was my first time working with a translator. I managed. We all managed! It taught me that I needed to plan meticulously for future talks. I would return. *Un Amigo Como Henry* was to be launched in June.

Having said *adios* to Marta and the guests, we went to our rooms to unpack. It was scorching. We were both elated by how we were treated. Blair had really lessened my anxieties by employing himself as my personal assistant, and calling me "Boss"! I told him he would get a brilliant reference from me any day! I couldn't have done without him. He was a rock. A real friend.

Jokes aside, we commented on one issue that neither of us could ignore. We discussed how "socially hopeless" we felt, trying to engage and integrate with people we had just met without the language. We agreed. How on earth does a child with autism cope, every day, not being able to understand our language and environment?

We set off for a walk, to relax and enjoy beautiful Zamora, and Beni came too. Alberto adopted his dog trainer role with Rocio and Bruno, who accompanied us for some "environmental practice" in that quaint town. Bruno had been trained intensively as a potential guide dog for about eighteen months, but learning to work in partnership with Rocio was just beginning.

Alberto led Rocio, allowing her to hold his left arm, while she controlled Bruno, who, like any guide dog, walked on her left. He wore his harness, but she had to master controlling him using his lead first. It was a lovely evening, and we made our way through the sleepy streets at a leisurely pace. We needed to; the town was busier than usual because their Easter procession was about to take place.

Zamora was festooned with ornate churches and cathedrals, many were hundreds of years old. In the main square, people sat outside in cafe bars and restaurants, drinking and eating unhurriedly. Blair and I adored it. We wandered through a maze of cobbled streets, slabbed pavements, tarred roads and twisting stairways and alleys. Alberto used them all!

Rocio worked on taking unexpected turns and avoiding jutting litter bins, lampposts, benches and the like. Everything, everywhere – things we sighted people take for granted. She worked hard to keep Bruno at a consistent pace, just a couple of paw lengths in front. Spatial awareness and the correct pace for both dog and student were paramount. We witnessed a common problem: as she went about her work, people couldn't resist interrupting and patting Bruno. Like all guide dogs, he was beautiful and well behaved, but when a guide dog is in harness, he knows he is working.

He must be fully focused on his master, be able to concentrate and guide the person safely. Never distract or interrupt the dog when working, as it causes confusion, which, of course, compromises the safety of the owner. I could see Rocio's frustration. Bruno was still learning.

It was really touching to witness them working together, giving Rocio similar independence to that given to Dale by Henry. How amazing man's best friends are! Man simply couldn't live without them!

Whilst strolling, we were interrupted by big storks shrieking. They nested in the rooftops, but a louder thrum was growing. Just as we neared the main cathedral, we heard the religious festival. The crowd was dense, desperate to see the spectacle. An effigy of Jesus was being borne from the cathedral to another church. The beat of the drum pounded in our chests, and the lament filled the air. All were dressed in black.

Rocio and Bruno were a couple of metres away. We were mindful of the impact the parade may have had on the dog. How would he cope with the sensory overload of the event, still under test conditions? We needn't have bothered! He took it all in his stride and later lay at his mistress's feet, content. We all were! At eleven o'clock, as is the fine Zamora routine, we went for a drink and tapas in a bar, bursting with every generation. Perfect.

For the rest of the weekend I relaxed, and had long working chats with Jane and Alberto. Blair showed video footage of DATA children. PAAT were thoroughly impressed. The wonderful hospitality, insight to the guide dog world and the friendship I gained that weekend helped me focus, be confident again.

When I got back, I even felt okay picking up the phone to Jamie, making arrangements to collect Amy. Looking around that house, I surprised myself. It was just a house. This wasn't my home any more. He could rattle about in it till it sold. It didn't seem to bother him, and it certainly didn't bother me. Maybe Amy and I were in the flat, and we didn't have the big rooms and gardens. So what? We had something more. I had something more. Freedom, I think. My new life had begun.

# 17

## Man's Best Friend

"If I sit down on a bench he is at my side at once and takes up a position on one of my feet. For it is a law of his being that he only runs about when I am in motion too, that when I settle down he follows suit."

— Thomas Mann, *A Man and His Dog*

My career path – if that's the right term for it – was progressing. So far there wasn't exactly money and a pension plan in it, but whatever it was growing into was fitting me very well indeed. I felt wanted and needed, purposeful, in a way that I hadn't been to anyone other than my children for years. I just kept hoping that all the trappings would follow, somehow, but for now, it was more than enough. Sadly, I couldn't say the same for Dale's situation, and his well-being worried me terribly.

He continued to slog away, trying to secure employment. Every week, he attended a job club run by the Shaw Trust, where he would apply for vacancies – librarian, museum attendant, leisure attendant – anything and everything. He was called for the occasional interview, but all his efforts were in vain. I hardly saw him, he rarely phoned. His mood was low, and who could blame him? The odd time he visited for a coffee and chat, he was passive, as if his entire zest for life had evaporated. All of his strategies to keep going were now running on empty. He had left Prospects Social Group because his peers there were painful reminders of his own plight. Fortunately, the one thing he had was a thriving social life outwith Prospects, so in that sense, the group had served its purpose.

To my relief, he managed to carry on without any obvious signs of regression. While this was reassuring, it still upset me to see my son so unhappy, with little hope of a decent future. One morning, I invited him over for a coffee and a chat. I suggested he increased his voluntary work with Barnardo's. Perhaps do some administration work for them, as he wanted to expand his skills in that area. Certainly, it could only help his chances of employment. He went along for an informal chat with one of their staff, and soon thereafter, on Monday afternoons he helped out with office work, appreciating the routine and normality of driving to and from work. He enjoyed the different environment of the office, despite more than a twinge of annoyance when a member of staff remarked that she was shocked to learn he could drive ... given he had autism!

This increased workload helped lift his mood, and more was in the offing. Barnardo's also wanted his help with a new Autism Social Group they were running in Inverclyde for school-aged children. Dale seized the chance! Certainly, it was voluntary, but he was keen to participate in all the necessary duties, and he was happy to attend staff meetings. He also continued volunteering at Barnardo's Thursday drama group, because he didn't want to disappoint the children there.

Life, for a while, was mundane, as the calendar flipped through the early months of 2012. Mundane wasn't the worst place we had been recently! Although Dale hadn't secured a job, there were no major setbacks or issues to grind us down. I spent my days writing and researching; Amy adapted to having two homes, and even Thomas the rogue had become accustomed to his new lifestyle.

By June it was time to return to Zamora. As I'd already made that trip with Blair, I felt sufficiently strong to go back alone. When I arrived at Glasgow Airport, it was a wild night, all howling wind and rain. Bin lids flapped, some even tipped over, and I was sure that my flight would be cancelled. It was called. Boarding, I was quick to fasten my safety belt, as the wings shook and the whole aircraft moved while we were still sitting, allegedly stationary, on the tarmac. Terrified, I began to think the plane didn't even need an engine! It was a rough flight, but we arrived safely. It felt really good to be in the sanctuary of that lovely hotel. Best of all, I was excited at the prospect of seeing Alberto and Jane again; they had become such dear friends.

My escalating confidence even made it possible for me to go to the hotel's busy restaurant, which was teeming with couples sharing romantic meals, all enjoying the ambience. A charming young waiter approached. I lifted my chin.

"Table for one, please." This was possible.

For the first time in ages, I was hungry and able to enjoy a steak with a glass of red wine.

After I had phoned Dale and Amy, I managed to snatch a few hours of sleep, which felt superb. I was still regularly blighted by insomnia, worrying about Dale or the responsibilities of my new life, and all the baggage of being a single mum. At 6 a.m., I prepared to leave, with the breakfast television news on in the room. I was shocked. All flights to and from Scotland had been cancelled the night before. A raging storm, with eighty mile-per-hour winds had caused a fatality and flights from Scotland were cancelled. I nearly hadn't made it to Spain, but for a change, fate had been on my side.

Greeting Jane again was wonderful. She understood my divorce situation and all the horrendous stresses I had been under. As we sat drinking tea and catching up, she explained her own exhausting but incredibly worthwhile times. She was working with families and loving it, but the majority of her work was done at home, and that brought its own problems. Her two daughters would meet the families and they pitched in; those young girls' understanding and tolerance was exemplary. However, one day, Jane realised that her eight-year-old daughter had perhaps met one family too many.

"Oh no, Mum, not the autisms!"

After we'd emptied the teapot, Beni arrived with copies of my Spanish book. He'd done a great job. The front cover showed a little Spanish boy with a beautiful golden retriever sitting beside him. Together, they were looking over lush, green plains. Later in the day, Alberto and I recorded a local radio programme, which was another interesting learning curve. I was becoming more adept at working with translators! That evening, I dressed smartly, readying myself for the Zamora conference and the launch of *Un Amigo Como Henry*.

It was a stifling night, and the grand room of Zamora Town Hall was filled with professionals, parents and interested locals. It was lovely to see the PAAT guide and assistance dogs in attendance with their owners. An attractive woman, Carmen, who worked for UNICEF, opened proceedings by reading an extract from my book. She delivered that piece with passion, as if she was appealing to the UN itself: Read it!

Alberto translated and I delivered my PowerPoint presentation, and may I say, with some aplomb! I was relieved that my confidence had held up, and despite the language barrier, I was able to engage with some of the audience. Alberto gave a terrific speech, which resounded in the hall and though I could only catch the gist of it, so much was clear from his communication. My name and Dale's sang out in praise. Then he produced a large gift bag and revealed two beautiful engraved glass plaques. I had to fight back the tears as Alberto read out the inscriptions: "Honorary (Patron) Member of PAAT. Presented to Dale Gardner, through your fight for independence you have been the inspiration and motivation for the work in the association of PAAT Zamora."

I had to compose myself again as he read mine: "Honorary Member of PAAT. Presented to Nuala Gardner for her dedication, commitment and support to the world of autism and the association of PAAT."

In response, I asked Alberto to translate for me. It was a privilege and a pleasure for me to be with everyone that night. Afterwards, I signed books, carefully asking the purchasers to write their names out for me, because I didn't want to deface their books with misspellings. At 11 o'clock, the night was over. Hardly! I was forgetting! In Zamora, it had just begun.

Staff from PAAT, with Carmen in tow, summoned me back to my hotel for a night-time feast. The meal and company were sublime. Carmen stole the conversation with her hilarious (and true) tales, gleefully translated by Alberto. A handsome young man joined us. Victor was physically disabled, and sat at the top of our table, because he used an electric wheelchair and needed room for his assistance dog, who lay beside him. Another physically disabled gentleman sat next to me. He knew a little English, which allowed us all to exchange a few words. Victor, who was the same age as Dale, had been born with a degenerative neurological condition, which in adulthood had increased his dependence on his devoted parents.

I tried to imagine how he felt, faced with the daily deterioration of his condition, having to rely on his parents to help him manage the most basic things, the things we neuro-typicals take for granted. Consider beyond the obvious aspects of caring for a disabled person's daily needs. Think about all those small, endlessly repetitive tasks: Victor needed doors pushed, drawers opened and closed, lift buttons pressed, newspapers opened, mobile phones and, well, everything really, collected for him. Every day, countless times, his weak grasp would loosen, causing him to drop keys, money, and that needed a carer with the patience of a particularly special saint. He required assistance to unzip and remove his jacket, put on and off his socks, little things in themselves perhaps, but things which mounted up over the days, weeks and years. His saint had to be physically up to the job, but of course he had no saint to hand. He had his parents, who were becoming physically and mentally exhausted. For Victor, that kind of dependence on his parents added another terrible burden to his condition's luggage. He became increasingly demoralised, quiet and withdrawn. He stopped going out socially, and his parents despaired, watching helplessly as their son's loneliness increased and his quality of life disintegrated. Desperate to help their son, they contacted PAAT. Perhaps that saint was on hand after all, one with a fur coat and a wagging tail. PAAT purpose-trained an assistance dog to do all those wearyingly repetitive tasks. Undoubtedly this transformed Victor's quality of life, giving him back his much-valued independence and offering his parents some of the respite they needed.

Is it possible that a human could have been employed in that role? Possible, but ask a person to pick up a pen, fetch a phone and do all these tasks countless times a day, and eventually it will take its toll. By contrast, the assistance dog will thrive, working for its owner, receiving the constant rewards of affection, as well as developing the strongest bond possible with its master. All guide and assistance dogs are trained intensively to be great at their job, and that can be measured, but there is so much more: the emotional well-being and companionship they give to their owners is immeasurable.

As we sat enjoying the delicious food and wonderful companionship into the wee sma' 'ours, it was in fact Victor who snitched back the conversation from Carmen, and his love of life shone out from him. It struck me that night that while there was two disabled people at our table, because we were all at one with integration there was no disability to be seen!

The next morning we set off for the two-hour drive to Madrid. I put on a tailored dress because we were going straight to a popular restaurant, where we would meet Rocio. She was translating for me, as a reporter from Spain's biggest national newspaper was doing a feature on my book. The finished article, which was to be tied in with a review of our meal, a weekly feature, would cover the entire back page. It was a pleasing device, adopted by the paper to give the story an informal feel. Certainly, I felt very relaxed! At the end of the meal, I thought I might roll home, having eaten more that week than I had in months! To complete the article, the photographer captured a lovely picture of me with Bruno.

We had an hour to spare, so I sat with Rocio and went through what she would be translating for me at the conference. I had already sent her an electronic copy to allow her to familiarise herself with my talk, and I had described the photographic resources I would be using, so she had created an excellent mental picture. Alberto produced a memory stick, loaded with pictures of PAAT children with their autism therapy dogs, and he popped that into my laptop to let us see them.

The first picture made my jaw drop. It was stupendous. PAAT had trained a golden retriever for severely autistic non-verbal twin boys. Both had bonded with and benefitted from the dog, in their own uniquely different ways. This particular picture of one of the boys had been taken by their parents when the twins met their dog for the first time. The body language between the boy and the dog spoke volumes, no words were necessary. The dog sat relaxed, and with its tail stretched out, and its back providing the perfect leaning post for the child, who laid against it, spine to spine, head to head. The trust and bond was beautiful. Both had their eyes closed. They were at one.

There was more to come. The next one, of his brother, hit home just as forcibly, yet for different reasons. Here was an image I had seen countless times before, "The Golden Pillow"! In this one photograph was PAAT's evidence to support Amy's interpretation and the Mira Foundation's research in Canada, of the power the right dog has with autistic children.[1]

Both these boys had had bolting behaviours with challenging tantrums when they were outdoors. I am well aware that keeping one such child safe is nigh impossible for parents, but two? Unthinkable. Now when the boys went out, they both had their leads attached to the dog and they stayed with that dog. They were calmer, and enjoyed going to the park, sharing their food and their lives with their dog.

One of the boys has dyspraxia, affecting his coordination, and he had not previously been successfully toilet trained. In their home, the dog wore its harness, which had a small handle on the centre to allow the child to support himself when mobile. This improved his walking balance and pace. The dog even accompanied the child to the toilet.

Lo and behold, a few weeks later that lad was successfully toilet trained.

It was wonderful seeing the children with their special dogs, proudly holding onto their coloured leads. Unsurprisingly, royal blue and red were the most popular. All the children were happy being with their dogs. One was brushing her pet, another was giving it a treat, and yet another little girl was simply content, with her dog lying on her bed beside her. All of those children gave their dogs appropriate eye contact, just as I had witnessed before with the children who had piloted my own programme. There were so many positive changes, but one issue stood out: none of those children was physically being attached to their dogs!

All the children were relaxed, just as Dale and Keir had been, and none ran away when outdoors. Parents reported their children's overall behaviour had improved. Social belonging and inclusion increased because the dog reduced the stress for the child when they ventured out. The animal's presence facilitated positive interaction with the public. Interaction with parents and siblings also improved, and the dog helped the children reach a resolution more quickly when the inevitable tantrums occurred. The whole family gained. Unquestionably, the children had bonded with their dogs, and the pictures were both humbling and gorgeous. Looking at them brought back vivid memories of a younger Dale with his Henry. I was in no doubt that I was once again seeing Henry's legacy. I stole a few moments, whispering, "Thank you, Henry. Thank you for everything. I love you."

Having said *adios* to Rocio, Alberto asked if I wouldn't mind visiting some parents, called Angela and Oscar, who lived in Madrid. Their daughter, Lucia, had had a PAAT Assistance Therapy Dog (ATD) for a year. Lucia was six with severe non-verbal autism, poor comprehension and challenging behaviours. Alberto wanted to see how she was progressing with their dog Tiffany, a three-year-old Labrador. Tiffany's calm nature and autism training were perfect.

Angela and Oscar loved Lucia so much that they couldn't bear to say no to her. Day after day, they tried to keep her as happy as they could by not challenging her autism. Instead, they submitted to it. PAAT had spent hours and days teaching them how to manage the condition, but despite this and all her teachers' efforts, nothing changed. It simply broke the hearts of these loving parents, seeing their daughter's distress when things didn't go her way. Unfortunately, that was almost every hour of every day. As a result, Lucia took ownership of her home environment. She needed to try to control everything in it, effectively using her parents as her remote control device, in an attempt to try to make sense of her environment.

The consequences were dire. Angela, Oscar and Tiffany were at the mercy of Lucia's ferocious and frustrated autism. Her lack of "theory of mind", known as "mind blindness", caused her endless distress, because she couldn't understand that her parents' thoughts, intentions and emotions were not the same as her own. She couldn't comprehend that others didn't know what she wanted. She therefore had no reason to communicate her wants. She found her parents unpredictable, and empathy was beyond her.

This beautiful, tormented child communicated the sensory chaos and confusion of her world. When inevitably it went wrong, she did that in the only way open to her, through intense high-pitched screaming, screeching and forceful crying. She cried until her throat was raw, throwing horrific and challenging tantrums virtually twenty-four/seven.

Alberto felt he needed to prepare me, as Lucia's suffering was soul-destroying to witness. Understandably, her parents were reaching breaking point. While this was a huge worry, there was the added concern of Tiffany's welfare. Lucia was sufficiently fortunate to attend a small school for autistic children in the heart of Madrid. The pupils there had different levels of autism, some verbal and some not. The educational approaches were condition-specific and the teachers' methods were the same as those used at Hinderton. Good practice has the same principles, wherever it occurs in the world.

Lucia's parents had completed a Hanen course, which teaches families how to engage with and help their child learn to communicate.[2] Those same methods were to be used at home and at the child's school, giving the needed consistency. Yet Angela and Oscar's desperate attempts to try to interpret her needs and communicate "for" her had made their daughter the autistic master of the home. Tiffany had made a difference when she was outdoors. Lucia stayed by her dog's side, where before she would have spontaneously run anywhere – into the line of a car, anywhere she desired – she had no sense of danger. She could now be motivated to move on through her dog. Tiffany had certainly enhanced their family life, because they could at least stroll together in the cool evenings, giving her parents some much needed respite. Indeed, Lucia couldn't bear to be stuck indoors.

When we arrived at their top-floor apartment, Angela greeted us warmly. As I entered the hallway, I noticed there were beautiful wooden floors throughout. I removed my shoes and went into the lounge, ready to meet Oscar and Lucia.

When I visit a family, I generally wear comfortable jeans and flat shoes, knowing I will be working on the floor or with them, in their garden, on their bed – in fact, anywhere and everywhere the child might lead. Slowly, calmly and patiently, as we play, the child allows me to interact with them, and – albeit on their terms – to share "our" playtime.

When Lucia saw Alberto, she screamed, cried out in horror while she manipulated both her parents to have them remove us from her home. We ignored her efforts, and sat silently while we watched her trying to control everything that was happening in her domain. She was distressed and in autism crisis, desperate to have her parents help her make sense of her environment. Oscar and Angela tried desperately to interpret her needs. They grabbed her favourite books, seized her box of social pictures, sieving through them, hoping, pleading, "Lucia, Lucia, what do you want?"

They tried everything to console her and to interpret her needs, but their efforts were in vain. Her screams intensified. Alberto and I remained calm. When she approached us, only one of us spoke, gently, quietly, concisely, in order to allow her to express her needs, or at least to show us what she wanted. When her efforts to control us proved unsuccessful, Lucia switched to her parents.

Alberto had been right to warn me. Witnessing this child's distress at being unable to communicate and hearing her vexed screams was devastating. Lucia had become the holder of her parents, using them as an autism remote control, programming them to channel her needs. I felt she did this to reduce the sensory chaos in her home. What I was seeing in that child's overload was what Dr Wendy Lawson has compared to "an untuned television".[3]

We understood why Lucia screamed. She had to try to drown out the overwhelming interference in her home, to enable her to survive the terrifying days that autism gave her. Her parents' efforts to try to tune into whatever she wanted in order to pre-empt the screaming was being lost in translation. There were times when she wanted her "programme" repeated for hours on end. She particularly liked to make her Papa draw a picture for her; she gestured, giving him a pen. Papa would duly start drawing, but then it would have to be a montage, endlessly of the same picture, before Lucia suddenly would decide to change the programme.

Throughout, we noticed Tiffany in the kitchen, lying on her comfy bed, resting quietly, with her big brown eyes wide open, and she looked so forlorn. She had been trained to cope with the extreme environment created by an autistic child, but the child should really improve with their dog so the home would be better for both! Sadly Lucia's home life hadn't got better and I shared Alberto's worry for Tiffany's welfare. The howling intensified and, throughout, Alberto was pleading, "Be at Lucia's eye level. Say her name, just once. One parent, one voice. Be calm, use concise words. Be consistent. Give six seconds to process, then repeat."

Such was their love for their child that they couldn't, or wouldn't, listen. I sat quietly, observing the signals of anguish broadcast by these parents. Simultaneously, I was humbled by Alberto's unstinting efforts to help them. Suddenly, Lucia lowered the volume and paused her screeching. There was an interlude where she looked out of the window, indicating that she wanted to go out.

In despair, Alberto asked, "Nuala, what do you think we need to do here? The dog seems miserable. These parents are exhausted, lost. I fear for their future."

I couldn't disagree, telling him that they needed to press the delete button, rewind and start again, right from the beginning. They had to act as if Lucia had been newly diagnosed. That despair and mental exhaustion was palpable. I too was afraid for their future. It was time to do something I'd done countless times before when I needed to help my own children. I took a risk.

"Alberto. Enough of this. It's time for some tough love. Can you translate for me, please?"

Beating heart battering on my ribs, I said, "Tell them if they want Lucia to be like she is now when she's sixteen – bigger, stronger, louder, more distressed, still unable to communicate – tell them to carry on with what they're doing now."

Alberto delivered my words with conviction. I could see shock unfold, and their anxiety increase.

"Tell them it's not too late, but they need to change. Right now!"

Lucia, like any child, with or without autism, needed strict boundaries to allow her to make sense of her environment. Reassuringly, he informed them how I had taught Dale; it had been hard and had meant our family had endured many of his challenging tantrums before he began to learn. Lucia needed to understand, like Dale, the two most important words of language were yes and no. Yes, brought good things and no means no . . . and is always one hundred per cent final!

When Lucia sought Alberto's help, he gave her clear body language, and then turned away with his hand up. That meant, "Lucia, Papa. Go to Papa."

When she approached me, I did the same.

"Lucia, Papa."

She gripped a cartoon video in her hands — her ultimate obsession — determinedly trying to make us put it on. Almost immediately, she learned that she wasn't controlling Alberto or me. So, she calmly approached her Papa, gesturing at him to put the video on. I took another risk. "Oscar no! Lucia do it. Alberto, tell Oscar to say, 'Lucia do it.'"

Her papa didn't give up, despite all Lucia's attempts to twist him. Then, just as he was about to concede, she confidently popped the video into the recorder, and she was delighted to see her cartoon appear on the screen. Immediately, I clapped my hands, and everyone joined in. She rewarded me with direct eye contact! I gave her a Makaton two thumbs up, with a tone of voice that communicated good girl! Seeing the smile on her face and her "acceptance" of our hand clapping showed us all the way forward. She seemed to understand. Now we were getting somewhere.

"Alberto, tell them now Lucia can do it. They should never do 'it' or anything else she can do . . . ever again."

I saw that Oscar and Angela were pleased by their daughter's astuteness, but with a worried tone Oscar asked, "What if she screams and tantrums?"

Alberto was firm.

"Let her. It will pass. She can do it. You are preventing her from being independent and making her own choices. Let Lucia communicate!"

We showed how our calm, child-led approaches were getting through and her comprehension of basic language was better with the reduction in sensory overload. Just as things were going well, she tried to get her mama to move the cartoon past a sequence she didn't like. For the first time, Angela turned away, putting up her hand. Calmly, she said, "No! Lucia do it."

And true to form, she did, with another jovial round of applause as a reward.

With Lucia settled, Alberto advised that it might be better if Tiffany were taken away for a trial period, just to let them start again and allow them to turn things around. Immediately, Angela broke down. She wept as if she was losing her second child, which, in a sense, she was. I held her in my arms as she cried, frustrated that I was unable to comfort her better because of the language barrier. Her grief was devastating. It broke our hearts, but still, we concluded that with the triumphs we had seen that day, these loving, wonderful parents just needed a little more time to adjust.

Throughout our visit, I sat on the floor and played with Lucia, with Tiffany joining in. The potential she had just flowed from her. She was such a beautiful, clever child. We advised Oscar and Angela to work closely with Lucia's teachers, because their approaches at home were now the same as those used at school.

We left the couple somewhat shocked, but also with the gift of hope. It was emotionally draining to be so forceful, but I felt humbled and privileged to be able to take those steps. After all, I was once where they were, twenty years earlier, when I had lain in the foetal position on my own kitchen floor. I was desperate, without hope. I was staring death in the face because I couldn't reach my son. Thankfully, Henry did what I could not.

Alberto had felt because I was a mother maybe Lucia's parents would accept my advice. I think he was right. Neither of us were in any doubts though. We were no miracle workers; Angela and Oscar had a mammoth task ahead. They would need every ounce of strength they possessed.

When I arrived back at my hotel room to change for evening dinner, I wasn't just emotionally wrecked! I'd stepped out, every inch the smart professional, and I'd returned, well, what we in the West of Scotland might term "complete mink"! Those expensive glossy tights were covered in ladders. I didn't give a toss! Smiling to myself, I unpeeled them and chucked them in the bin. Every shred had been worth it, playing with Lucia and Tiffany. For the first time in a long time, it felt great to be doing work I truly loved and for which I was respected.

At 10 o'clock, it was a stiflingly hot evening, with Madrid's pavement cafe bars swarming with people, chilling out, eating and drinking as if the night was young. For the Spanish it was! Beni and Alberto wanted the coolness and peace of indoors, but I wanted the luxury of being able to soak up the atmosphere, with the rare opportunity to sit in the perfect climate and to eat outdoors. After all, I'd come from Gourock, a place not known for a lot of late-night outdoors dining . . . for some reason! As we waited for our meal, I could see Alberto was still stressed about his day and the emotionally draining work he was trying to achieve through PAAT.

"Alberto, have a beer with me. Relax, we will get there! Slowly, things are changing."

Checking his phone to view the week's activity on PAAT's website, he showed me. "Nuala, look! Two hundred enquiries this week. Desperate stories from parents wanting an ATD. We have virtually no funds! Demand is overwhelming."

He forced himself to lighten up.

"Nuala, I am so depressed, I could kill two guide dogs."

How Beni and I laughed!

"Alberto, chill. Eat your meal! Drink your beer."

His passion for his work never faltered, although throughout that dinner his phone didn't stop. Taking his last bite, he checked his phone again. Two texts had come through. Reading them shocked us, given the joke we'd just shared. The first was from Rocio who had been told that her first beautiful guide dog, Macey, whom she loved so much, had died earlier in the evening. I felt for Rocio, because I completely understood that the bond a visually impaired person has with their dog is one of the strongest known. Macey was as special to Rocio as Sir had been, and still is, to me. Like Sir, Macey had transformed Rocio's life and given her true independence.

If that news wasn't bad enough, the other text was equally alarming. It was about another guide dog Alberto had recently placed. The client wanted Alberto to know that his guide dog, Rey, was critically ill, and vets were trying to save its life. Rey was a stunning three-year-old white German Shepherd, who was extra-special to Alberto. Out of the hundreds of guide dogs he'd trained, Rey was the best worker he had ever known. He had changed his owner's life. Prior to having his dog, that man's quality of life was limited and his independence dreadfully compromised. The client was on holiday when Rey had become dangerously ill, with a life-threatening blood disease, an infection spread by mosquito sand flies. Only a miracle could save him now. It was a matter of waiting. The vets had done all that they could.

The next morning, we were pensive. To try to comfort Rocio, we emailed her a poem, one which is really special to me, adapting the words so it related to Macey. She replied, saying it had helped her, but she was truly broken by her beloved dog's passing. She meant the world to her. I understood Rocio's grief entirely. Six years after Sir's death, I still see him, running through my thoughts and dreams. I know he's always going to be there for me.

# 18

## New Horizons

With thoughts of Rocio and Macey, we prepared for the task ahead. Alberto and I cross-referenced our plans, our moves in cyberspace. No small concern, as we had experienced difficulties in Zamora with the technical aspects of our presentation and we dreaded a repeat of that. We looked at each other and nodded. We scrubbed up well! Time to go!

The conference was in the Circulo de Bellas Artes in the National Library of Spain, an imposingly beautiful nineteenth-century building which houses a remarkable collection of books, paintings and other treasures . . . and today, er, me! As I climbed that ornate central staircase, catching glimpses of opulent rooms through dark doors, and as I breathed the heavy air under gilded cornices and traced a daring finger along carved marble, I wondered, how did I get here? I stopped to look from the tall windows over Madrid, which was golden and beautiful as far as my eye could follow. If breathtaking smacks of cliché, I can offer no apology. It was more than enough to take anyone's oxygen supply, and somehow, I was there, in all this splendour and with a sense of purpose. I knew who I had to thank for that.

Tempting though it was to stand and muse on the wonder of it all, as my eyes began to fill, the splendid room was also filling rapidly. Professionals, parents and dogs arrived, and in amongst the masses there was a familiar face with a companion! Bruno, paws tick-tacking across the marble and full of glee at Rocio's side, communicated in his inimitable, language-crossing style: "Hello, everyone! New guide dog in the room."

They were soon followed by Marta, lovely and as strong as ever, then Jane with Oscar and Angela. What *holas* we kissed! Joaquín was a constant, industrious presence, oiling every linguistic and operational wheel, determined to ensure smooth running. Fundación Quinta was supporting my Spanish book launch.[1]

Alberto opened the proceedings with his customary exuberance. With the confidence-building Rocio and Bruno beside me, I launched into my talk. We co-ordinated as if we had known each other for months rather than for days. I was both relieved and pleased to see her smile when she recognised images from my PowerPoint. Bolstered and affirmed by the laughter from the audience, I relaxed into the rhythm. I stood confident and secure in the certainty that inclusion should be everyone's right, and not a privilege for the few.

When the conference ended, the passion for the cause fired the room. Marta, Angela and Oscar confirmed that they had learned new ideas and were inspired; there was so much to carry forward for their own children. Jane spent time talking with Angela and Oscar, who now seemed far more relaxed and enthusiastic. It was as if Lucia had been newly diagnosed; they were so eager to learn. Before they left, they bought three books, two for family and a copy for the school, which I thought astute. I signed them all. We hugged and hugged. As parents we were forever connected. When I watched them carry off those books, I hoped Henry would help them in turn, as he had me. They now had their own Canine Guide to Autism for Lucia and Tiffany.

I felt it was the best presentation I had ever delivered. The tummy-filling nerves had ceased, and I checked the time. It was three in the afternoon, lunchtime in Spain! Along the sunny pavements with staff from PAAT, Marta and Joaquín, we crocodiled into a traditional tapas bar. Alberto, never quite managing to settle without more work, grabbed the time to walk with Rocio and Bruno to pursue some guide dog work. Marta and I chatted, surprisingly fast and furiously, using Makaton signs to bridge the language barrier. We clicked like a pair of schoolgirls.

As usual, the food and the company were outstanding. This was bliss. Just as I finished eating, Alberto delivered his bombshell. I was to record an interview for Spanish television. Suddenly, that extra plate of patatas bravas seemed a little less wise!

Lunch finished, we made our way through central Madrid to a disused kindergarten. Fundación Quinta had raised funds to renovate it to be fit for purpose as a recreation and rehabilitation centre for adults with autism. Joaquín showed me around, explaining the refit. It was amazing. There were areas for clients to enjoy art and music and to use computers. A major objective was for them to be able to learn new social and independence skills, so a large kitchen featured. The gardens were private and secure. In a grove of mature trees there was an old wooden play lodge. Although modest, it was large enough to allow for the potential creation of separate rooms, a lounge and kitchen area, with the built-in opportunity for adults to practise their independent-living skills in a realistic environment and with adequate support. I was more than impressed by what they had achieved. No similar facilities existed in Madrid. Looking around, I promised Joaquín that on my return to Scotland, I would send a framed copy of Henry's portrait for the centre reception. I wished I could have done more. So many adults in Dale's generation had already missed so much.

Fantastic though that was, I knew I was only seeing the outline. I hoped I would return someday to see the centre bustling with people, because I understood the enormity of the task and the dedication needed to fully establish the project. Buildings are important, but people carry the story. For charities everywhere, from here to our own SA and NAS, people are the lifeblood. Parent power and supporters have improved, and continue to improve, education and awareness of autism. That is why it is where it is today.

That tapas-turning television interview went smoothly, and Joaquín pleaded with viewers to support the centre. Afterwards, Marta invited Rocio and me to her home to meet Jorge, her parents and her daughter.

What great people they were. I saw in that couple a mirror of the support system that once my mum and dad had been for me. She drove us to collect Jorge from her school, which thankfully was an excellent, autism-specific provision. Despite the language barrier, I could see that the teaching practices were highly developed. Marta pointed out her son. Oh boy! He was Dale at the same age – such a handsome boy, with those classically Spanish brown eyes. I had heard so much about how he had improved, and it was great to meet the person to match the tale. Marta had worked hard with him. I knew that. Between them, what memories they stirred.

I may have been in a different country, but watching this mother interact and communicate with her child, I saw the same rules of engagement, the same approaches. This was bigger than Esperanto. Whilst not diminishing the individuality of the people affected by ASD, there is a universal bond. From Jorge to Amy, Dale, the A-Team, to the young men at Struan, the obsessions, the sensory issues, the difficulties and the truths unite them beyond language and borders. This is an international community. It is fine and noble to consider these matters, but the day-to-day experience of autism at home and abroad leaves little room for such musings! The car stopped, and immediately Jorge ran into a shop, with Marta tearing after him. Not only that, but Bruno's training needed some fine-tuning. I was pleased that Rocio felt confident with me, as she held onto my left arm for guidance. I reached back into skills I had first learned when I worked in an eye ward twenty-five years earlier.

I guided her into the shop, warning her that it had two deep stairs downwards. With Jorge now happy, we made our way to Marta's home, which was accessed by a narrow lift and was a bit of a squeeze for two adults, let alone for the additional presence of Bruno! Throughout, I was Rocio's eyes. Marta's parents treated me like a celebrity, insisting I put my feet up on their sofa, and proffering cool drinks, all more than welcome in the blistering heat of Madrid. Her mum had started reading my book, and gestured how much I had captured Dale's autism. She too caught the Jorge/Dale connection. Rocio sat beside me, while Bruno lapped up his well-earned drink.

Jorge decided it was now playtime for the dog. His owner didn't demur, so he launched into a game of fetch, using his favourite cuddly dog toy. Bruno couldn't believe his luck! The game was set to last a while, until the lad burned him out. He collapsed in an exhausted sleep at his mistress's feet. In the meantime, I retrieved pictures from my presentation for Marta's parents. Sometimes images speak where words cannot. As I came to the photo of a sleeping black Labrador, Jorge came back into the lounge, hoping to rouse the shattered Bruno. I couldn't resist. I showed him the sleeping black Labrador on the screen, which he took a fleeting interest in, then I signed, "Jorge, no!"

I indicated that the dog was sleeping. He regarded him momentarily. I signed sleeping, in the hope that he would leave Bruno be. To my relief he did and, calmly, he went to his own room. Ten minutes later the doorbell rang, and in came Alberto with Beni, waking up Bruno, who was, after all, up for another round of hilarity. This time, just to make sure the play was mad enough, Alberto joined in, and they had the time of their lives. For a time. Somewhere in the party, Bruno had toddled off. Silent, amidst that entire boisterous riot, Marta stood at the lounge door. She looked astonished, and asked her parents to come to their grandson's room. Rocio sat quietly, but I noticed that she was smiling. "Oh, Nuala, you must go and see what has happened."

When I witnessed the cause of the excitement, I nearly blurted something out, but Alberto stopped me; reminding me, "Nuala, don't say anything. You'll spoil the book for them."

Bruno lay down on the floor asleep. Jorge had removed his favourite duvet from his bed, tucked him in, and left him to sleep. He dozed, blissful as a baby. I was back in another country, twenty years before with Dale and his puppy.

It was a phenomenal evening. We set off for a walk to meet up with Joaquín and his son Quinto. I was really looking forward to meeting him at last. Joaquín had told me so much about him. I wasn't dressed for a casual walk, but no matter, I was ready to stroll. Again Alberto used the evening to do more guide dog training until Jorge stole Bruno, for his second starring role of the day as his autism therapy dog. Once more, there was that natural bond and that magic happening between the pair. He was focused and lead by Bruno, at all times, just as all the other PAAT children had been. My Makaton wasn't quite enough at this point! I asked Rocio to translate on my behalf for Marta, to let her know how much Jorge would thrive with a dog. Already, he had a natural connection with Bruno, just as Dale had had when he first met his Henry.

Madrid's river walkway is scenic, a real feast for the senses. I would like to tell you I could have walked there all night, but I'd be lying. My dog-walking flatties might not have done much for my outfit, but I'd have given a lot of Euros for them that night. Stilettos and walking do not equal tranquillity. I did my best to disguise my tortured soles, but in every other respect we had a blissful, if needfully leisurely, walk. I was glad that I managed to stumble on, because on the banks of the Manzanares I received the compliment of a lifetime. Quinto seemed to like my bright red dress, because he regularly gestured that he wanted a hug from me, saying, "Amor." I signed, "Nuala amor Quinto."

I couldn't resist kissing his hand. It was so easy to take this endearing lad to my heart, with his loving personality and, of course, those eyes again. His vocabulary was limited and my Spanish almost non-existent, but he didn't need words. Friendship and affection just shone from him. This never ceases to amaze me, so many autistic children and adults I have met have been extraordinary people. If only we neuro-typicals had those same innate qualities. Wouldn't it be great to be truly non-judgemental and accept those we meet at face value? People on the spectrum, to differing degrees, want to fit into our scary world, to be accepted. They have no agenda at all to cause deliberate hurt, to deceive or to cause upset. Instead, they offer unconditional friendship, and for that alone they deserve our unstinting respect. How could anyone harm Quinto, or the legions of others who share his vulnerability? Yet we can never drop our guard, and it is an ongoing source of added distress to families that that horror does exist.

Back at home, we live with the spectre of episodes of horror, like the BBC's traumatic screening of a Panorama investigation *Undercover Care*. This programme investigated the systematic abuse of adults with a range of learning disabilities and autism in a Bristol care home. We watch Peter Mullan's portrait of how the differently fragile were treated in the Magdalene Laundries. The extent of the Jimmy Savile scandal will likely never be known. The Panorama team stated that they believe their investigation only grazes the iceberg. If that makes you shudder, then it should. How much more frightening must that be then for those who know that their precious and deeply fragile children must at some point be in the care of such places and people, even when they are no longer around to watch over them, especially when they are no longer there. Is there any greater fear? Every one of us has a role to play in keeping our world family safe.[2] Martin Luther King Jr says it all: "Our lives begin to end the day we become silent about things that matter."

The most beautiful of all the goodbyes I received at the end of that glorious walk was a last hug and *amor* from Quinto. It was worth every blister on those red-roasted feet. I felt a little sad, wondering if I would ever see them again, but still, I was so happy to have known them. I went back to my luxurious hotel to steep my most unglamorous feet.

Rested, and more appropriately shod, the following morning Beni showed me the sights of Madrid before we set off together for another presentation in the kindergarten building. Teachers from Jorge's and Lucia's school and other professionals in the field were already impressed by our work. One head teacher informed me that every Friday trained dogs visited the school for "canine therapy". The children engaged with and responded to those dogs, and there were lots of little breakthroughs being noted as a result of playing games with the dogs. Incredibly, that deceptively simple strategy addressed the triad of impairments all at once!

As the evening ended, we set off for the long drive back to Zamora. My feet, though more cosseted by now, remained a background issue! I kicked off my shoes, relaxed across the back seat, and was relieved that all had gone well. As ever, Alberto didn't manage to relax! His phone was a hotline with texts for PAAT. At midnight, Angela called. This was the bad news call we'd all been awaiting. Or was it? As Alberto listened, he gasped with relief, giving me thumbs up. I had never seen him so happy before. Something good had certainly happened. He turned. "Nuala, things are going to be all right. It has taken your visit, as a mother, to get through and to say what we all have been trying to tell them."

After our presentation, Angela had managed to steal some time, and she had read half of my book in a single night. Now, she understood what they needed to do, and how they could use Tiffany to help Lucia progress. They bought a projector to make pictures of characters from her favourite video. Those images were going to be used in a print to create a scarf for Tiffany to wear when she went out. This visual resource would help her learn that going outdoors had a beginning and an end, and encourage her to bond more with her special dog.

They had already used the morning to sort out the chaos of that social picture box. Again, the images would be projected onto the wall to give Lucia clear messages about what was going on in her home environment. At last that little girl would have a meaningful structure in her routine. She would be able to learn, and would have the means to communicate her needs. Both of her parents were now managing her as we had demonstrated they should. They were adhering to the adjustments in order to engage with their precious daughter. Lucia was no longer remote controlling her parents, and home life had changed for the better for all of them. Angela was positively laid-back, confident with hope for their daughter's future and, indeed, for theirs, together as a family. At last they were aware of how to use Tiffany as their educational facilitator to help Lucia communicate at her level and on her terms. As I told Alberto, if my week's visit had achieved nothing else but to help this dear family, then that alone was worth every moment and mile.

"Nuala, your visit has done so much, and now *Henry* is in Spanish, things will begin to change for parents."

As Beni drove into the small hours of the night, we felt great. It was intense, certainly, but yes, it was brilliant! We arrived at two in the morning. Despite the hour, we had a treat in store. Jane had laid a tempting table with a feast and red wine. We were to chill. Poor Beni nearly fell asleep at the table, being so exhausted by the drive, but somehow he managed to rally. Overloaded with our passion for our work, we never tired of talking about it. Jane had so many mixed emotions; she was happy for Lucia's parents, of course, but that was tinged with sadness with the news about Rey. She personally had invested a lot in his training, and he was such a brilliant guide dog. We sat for an hour before we all headed off to bed. I had to catch an early flight in the morning.

The next day, I gave Beni a hug and a last heartfelt *adios*, then I exchanged the same with Jane. I was leaving behind a much-loved friend, whom I knew would always be part of my life. I could only hope that I would see her again someday. At Valladolid Airport I had a final, inspirational chat with Alberto, before we made our own farewells.

Impishly, I couldn't resist quoting the famous words of President Barack Obama. "Alberto, adios. Yes we can!"

During the flight I tried to sleep, but my mind was active, re-reeling the thrills of the last few days. I managed to rest my eyes at least, and even those still-throbbing feet. I was exhausted. I couldn't stop thinking about how fortunate I was to work with Alberto Alvarez-Campos and Jane Kefford. They are the most amazing people and professionals and they care so deeply for both their clients and their dogs. They really believe in them. In turn, I will forever be grateful to them for believing in me and in my own work.

I say this because, whilst our programme gives the child the condition-specific transitional care and education required to provide a platform for meaningful communication and bonding with their dog, PAAT's work allows the children a similar experience and education with their dogs as Dale had had with Henry. Their dogs will facilitate and "lead" the children through all the transitions in life . . . right up to its demise. Hopefully, at long last, society will learn from these children and their special dogs, and encompass them. Let's hope it keeps on encompassing them right through to their time as adults with autism.

Never mind those feet! Arriving back at my flat, I felt better than I'd done in years. My confidence had soared, and I realised that I hadn't suffered a single panic attack in months. At last, my emotional healing had begun, and while it still had a long way to go, it was certainly gliding in the right direction. No one comes out of a three-year downward spiral towards a beckoning oblivion without sustaining some serious scarring. I'd never again be quite the same confident, strong woman I had once been. Perhaps, however, I was on the threshold of being a different one. I had my beloved children, good friends, and the solid support of Dr Grose. I was determined my scars wouldn't scab over and spoil my future. My future lay here in Scotland, and there was a great deal of work to be done.

In August, in order to help increase Dale's chances of employment and then to provide adequate support if he were to secure a job, the Shaw Trust referred him to SAMH (Scottish Association Mental Health).[3] SAMH put him forward to be assessed for a temporary Christmas job at a local, but major, online supply base. Dale passed their procedures comfortably, but he failed to obtain one of the 1,000 jobs on offer. While he was disheartened, SAMH were also disappointed and confused about why he hadn't been offered a position. They were confused? I wasn't exactly clear about that one either!

A month later, three and a half years after leaving college, with exceptional support from SAMH, Dale finally secured his first job. It was a six-month temporary contract, and he declared his autism.

Legally, a client doesn't need to make that disclosure, but the flipside of that is if they are not informed the employer cannot reasonably be expected to support adequately in line with the DDA or Equality Act. Some applicants decide not to declare at application stage, for the understandable fear of being discriminated against.[4] They then inform their employer when they are safely appointed. At that stage, of course, the employer's legal requirement to make the necessary adjustments in the workplace becomes enforceable.

Dale went through the recruitment process, and he impressed the interview panel, which conscientiously adhered to his requirements. He needed no other support at his interview. His experience of volunteering for Barnardo's and doing clerical work gave him the skills he needed to start his new job as an administration assistant. It was based in an arts centre, twenty-five miles from home. Ironically, he had to take the same bus that the Largs nursery position would have required him to use. He settled in well and SAMH received positive feedback from the centre's staff. Naturally, his computing skills were superb, and as ever, he was always punctual and he fitted in well with the team. He used his initiative, and was unfailingly courteous and helpful with both staff and the public. My only real regret in all of this was that it had taken all those years of facing unfairness for Dale to get behind that desk and be given that chance.

In the bitter cold of February 2013, a beam of Spanish sunshine was to warm my heart. Alberto called with incredible news. The CEO of Guide Dogs Queensland in Brisbane, Australia, had asked Alberto and Jane to move their family to Australia for employment. More, they could establish our programme with the charity there. I was thrilled that our work was reaching still more families. We both saw the potential for that success to be replicated on the other side of the globe for many, many more. His next words left me speechless. "Nuala, we will try and get you over to Brisbane, because your experience is vital."

I thanked him for his faith in me. Still, Spain had felt far enough away. It was hard to imagine my great friends being in another hemisphere.

There was something else I needed to know. "Did Rey win his fight for life?"

Alberto reassured me. He had pulled through, but alas, would be chronically sick for the rest of life. He had sustained significant damage to his kidneys and liver, and such was the level of his debility that he could no longer work as a guide dog. The client had been devastated that he had lost such a superb dog and companion, and with him all that independence and well-being that Rey had gifted. They had only had one year together. The client was in the process of obtaining a new guide dog, and Rey himself was now in retirement and was being cared for by another family. At least there was more positive news.

I asked about Lucia and his reply made my day! Her parents had taken on board everything we could have hoped. They had sought professional help after researching the possibility that her autism had worsened because of gluten in her diet. Certain studies link gluten to adverse metabolic reactions in autistic children, finding that it gives them acute digestive and bowel problems. Her parents implemented a gluten-free diet and rapidly they noted signs that her autism had improved, although she still didn't speak. Non-verbal autistic children can obtain speech at any age. Lucia was still very young, so there was every hope that her spoken language could come yet. Her parents' structures and strategies ensured that she was connecting better with Tiffany. In every way, family life was moving in all the right directions.

Inverclyde, Ireland, Germany, Spain, and now Australia! The world was getting smaller, and I could get to like that! There's nothing like the thought of sunny Zamora when the hail is battering at your already draughty windows and a gale-force wind is howling in from the Clyde! I didn't have any Spanish red in the cupboard, and maybe that was just as well! The trusty teapot was around though, and the kettle not far off the boil.

I was growing into this flat. It could use some of those gorgeous ceramic plates I'd seen in Madrid to bring a measure of Mediterranean warmth into this cold Scots kitchen. Madrid. It was like a dream. How did I get there? Me, Nuala, wee lass from Renfrewshire! What was that all about? That library, all the ornate carvings and cornices, and the light flooding in through those massive windows. All these paintings that I never would have known existed, far less stand beside. Certainly, there were dark corners, heavy doors with who knows what behind them, stairs going up as well as down, but now that I thought about it, that was a bit like my life, really. What was that noise? The kettle must have boiled ages ago! Again, someone's been knocking at the door. Who would be out in this filthy night? Again that knock. Should I answer it?

It could be Amy's pal's mum, with news of the riding group. It might be one of my friends, with a warming bottle of red to share. What if it's Dale, with that very lovely lass, and some cake to go with the tea?

Or that secret, special man for me.

Or it could be a wee opporchancity, as the great Chic Murray might have said.

Possibly, there's the risk that it's something else. Possibly, but unlikely. Risk. There's always risk when you open a door.

Will I open that door? Too damn right I will! The future, whatever it is, is behind it, and I'm striding out to envelop it. Anyway, I've a guardian protector by my side, and he's never let me down. Before I answer the knock, I give thanks for an angel with a glossy golden coat, four legs and a wagging tail.

# Postscript

There is no real way of adding up Henry's legacy. It is incalculable, but my hope is that, in some way, if *A Friend Like Henry* shared what that beautiful dog had done for Dale and our family, then this book's obligation would be to show that his gift was ever bigger and more enduring than any of us could possibly have imagined.

There are so many thanks to be given at the end of any journey, and this journey has been more filled with people and presences than most. It would be impossible to acknowledge them all, but there are some we need to catch up with before we leave them.

Spain and all the wonderful people from PAAT remain a huge highlight on my personal map. In March 2013 I presented my work at the first International Congress of Health Professionals in Animal Assisted Interventions in Lleida.[1] It was both a thrill and an honour to share a platform with contributors of the calibre of Dr Aubrey H. Fine, an eminent psychologist specialising in research into the unique bond animals share with humans. He spoke magnificently on his work with people with autism, sensory loss, bipolar disorder and more. Some of Dale's story will be referenced in his latest book.

Then there was the experience of hearing the great Mylos Rodrigo Claverol present on her innovative work with her own trained dogs in an animal therapy situation. In her role as a family and community medicine specialist, her pioneering approaches are already changing lives for people with dementia. I had seen a fraction of this rainbow of hope many years ago when I visited my own father in a care home.

Henry made more than a little difference to those elderly residents. In Mylos, I saw that rainbow reach into infinity. The strategies she is using with dogs to reach and teach those burdened by Alzheimer's and similar afflictions also have significant parallel applications in autism. Paco Martín Zarzuelo opened our ears and hearts with the possibilities seen in his own groundbreaking research, using electronic devices and animatronics, the technique of operating lifelike robots. Using dogs, with attached iPads, modems, PECS and the like, he is witnessing improved focus, motivation and communication in his user group. Here was an update of what Jim Taylor had described to me all those years ago when we "spoke" through Henry. Yes, he urged, do it. Use the animal as an appropriate, non-threatening buffer zone!

There were so many more. Francisco Javier Lozano Olea and Eva Doménec Elizalde of the Animal Assisted Interventions (IAA) Unit. Sant Joan de Deu Hospital in Esplugues were working with their dedicated team to help alleviate fears for children in oncology wards and similar units. Their dogs are trained to wear theatre hats, gowns and even mock IV drips. They receive placebo drugs to help the children accept and relax in their treatment. This strategy is already so successful that they are seeing a significant reduction in the level of sedation required by the children in the traumatic post-operative recovery time.

From the UK, Clair Guest, of Medical Detection Dogs /Cancer and Bio Detection Dogs, lifted the lid on the work of the dogs she is training to quite literally sniff out cancers. With 300,000 sensory receptors on the canine nose and a sense of smell 100,000 times greater than the human one, and with that specialised double sniff at a patient's breath, those highly trained dogs can detect cancers, including those in the breast and bowel, at a remarkably early stage. The dog's ability to discover cancers so soon in deep tissue is 95 to 97 per cent accurate. Clair herself owes her life to her dog who continually licked her neck, alerting her to changes occurring in her own deep tissue where cancer cells were growing.

A hard act to follow! Follow I did, though. Once again, I was proud to share a podium with the amazing Alberto, on his last major "gig" for PAAT before uprooting to Brisbane. At my side, and making my Scots tongue accessible for Spain and beyond, I had the lovely Rocio. I am forever in her debt and in Alberto's and in Jane's too. Australia is fortunate to have them. Maybe one day I'll see them there. I hope so. *Gracias* to all of you.

What of my one-time companion in Spain, Blair? DATA is expanding by the minute. Keir, who piloted his programme, is thriving with Blair's innovative and empathetic approaches, and so many more have joined him. Late summer 2012 saw Blair stage a stunningly successful DATA dog agility competition and show, complete with qualified judges and rosettes awarded. It will not be the last such event for DATA. In the mainstream dog agility circuit, human noses are sniffing this new air. Blair's brilliance and daring is earning him the reputation he so deserves.

What of autism in the big world? How much has really changed for the majority? No question about it, things are moving, but there's still too far to go. If we fail to ensure all with ASD receive their right to a good, appropriate education, which is clearly their best chance of independence and their pathway to a proper quality of adult life, ultimately society will pay the price. Financially alone, research shows (2008 by the London School of Economics and Political Science) that autism costs the UK £27.5 billion a year. Inadequate help in the early years results in substantially greater ongoing adult support. The National Audit Office has assessed this hidden cost at around £2.3 billion a year, in Scotland alone. Best value it is not! The government has identified the importance of early diagnosis and condition-specific education. Let it act upon that and quickly!

The NAS reports that two-thirds of adults with autism in England receive insufficient support. One in three adults will experience severe mental health difficulties as a result. Mental health problems are not an inevitable consequence of having autism. With the right help these issues are preventable. Consider the ongoing cost to the NHS for this alone, or the long-term financial implications of supporting adults in residential care, who, with the right education and support as children, might have enjoyed significantly greater independence. Some, like Dale and his friends, might be contributors to society rather than being dependent upon it.

Every year in the UK there are 600 to 700 newly diagnosed children with autism. For these new families, this story gives something they hardly dared to have before: hope! I commend the relentless work of the NAS and Scottish Autism in trying to plug the gap in services, but the demand far outstrips the supply.

Nearer home, as I write, I realise it is now a full nine years since Henry died. Life is as normal as our life could ever be. We are all content and prospering. Amy is settling into her first year of secondary school thanks to the Rolls-Royce of transitional care given to her by her school's autism outreach service. Such is her desire to be like her peers that she wears a full school uniform, including a shirt and tie and, for the first time in seven years, a school skirt! Her school is newly built and huge. Many of the teachers there had already taught Dale and they remember him well.

Amy is taking a similar pathway to the one that her brother had earlier walked for her. Just as Dale had been fortunate in having the perfect friend and role model to guide him towards adulthood, so she has her own heroine friend in the form of Regan Boyle. Regan has known my daughter since she was four, when they were both at Moorfoot Nursery. While the friends from the Famous Five come and go, Regan has remained committed to Amy throughout all the intervening years. To this day, if I were asked to design the perfect friend for Amy, she would be Regan. I am as proud of that smashing young woman as I am of my own children.

Amy, at thirteen, is halfway to becoming every bit as successful as her brother. It wouldn't surprise me if, in the future, she were to take the computer industry by storm, like so many of her ASD peers before her. She has the added talent of being able to blend her autism with a wicked sense of humour and an affectionate personality.

Five years of continually addressing her inability to express her negative feelings appropriately has paid off. There are days when, inevitably, things don't go her way, but the time of "I'm going to kill a horse!" is passing.

As for Dale, his job at the arts centre ended in March 2013. With a heavy heart, he gave his colleagues a card and chocolates, and he wished them all well. He had loved working with them. Determined to work again, he began to volunteer with REACH, a new autism non-profit organisation in Inverclyde, which had been founded by a local mother, Vicki McCarthy. Vicki's teenage daughter, Kira, was diagnosed with Autistic Spectrum Condition aged four, and received that all-essential, condition-specific education, together with other intervention therapies. These measures allowed her daughter to blossom, communicate and enjoy the same quality of life that her contemporary Amy has. Both girls attend the same drama group, and one night after a sparkling show, Vicki and I were chatting. As ever, she was keen to catch up with Dale's progress. What started as a friendly, post-performance natter between two mums was to have seriously good consequences. I heard more about her story. Through "The REACH Way" (Relationships, Education, Action, Community and Health) Vicki is striving to improve so many aspects of autism in a multi-disciplinary way. A significant part of REACH's work is in providing employment for adults with ASD and AS who assist with the administrative dimension of their organisation. As soon as I mentioned Dale was seeking work again, Vicki arranged to meet him.

We wanted to help however we could. REACH is becoming increasingly significant for not only the Inverclyde ASD community but for the local community as a whole. It is working with Prospects and other agencies to try to secure funding for stable wages for all their workers. While there was no salaried post available to him, Dale was keen to be part of this, and he seized the opportunity to work on a voluntary basis with another adult with AS.

These are exciting times. REACH is housed in a building which has needed significant renovation to be fit for purpose. Once completed, our community will celebrate the wonderful, socially inclusive aspects of that charity in a space which will offer opportunities to children, adults and whole families alike.

Of course, REACH has a scope beyond those walls. Through it, our local cinema now offers autism-friendly screenings. There are no adverts, the lights dim just as the film commences, and there is a relaxed atmosphere which makes it possible for these families who were previously unable to see anything on the silver screen to enjoy a night out together. I am dumbstruck by Vicki's vision and stamina. Dale may well have found his perfect vocation after all those struggles, right here on his doorstep.

For the first time in the three challenging years that pushed Dale to the limit, he is settled and content with his life again, so much so that his wee band-playing with his friends was not quite enough! He is now very involved in the Glasgow rock scene. The lads in his current band knew nothing of his autism. They simply heard him play and wanted him as part of the outfit. Dale is approaching twenty-five, and undoubtedly he has become the kind, well-adjusted, responsible and independent young man I sacrificed great chunks of my life to see mature. I'd do it all again.

Jamie is thriving, and living nearby. Whatever our problems have been, and perhaps still are, we have both moved on, and splitting up was the third best thing that ever happened in our marriage. I think we'd both agree on that. The two best things that ever happened, unquestionably, were our children, and however bad the bad times were, we have them to show for our years together. I know he's every bit as proud of them as I am. Yes, we've both moved on from each other, but neither of us will ever move away from the two most precious people we could ever have created. That's not the worst thing in the world.

My thanks could not be complete if I mentioned only the two-legged contributors to this book. From Greyfriars Bobby to dogs who sniff out cancers and find bombs, and those who rescue people who just survive in disaster zones, to those who are the eyes and ears for their humans, to our own terrible but lovely Thomas, and most of all, to the late, great Sir Henry, I raise a glass and the biggest, most succulent of bones.

Thank you!

Nuala Gardner
July 2013

# In Their Own Words

*The implications of literal meaning in autism,
and some not so shaggy dog tales from friends.*

Amy

Aged four, Amy had limited vocabulary and comprehension of language, or so I thought. At Alton Towers we waited to board the rollercoaster Oblivion, notorious for its terrifying vertical drop. I held her in my arms. It was helpfully signposted that parents could take turns at the start of the ride to allow for a "child swap", and a staff member clarified that in a loud voice as we approached the start of the ride. Despite her already well-known complete absence of fear, she screamed and became seriously distressed. Five years later, in Disneyland Paris, she took great delight in preparing to board the Stars Wars ride: "Nuala, am I going on this ride with you?"

"Yes, you're big enough now."

"Oh good, Nuala. I thought you were going to swap me for a different girl to take home."

\*\*\*

In my car with her friend Shannon, when both were aged nine.

Shannon said, "We drove all the way from Belgium to Scotland."

Amy replied, "Shannon, you're too young to be driving!"

\*\*\*

The teacher wrote on the whiteboard for the class to copy as homework: "Please write these numbers in words: 1.5, 2.5 and a continuing sequence of decimal numbers."

Amy did that exactly . . . completing her homework on the spot.

\*\*\*

Friends in the playground were telling Amy that Justin Beiber was really hot!

"Why doesn't he take off his jumper?"

\*\*\*

In The Body Shop:

"Nuala, I thought you could buy parts for your body or bodies in that shop!"

\*\*\*

Teaching sex education, and stressing the importance of the issue, I asked, "Amy, do you know what 'consent' means?"

"Yes, Nuala, it means you have to get them to fill in a form.

\*\*\*

Having discovered that her school bag was broken, I blurt out, "Oh, Amy, the zip on your bag is gone!"

"No, Nuala, it's still there!"

\*\*\*

A teacher asked her pupil to go back to the classroom and bring her back the green cardigan. When the pupil returned, he brought a green basket. He did not know what a cardigan was, so he looked for the nearest green object.

\*\*\*

Another teacher exhorts an AS child to pull his socks up. Naturally, the child does exactly that! This one had dire consequences in one classroom, where the uncomprehending child was excluded for what was wrongly interpreted as insolence.

\*\*\*

When Amy was aged eleven, I explained to her that she had been a test-tube baby and as an embryo, she had been in a freezer for three months.
   "Nuala, that's why I don't feel the cold!"

\*\*\*

**Delayed Echolalia**
The five-year-old Amy repeated a slogan she had heard a comedian use on TV. Of course, this clearly-enunciated performance happened while we were waiting in a long queue to see Santa Claus.
   "Jamie, look, it's a f\*\*kin' squirrel. What a f\*\*kin' liberty!"
   Never underestimate that. A child with autism is always listening.

\*\*\*

After so much chat from his sister, here's a final, and quieter word from Dale, then aged ten.
   At his Aunty Lorraine's, he accidentally spilled some juice on the carpet. He approached Lorraine, anxiously, seeking her out to help him clean the mess. She emphasised, "Dale, I'm so happy you told me, which was really good."
   "Well, your face doesn't look it!"

\*\*\*

## Jonathan Glass

This book has detailed Dale's many challenges and barriers when trying to find work, but there is hope. Here is Jonathan Glass's experience. He has a diagnosis of AS and is twenty-four years old:

Because my UCAS application for entry into the University of Glasgow was completed whilst I was still in secondary school, my university of choice knew of my Asperger's diagnosis before joining, so I didn't get a choice about whether to declare it or not. In August I was invited to meet my Advisor of Studies to discuss course options. She ensured I knew where the Disability Service for the University was, and gave me a point of contact to meet. She was initially helpful, and showed me where my classes were.

My University experience was mixed; ironically, the staff I got the fairest and most compassionate treatment from were lecturers in my own department, Urban Studies. It was a small and close-knit learning environment. The Link workers from the National Autistic Society spent an hour a week with me after securing funding from SAAS. I was advised to quit by the Disability Service at the end of my second year, because my grades weren't great and my attendance was slipping. There was no attempt to try to help me or to prevent me from feeling isolated. I'm glad I didn't quit, as I gained my masters degree with an Honours entitlement, after four years of hard work. My friends knew of my disability, because I got extra time in my exams, and they were supportive. In fact, I met several of them, thanks to my disability, as we met during that extra time before the exams!

After graduating, I started a postgrad at another university, which I hated. The course description was different from the course content, and there was little or no support for me. With no funding for an NAS worker, and little in the way of a fixed contact in the department, I found that staff were actually bordering on rude when I raised my concerns. I left after paying £2,000 for six months of study.

I decided to continue working part-time in retail until I could find a full-time job in my own specialism. Several months had passed and I was getting desperate. I was even considering going into a retail job full-time, just to have something to do with my days. I had kept a close eye on various railway websites, as I had always loved trains, and part of my degree was studying transportation policy, so I was more than qualified in that area. Luckily, a management grade role came up within a train company, doing what every autistic boy who has grown up with *Thomas the Tank Engine* dreams of doing – planning train timetables! I get to help plan trains, resource them with train crews, and help make a difference to improve our railways.

I was lucky. I didn't originally get the job, but I made such an impression on the interviewers because my knowledge was "Greater than theirs"!

When my present post arose, I was offered it unconditionally. I'm getting paid a nice wage and because of my inborn attention to detail that "useless" train knowledge is now essential to my work! I know most folk with AS never get this chance, so I'm very lucky indeed.

Jonathan Glass, March 2013
"The Power of the Dog"

## Amy Barclay

Over the last year, as a family we'd found ourselves virtually housebound. Our four-year-old eldest son, Noah, diagnosed with autism when he was aged two, had become increasingly difficult to manage out in public. We'd reached the point when he was too big for a conventional pushchair and he was a "bolter".

My son has no understanding of danger, no negotiability. In fact, most of the time we were unable to engage with him at all. He couldn't tolerate wrist straps or hand-holding. He'd begun unclipping his buggy harness at lightning speed and would run in front of traffic. We couldn't calm him enough, or teach him how to behave safely near the roadside, and we realised that our only option was to use a wheelchair because it provided sufficient restraint to keep him safe.

Then we got our dog, Beano. We'd researched the benefits of pet therapy and read *A Friend Like Henry*. We knew it wasn't just about getting a dog or even getting the right dog. It was monumentally about getting it right for Noah, preparing him before the dog arrived. Transition was the key. After all, we had come to live and breathe by visual timetables and communication aids in order to help Noah understand his environment and what to know and what to expect from his day. By fate we found Nuala, and suddenly we found in her the amazing support we needed. She sent us numerous resources, including an entire step-by-step transition programme with helpful visual aids for our son. These were developmentally appropriate tasks, which helped him understand that a dog was coming to live with us, and it would be his. Not only that, but that he would have to care for it.

Nuala worked closely with us through the entire run-up to getting Beano (and after), making sure we had every bit of support we needed and making the whole process seamless. We were excited and nervous when we introduced Noah to Beano, who at the time was a nine-month-old yellow Labrador. We had sourced him from Gun Dog World. Life for Noah was black and white; in a split second he would make a decision whether something was right or wrong. We knew that his first meeting with Beano needed to be positive for the relationship to stand any chance of success. As we walked that dog into our home for the first time, Noah's response blew us away. An enormous, beaming smile greeted us (or rather, greeted the dog), with the words, "It's a Beano."

All those weeks of preparation had been invaluable. The following morning was our first attempt at going out for a walk, and we couldn't have been more stunned at the outcome. Our little boy walked calmly and contentedly, with his hand resting on his dog's back, from start to finish. Every time Beano stopped walking, so would Noah. He stopped at every kerbside, and did not budge until Beano was instructed to cross. Within a few outings, Noah began to abandon his previously "inseparable" comfort blanket. He began stuffing it into the shopping basket of his little brother's pushchair, in favour of Beano's backpack.

After a fortnight we began getting positive feedback from nursery about changes in Noah's behaviour. He'd become tactile. When his teachers helped him with a task, they found he would stroke the back of their hands or arms, the same way he petted Beano. As time passed we could see he was learning valuable life skills through his hours of play with his dog.

It was evident that he was coming to understand things like turn-taking, cause and effect and such like. Through simple games like fetch, and by giving Beano commands – well, no wonder his speech and levels of engagement improved. My son was transferring these newfound skills into other aspects of his life. As well as that, he became able to play with his little brother much better than he'd ever done before. He was starting to understand sharing and patience in small amounts, where previously he'd struggled with those concepts.

Personal care instantly became easier. If Beano was having his hair brushed, Noah would tolerate having his brushed too. Every time my son's teeth were brushed, Beano's were done too. In fact, Noah would sing his version of our household's teeth-brushing song, to encourage his dog. As time passed, one of the most significant changes we noticed was his ability to sit still and, consequently, this made possible his newfound love of books. In the past we'd been lucky to see him stay in one place for more than thirty or forty seconds. Before his dog came into his life, Noah has been at nursery school for a year, but attended only short sessions, as he couldn't cope with "sit-down-on-the-carpet time".

Within a very short time, his sessions had been extended to include "carpet time" and now he's enjoying stories and singing time with the rest of his class. We regularly find him cuddled into Beano, with a little pile of books beside them, and one by one, he will read his version of the stories to his furry friend. The success of this friendship has far exceeded all of our expectations, in a way we could never have imagined.

All of a sudden, we've been given the tools to do what we've been watching other families do (and take for granted) for years. We are making huge steps towards improving Noah's chances of coping with early education and life, and simply becoming the happy little boy that we want to see. We will be eternally grateful to Nuala and Blair Cochrane of DATA, and all the others who have helped us, because we were at a crunch point, where life could have become really difficult. Instead, Noah (as an individual) and we (as a family) are thriving. We look at the bond he has with his dog and it melts our hearts.

And how long has Beano been with us as I write? Sixteen weeks! We are looking forward to watching them grow together.

Amy Barclay, Noah's Mum
March 2013

# Endnotes

*Preface*
1. NAS *Communication* magazine. 2005.

*Chapter 1*
1. The DDA 1995 was reviewed and is now the Equality Act 2010, which is still in place at the time of writing.

*Chapter 2*
1. Quote from Scottish Executive parents manual *Next Steps*.
2. Quote from NAS *Communication* magazine. Summer 2006.
3. In April 2007 NAS launched a report called "Missing Out". It revealed children with autism from black, minority and ethnic communities experienced "double discrimination", meaning that their disability and their ethnicity isolates and excludes them from having the right education to allow them to reach their full potential, as any other child. The report states, "24% of BME children with autism were excluded from school." Parents from BME communities were significantly less satisfied with their child's academic and social progress compared to their white British counterparts. The report recommended that "schools must address bullying on the basis of race, disability within anti-bullying procedures" and "all professionals working with children with autism from BME communities should receive training in autism and cultural awareness." (http://www. autism.org.uk)

*Chapter 3*

1. Carly Fleischmann finds "her" missing piece of jigsaw: http://www.youtube.com/watch?v=vNZVV4Ciccg.
2. National Audit Office research 2009 revealed that 80 per cent of Atos doctors said they needed more training to help people with autism.
3. Don't write me off (http://www.nas.org).
4. All statistics sourced from http://www.nas.org.

*Chapter 6*

1. Children on the higher end of the spectrum and those with AS are more vulnerable in mainstream school with 47 per cent of parents reporting their children were bullied (http://www.autism.org.uk, Make School Make Sense, 2006). Over 50 per cent of adults with autism have been bullied and experienced harassment since they were eighteen (http://www.autism.org.uk, We Exist campaign).

*Chapter 7*

1. "Doggy Business" page 39. NAS *Communication* magazine. Winter 2007.

*Chapter 8*

1. *Greenock Telegraph*, Friday, 3 April 2009.

*Chapter 9*

1. Hinderton School: http://www.hindertonschool.co.uk.

*Chapter 10*

1. Source: http://www.talkaboutautism.org.uk.
2. *The Transporters*. http://www.thetransporters.com.
3. Tammet, Daniel. *Born On a Blue Day*. Hodder & Stoughton. 2007.
4. Pets As Therapy, http://www.petsastherapy.org/.

## Chapter 11
1. Dr Temple Grandin, http://www.templegrandin.com.

## Chapter 13
1. Issacson, Rupert. *The Horse Boy*. Penguin/Viking: London, 2009. Horse Boy Camps in the UK. www.horseboyfoundation.org.uk.
2. DATA – http://data1.moonfruit.com.
3. The YouTube video is a CBS newsreel of a boy named Parker, who is a child with autism. His behaviours and life are transformed when he gets a golden retriever service dog called Candy. It is a moving story, one worth taking time to watch. You can find it by searching "North Star CBS news story" or visiting the link: https://www.youtube.com/watch?v=QeKj3vjnD7M.

## Chapter 16
1. http://www.familyfund.org.uk.
2. http://www.iancommunity.org/cs/autism/icd10_criteria_for_autism.
3. "Early Bird Program." http://www.nas.org.

## Chapter 17
1. Research Mira Foundation. Quebec, Canada. 2010. http://www.mira.ca/en/r-amp-d/10/autism_101.html, http://www.mira.ca/en/r-amp-d/10/autism_101.html
2. Hanen Programme: http://www.hanen.org/Home.aspx.
3. Lawson 1996 source: Scottish Executive parent manual *Next Steps*.

## Chapter 18
1. http://www.fundacionquinta.org.
2. Panorama's evidence allowed a full criminal investigation to take place. Following investigation by the Care Commission, Winterbourne has been shut down. Twelve staff members were arrested.
3. http://www.samh.org.uk.

4. A survey in Scotland by the NAS We Exist campaign revealed over half of adults with autism have been subjected to bullying and harassment since they were eighteen (http://www.nas.org).

*Postscript*
1. http://www.iaacongresolleida.com/english.html.